Homicide, Race, and Justice in the American West

Clare V. McKanna, Jr.

Homicide, Race, and Justice in the American West, 1880-1920

The University of Arizona Press

TUCSON

The University of Arizona Press
Copyright © 1997
The Arizona Board of Regents
All Rights Reserved

♾ This book is printed on acid-free, archival-quality paper.
Manufactured in the United States of America
02 01 00 99 98 97 6 5 4 3 2 1

Library of Congress Cataloging-in-Publication Data
McKanna, Clare V. (Clare Vernon), 1935–
Homicide, race, and justice in the American West, 1880–1920 /
Clare V. McKanna, Jr.
p.   cm.
Includes index.
ISBN 0-8165-1708-8 (cloth : acid-free paper)
1. Homicide—West (U.S.)—History. 2. Violence—West (U.S.)—History.
3. Criminal justice, Administration of—West (U.S.)—History.
4. Discrimination in criminal justice administration—West (U.S.)—History.
I. Title.
HV6533.W46M34   1997
364.1′523′0978—dc20   96-35638
                              CIP

British Cataloguing-in-Publication Data
A catalogue record for this book is available from the British Library.

In memory of my father,

Clare Vernon McKanna

(1911–1951)

Contents

Illustrations

Maps

Tables

Acknowledgments

I owe a great deal to many people. Four historians provided critical readings of this manuscript. Professor John R. Wunder, Center for Great Plains Studies, University of Nebraska-Lincoln, proved to be a marvelous critic, a forceful mentor, and a good friend. He was always there with encouragement and nononsense evaluations—chapter after chapter. Professor Roger Cunniff, Department of History, San Diego State University, a good friend, provided the concept of convergence that distinguishes the American West. His insightful reading at a critical stage of manuscript preparation enabled me to refocus on the real issues that defined lethal violence in the West. Professor Sidney L. Harring, CUNY Law School at Queens College, City University of New York, and an anonymous reviewer provided critical analysis that immeasurably improved this book. Ms. Ona Siporin, assistant editor of the *Western Historical Quarterly*, offered a thoughtful, penetrating evaluation for an essay that forced me to rethink and reshape the book. Thanks also to Alexis Noebels for her fine editing. A special thanks to Bardy Anderson, Graphic Artist, San Diego State University, for designing and completing the maps and figures.

Rose Marie Wheeler, County Clerk, Las Animas County; Sara Murphy, Trinidad (Colorado) Public Library; David Hoober, Director, Arizona State Archives, and archivists Jean Nudd and Carolyn Grote; archivist Steve Wolz, Nebraska State Historical Society; and Rudy Tesar, Clerk of the District Court, Douglas County, Nebraska, offered access to county records. A special thanks goes to Coroner Thomas R. Haynes, Douglas County, for personally locating the coroner's logs and generously providing office space for their inspection.

The Center for Great Plains Studies, University of Nebraska-Lincoln, provided two graduate-student travel grants in 1990 and 1992, and the Department of History, University of Nebraska-Lincoln, bestowed a Landis Fellowship in 1993. Their support is greatly appreciated.

A special thanks to Professor Linda Parker, chair of the Department of American Indian Studies, San Diego State University, who offered support and encouragement.

Finally, thanks to a true friend; without her assistance this project would have failed. In appreciation, I dedicate this work to Mary Beth Shoning-Klauer.

Homicide, Race, and Justice in the American West

Critical Convergences in the American West

The Roots of Lethal Violence

This is not a traditional story about cowboys and Indians or gunfighters in the American West; instead, it is a study of lethal violence and the treatment of racial-minority defendants by western criminal justice systems, placed within a "new" western history paradigm. In the past, historians of the American West have portrayed violence as essentially episodic, involving gunfights in cattle towns, range wars between cattlemen and sheepmen, and vigilante movements. However, their sources and their traditional narrative style of history have left these authors unaware of the obvious. A common form of lethal violence occurred daily in the American West: homicide—committed by ranchers, farmers, cowboys, coal and copper miners, bartenders, cooks, butchers, gamblers, pimps, police officers, sheriff's deputies, town marshals, Baldwin-Felts detectives, coal mine guards, roisterous drunks, teenagers, old men—and occasionally house-wives and mothers. Homicide was commonplace in the West, and so was the mistreatment of minority defendants. Using quantitative methods and sources such as coroner's inquests, criminal registers of action, criminal-court case files, prison registers, and census data, this study documents this "other" violence in western society and examines its impact on minorities.

The Problem

In 1983, Richard Maxwell Brown complained that "there is no overall explanatory paradigm of western history that includes violence within its framework," and he suggested that "what is needed is a new conceptual framework for future research and writing on western violence."[1] In 1987, in a discussion of whether violence in the American West was more pervasive than elsewhere in the United States, Robert M. Utley suggested that "the debate remains unresolved, mainly because of an absence of reliable statistics from earlier times."[2]

This study, by focusing on lethal violence between 1880 and 1920, addresses two important questions: Was the American West violent? And were minority defendants treated fairly by western criminal justice systems? An examination of criminal records in Douglas County, Nebraska; Las Animas County, Colorado; and Gila County, Arizona, three disparate sites, offers an excellent opportunity to explore the interrelationships between race/ethnicity, gender, alcohol, and weapons to measure violence levels. In these three counties, as elsewhere in the West, the convergence of rapid population growth, ethnic diversity, alcohol, the gun culture, and the boomtown effect led to social instability that appeared as a subculture of violence within black society in Douglas County, and as more pervasive regional cultures of violence within Las Animas and Gila counties.[3]

A Lethal-Violence Paradigm

All three counties experienced high levels of lethal violence, and communities within these counties exhibited a variety of complex factors that had converged quickly between 1880 and 1920, creating the conditions for high levels of violence. First, southern blacks (Douglas); Mediterraneans, east Europeans, and Hispanics (Las Animas); and Apaches (Gila) were confronted by established northern European elites who controlled the power structure. Second, rapid industrialization caused by coal and copper mines, railroads, and meat-packing companies brought about the exploitation of labor. Finally, a clash of differing value systems—including rural versus urban, southern versus northern, and Apache versus European—increased tensions.

The convergence of these and other complex factors helps to define the American West.[4] It also provides a simple paradigm for measuring lethal violence, because as this study demonstrates, it is this rapid convergence of diverse cultures, industrialization, and differing social systems that best explains high homicide rates in the American West. Rapid population growth transformed Omaha, Nebraska; Trinidad, Colorado; and Globe, Arizona, into vibrant multicultural communities that the northern European elites found difficult to control. When stress levels between the various groups increased, some people turned to violence. The propensity for carrying handguns and drinking alcohol also increased the likelihood of violence.

In the American West, virtually every state and territory had regions where diverse factors converged quickly. If one were to survey homicide rates in other counties in California, Montana, Wyoming, Arizona, Oregon, North Dakota, Kansas, Washington, South Dakota, and Idaho where such factors existed, it is likely that similarly high homicide rates would be discovered. It is the thesis of this study that high levels of lethal violence in the three counties studied denote social instability—especially within Las Animas and Gila counties. It will be demonstrated that a subculture of violence existed in Douglas County, and that regional cultures of violence emerged in Las Animas and Gila counties. Further, it will be proven that minority defendants, especially blacks and Apaches, suffered under white-dominated criminal justice systems.

Images of Violence

Hollywood's visual images of cattle-town gunfights and Indian massacres have colored our perception of what the American West was really like. Whether it was *Shane, High Noon, Fort Apache,* or *Little Big Man,* violent images have been pervasive and have left indelible impressions in the minds of Americans. Many of us grew up on John Wayne movies and graduated to the Clint Eastwood genre. In virtually every film the first image was the cowboy on a horse. Soon, in the background, Indians appeared—threatening wagon trains, settlements, or troops of U.S. cavalry. In many films, violence became the main focus in telling the story, pitting white hats against black hats.

Most recently, *Unforgiven* accentuated the stark realism of violence in its portrayal of a brutal sheriff and the prostitutes who hire gunmen to kill two offensive cowboys, and in its vivid, violent scenes leading up to the actual killings. In one chilling scene, Clint Eastwood, as gunman William Munny, is standing over a prone, wounded Gene Hackman, the sheriff, aiming a rifle at his head. Hackman says, "I don't deserve this, to die like this." Eastwood retorts, "Deserves got nothing to do with it." Eastwood then cocks his rifle and fires point blank at his helpless victim.[5] This scenario dramatically asserts what every previous western film had suggested: The West was violent. Or was it?

The Debate

There is a significant difference of opinion as to whether the American West was violent or not. A discussion of this dichotomy, beginning with those historians who perceive the West as violent, seems in order.[6] In 1969, Joe B. Frantz's "The Frontier Tradition: An Invitation to Violence" appeared in a collection of essays commissioned to examine the reasons for the urban riots that exploded throughout the United States after the assassination of Martin Luther King, Jr.[7] In a wide-ranging discussion of outlaws, vigilantes, cattle-range wars, sheepmen versus cattlemen, and racial hatred in the American West, Frantz concludes that "every frontier state went through its period of lawlessness and its corresponding period of mobocracy designed to bring the lawless element under control."[8] He further observes that guns provided "an invitation to violence."

In *The Gunfighter: Man or Myth?* (1969), which examines the role of gunmen in the West, Joseph G. Rosa notes that "the gunfight was a fact; the fast draw, a fantasy."[9] Rosa examined lawmen, cowboys in cattle towns, gunfights, and methods employed by gunmen. He claims that from "1870 to 1885 forty-five men died by violence in Abilene, Ellsworth, Wichita, Dodge City, and Caldwell, most of them cowboys and gamblers shot by town marshals."[10] Rosa's study, however, is mainly anecdotal and fails to provide any meaningful statistics to document what he considers to be the violent nature of the American West.

In 1970, Harry Sinclair Drago's *The Great Range Wars: Violence on the Grasslands* examined the Lincoln County war in New Mexico, the Pleasant Valley war in Arizona (a feud between the Grahams and Tewksburys), the Johnson County feud in Wyoming, and vigilantes in Montana. Drago weaves a tale about violence in the West but fails to place the events into perspective. In his discussion of the 1880s Pleasant Valley war, in what is now Gila County, Arizona, Drago suggests that "Globe was . . . only four years old and too lawless itself to give any thought" to the Graham-Tewksbury feud.[11] At that time, Pleasant Valley was not part of Gila County, and consequently the sheriff would not have had jurisdiction. Without statistics, the reader is left to wonder just how violent these areas really were.

Richard Maxwell Brown has provided one of the best-known studies on vigilante movements in the American West. His *Strain of Violence* chronicles the rise of vigilantism in South Carolina among Regulators during the American Revolution, and its dramatic explosion in the West. Brown counted more than three hundred vigilante movements that reached their zenith, in terms of supporters, in San Francisco, California, and then spread to Montana, Texas,

Wyoming, and throughout the West.[12] The San Francisco vigilante movements were characterized by leadership among the business community, while those in other regions were motivated by a variety of factors, including racism. Although Brown provides statistical data on the movements and their victims, he fails to develop violence-level ratios. Nevertheless, one is impressed by the sporadic violence created by vigilante activities in the West.

In his 1983 "Historiography of Violence in the American West," Brown claims that "the popular image of the history of the American West is focused on violence," but that it is exaggerated.[13] He suggests that professional historians have avoided the study of violence because of the "dichotomy between the Wild West and the Workaday West."[14] Historians such as Frederick Jackson Turner ignored the Wild West and wrote about "the Workaday West of farm fields, ranch lots, mine shafts, millrooms, city streets, and legislative halls."[15] Brown focuses his discussion on what he sees as three categories of violence in the West: crime wars, land and labor wars, and racial and religious wars. He found that the historical studies of violence in these three categories lack any standardized paradigm.

In his most recent essay on violence, Brown discusses the concept of "no duty to retreat," "the Code of the West," and the dichotomy of what he calls the "Western Civil War of Incorporation," which pitted groups of gunfighters against each other.[16] In a spirited discussion, Brown claims that at the Mussel Slough gun battle in the Great Valley of California, Walter J. Crow shot and killed five settlers in an attempt to maintain the supremacy of the incorporation values of the Southern Pacific Railroad.[17] In a comparable dispute, the gunfight at the O.K. Corral, the Earps were trying to incorporate the values of the "entrepreneurial, Republican" forces in Tombstone, Arizona. Finally, Brown views the Ludlow massacre as an example of a confrontation between the incorporation gunfighters of the Colorado Fuel and Iron Company and the anti-incorporation gunfighters of the Western Federation of Miners.[18] Brown classifies forty-two episodes in the American West between 1850 and 1919 as "Western Civil War of Incorporation" disputes, and he concludes that "mining, mill, and cattle towns were frequently violent places, but there were also many communities in the West where violence was rare."[19] It is an intriguing discussion, but Brown provides no statistical data to measure violence levels in the American West.

Other scholars claim that violence was not common in the American West.[20] Although his is not primarily an examination of violence, Robert R. Dykstra has provided the most enduring study claiming that the American West was not violent. In *Cattle Towns,* Dykstra observes that during the cattle-drive period,

Abilene, Dodge City, Ellsworth, Wichita, and Caldwell were not especially violent.[21] Although it has been acclaimed by some reviewers as a major quantitative study, Dykstra's methods lack statistical sophistication. In his chapter "The Adjustment to Violence," Dykstra provides one table that chronicles only those homicides that occurred during the cattle-drive periods for the five cattle towns he examined in Kansas. His raw data, taken exclusively from newspaper accounts, fail to provide any relationships of homicide rates among the five towns. Without further documentation, the reader hasn't a clue what the homicide rates might have been for each town; however, by using population figures to establish homicide rates per 100,000, it can be shown that they were very high. For example, closer analysis of Dykstra's own data indicates that the homicide rates in Abilene for 1870, 1871, and 1872 (the peak period of the cattle drives) averaged 76.6 per 100,000, while Ellsworth recorded the highest rate for a single year in 1873: 421.9 homicides per 100,000. Wichita averaged 91.3 per 100,000 for the period 1871–74; Dodge City reached 160 in 1878; and only Caldwell maintained a modest rate of 8.9 for the period 1879–85.[22] Despite these high homicide rates (which, because of his methodology, he may not have known existed), Dykstra naively claims that "the average number of homicides per cattle town trading season amounted to only 1.5 homicides per year."[23] By listing only this raw data, he fails to establish a measurement for his statistics. Today, researchers use the homicide rate per 100,000 population as their measurement criterion, and there is no reason that it cannot be applied to the American West in the nineteenth century. In fact, this study confirms that it is the logical way to accurately measure levels of lethal violence in the West.

In *The Western Peace Officer* (1972), Frank Prassel suggests that "most western areas were really very peaceful when compared with urban centers in the East."[24] Prassel admits that "women, liquor, gambling, and firearms" contributed to violence on the frontier, but he concludes that "as a place of wild lawlessness the frontier's spectacular reputation is, therefore, largely without substantiation."[25] Prassel provides few statistics (and these are unreliable) to support his thesis. For example, in his chapter "Wild and Unsettled Portions of Our Territories," Prassel offers two tables to suggest that the West was not violent. One table covers crime in Denver, Colorado, for 1873, and another describes crime in Arapahoe County, Colorado, in 1882, but he fails to provide any analysis of violence, even for those one-year periods. Prassel provides five tables in an appendix, but these fail to show relationships of violence in eastern and western cities. He offers only anecdotal comments that provide no real discourse on violence levels in the American West.

In *Frontier Violence: Another Look,* published two years later, W. Eugene Hollon claims that "frontier lawlessness was primarily the result, rather than the cause, of our violent society. The truth is, our frontier heritage produced much more of what is good in the American character than what is bad."[26] It is remarkable that Hollon devotes more than two hundred pages to describing vigilante activities; gunfights in cattle towns; range wars in Texas, Wyoming, and Montana; and violent attacks on ethnic minorities throughout the American West—every imaginable form of violence—and then suggests that the frontier was not really violent. Basically an anecdotal survey of western violence, Hollon's book offers no statistical documentation to support his thesis that the American West was not as violent as eastern cities.

In 1981, Lawrence M. Friedman and Robert V. Percival published their comprehensive study of crime in Alameda County, California, which revealed "only four homicides in the county in 1893," or a homicide rate of 4 per 100,000.[27] Despite being heavily quantitative, Friedman and Percival's study provides only anecdotal observations and fails to establish homicide rates (either in tabular or graphic form) for the four decades studied. They concluded that "homicide was not particularly common in Alameda County."[28] In fairness to the authors, their study is concerned principally with crime in general and the operation of the Alameda County criminal justice system.

In his 1984 study of crime and violence in the boom and bust gold towns of Aurora and Bodie, Roger McGrath found high homicide rates.[29] In a critical review, Robert R. Dykstra claims that McGrath's use of statistics is "unsophisticated," and he criticizes his comparison of homicide rates of Aurora and Bodie with those of modern cities.[30] Another historian judged McGrath's study weak "because it relies primarily on traditional literary sources and lacks a quantitative research design."[31] McGrath found homicide rates of 116 and 64 per 100,000, respectively, in Bodie and Aurora. Although these homicide rates are extremely high, they may be unreliable. McGrath's study of the two gold camps covers a limited time span, from 1861 to 1864 in Aurora and 1877 to 1882 in Bodie. In other words, he examined only a combined ten-year period for the two gold camps. Despite finding high homicide rates, McGrath suggests that "in most ways the towns were not violent or lawless places."[32]

New western historians have spent very little time discussing violence. In *The Legacy of Conquest,* Patricia Nelson Limerick does place violence within the context of the conquest of Native Americans and Hispanics, and the brutalization of racial and ethnic groups, but she provides no framework for personal violence in the American West.[33] Richard White, in *"It's Your Misfortune and None of My Own,"* discusses the context of violence in the West and suggests that "the violence practiced by men against other men is fairly well documented. Two studies of largely male towns, one an examination of cattle towns . . . and the other a study of two California mining towns, address the question of crime and male personal violence."[34] He is, of course, referring to the studies by Dykstra and McGrath. Repeating Dykstra's earlier error, White claims that "during the peak years of the cattle towns, the average number of homicides was only 1.5 a year for each town." He further suggests that "gun control and regular police forces were, by and large, successful in curtailing violence."[35] White's discussion of violence in his chapter "Social Conflict" is flawed by historical inaccuracies and the misuse of statistics.[36] In his defense, however, it was not his intention to focus on violence or any other single topic, and he has provided the reader with an excellent synthesis of new western history. In essence, a survey of the debate on violence indicates that neither traditional nor new western historians have really explained violence within a proper framework. However, by using a lethal-violence paradigm and social-history techniques to examine homicide, it is possible to measure lethal violence in the American West.

Homicide Methodology

Defining homicide is not an easy task. Generally, homicide means the killing of a human being by another. In the past, the terms "homicide" and "murder" have been used interchangeably. In this study, however, "murder" is a legal term used to define whether the defendant was convicted of murder in the first or second degree, and "homicide" is broadly defined as any killing of one human being by another that cannot be clearly identified as accidental, which is the general definition applied by coroners.[37] These distinctions are important because many homicide studies use criminal indictments or informations as the measure of homicide occurrence, but by doing so exclude from their analyses many actual killings such as lynchings, duels, police shootings, and blood feuds. Using only criminal indictments also creates methodological problems stemming from the American West's transient population, lawless elements that lynched victims with impunity, the concept of self-defense,[38] and inefficient law enforcement. In all three counties, coroner's records offer an important source of data for explaining homicide.

The common practice of carrying concealed weapons on the western frontier helped to create a situation that virtually assured a high homicide rate. Equally important is the fact that prosecutors, judges, and juries usually accepted this behavior and would not always prosecute or convict local citizens accused of murder.[39] Therefore, this study is based on coroner's inquests coupled with court case files and newspaper accounts, a method that assures a fuller accounting of the actual homicides.[40] It is believed that about 90 to 95 percent of all homicides committed in the three counties are represented in the data sample.

Historically, homicide in the United States has been a crime dominated by males. Females seldom committed homicides and were more likely to be victims than perpetrators. Eric Mottram notes that "most homicides in America are committed with handguns in the hands of people who are not habitual criminals, but are acting under impulse during quarrels with relatives and friends. Social disorganization among men . . . is a major cause of destructive violence."[41] James Buchanan Given describes homicide as "a social relationship. For a killing to take place, at least two people must interact, if only for a single moment. . . . murder is patterned by the prevailing relationships—affective, economic, political—that exist within a society."[42] This brief human interaction provides an opportunity to examine the complex interrelationships of gender, race, homicide, and justice. The socialization of the killer and victim can be studied by examining coroner's inquests, court records, newspaper accounts, and census data. These sources create a composite picture that makes it possible to evaluate the treatment of diverse defendants charged with murder.

As a starting point, coroner's inquests contribute basic data about the crime, including race, gender, time, age, occupation, location, relationship, and cause. They are the best source of homicide data at the county level.[43] Registers of criminal action record the date of the indictment, name of the defendant, court case number, attorneys, judge, and a variety of other information, including the final disposition of the case. Preliminary hearings sometimes provide the only factual testimony by witnesses. Trial transcripts are seldom available unless the case was appealed. If, however, the perpetrator received the death penalty and the case was appealed or a pardon was requested, a complete transcript is on file with the governor's office or pardons board.

When a homicide occurred, a county coroner held an inquest over the body of the victim.[44] He usually selected six to twelve men to act as inquest jurors and then called witnesses to testify. After the inquest the coroner filed his report with the county clerk, and if he knew the name of the accused, he had power to issue a warrant of arrest. When law enforcement authorities apprehended the suspect, the defendant was questioned by the sheriff or arresting officer. Preliminary hearings usually were held in a justice or other inferior court. Since the defendant was not entitled to an attorney until the trial phase, this hearing could be crucial. Defendants were fair game, and prosecutors took advantage, subjecting them to penetrating examination that sometimes ended in an admission of guilt. Many of the plea bargains by racial minorities were entered because of damaging statements made by defendants during preliminary hearings.[45]

After the preliminary hearing the defendant was usually jailed to await a grand jury indictment or the filing of the prosecutor's information. At the arraignment, if the defendant asked to be represented by an attorney, the court would appoint one from a pool of lawyers waiting in the courtroom. A typical early-twentieth-century murder trial averaged between five and seven days.[46] When a guilty verdict was returned, the judge set a sentencing date. With the pronouncement of sentence, the defendant returned to the county jail to await transportation to prison or, in case of the death penalty, execution.

By comparing indictment data from Douglas, Las Animas, and Gila counties, it is possible to determine whether discrimination against minorities occurred in their criminal justice systems, and whether certain minorities were treated differently in one or all of the counties. Data analysis included a cross-comparison by ethnic identity as well as by county, and a comparison of homicide-variable data on victim and perpetrator (race, gender, time, age, occupation, location, relationship, and cause) may help to reveal why certain ethnic groups committed interracial killings while others did not.

Points of Convergence

An assessment of whether racial bias in criminal justice systems was endemic or prevalent only in isolated areas can be made by selecting counties that include the rapid convergence of diverse cultures, industrialization, and differing social systems from three different states in the American West. The time frame (1880–1920) is also important because many convergences occurred throughout the West during this era.

Douglas County, Nebraska, displays significant urban influences shaped by Omaha, a major railroad and stockyard center. The Great Migration of blacks from the South had an important impact on Omaha, a rapidly growing urban center situated on the Missouri River on the eastern flank of the Great Plains. Housing and employment discrimination were common and severely restricted black mobility. Within a decade the black population in Douglas County jumped from 811 to 4,665 in 1890 and thereafter remained stable until the First World War era, when it doubled to 10,315 in one decade. These figures reflect the out-migration of blacks from the South, who often brought with them experiences of racism and violence. Although never more than 5 percent of the total population, they are overrepresented in homicide statistics.

Las Animas County, Colorado, exhibits a more complex ethnic composition. The economic prosperity from coal mining was accompanied by a rapid influx into small towns of diverse ethnic groups, primarily Hispanic, Italian, Greek, and eastern European immigrants. Population within the county doubled from 8,903 in 1880 to 17,208 by 1890, and then jumped 50 percent within the decade following 1900. Trinidad, centrally located in the Purgatoire River valley, became the county seat and the center of economic activity. The evolution of the Colorado Fuel and Iron Company's management of company towns such as Starkville, Primero, Segundo, Valdéz, and Ludlow (averaging about 800 to 1,400 inhabitants each), coupled with company-controlled marshals, the operation of company stores with high prices, and the lack of competition, engendered deep-seated animosity toward mine operators. This adversarial relationship between the miners and northern European elites who aligned themselves with Colorado Fuel and Iron and other coal companies—best exhibited by the mining strikes of 1902–3 and the Ludlow massacre of 1914—may help to explain high violence levels in this region.

Gila County, Arizona, provides another dimension for examining homicide. In this county, the displacement and eventual control of Apaches by white society added to the volatile ethnic mix. Gila County is located in southeastern Arizona just ninety miles east of Phoenix. Globe, the county seat, is situated between the Apache Mountains to the north and the Pinal range to the south. East of Globe, portions of the San Carlos and Fort Apache reservations fall within the legal jurisdiction of the county. After the discovery of rich copper deposits in the mountains around Globe, the white population increased quickly from 2,021 in 1890 to 4,973 in 1900, and it doubled again within a decade. A region of intense conflict between whites and Apaches, Gila County offers an excellent chance to examine the treatment of Native American defendants accused of homicide. Together these three counties provide an opportunity to examine homicide, race, and justice in the American West.

Organization

This study is organized into a major summary and comparison of the homicide data for the three counties, three case studies, and a final discussion of violence levels in the West. Chapter 2 offers a comparison of aggregate homicide data within the three counties. Here the focus is on gender, race, time and place, cause, homicide scenarios, weapons, homicide rates, and accused/indicted ratios. Chapter 3 examines the black experience in Omaha, Nebraska. This chapter includes a discussion of the migration of blacks into Omaha, the formation of a black community, practices of discrimination, criminal problems within the ghetto, the impact of alcohol, and an evaluation of indictment data. It will be demonstrated that a subculture of violence existed among Omaha's black population and that racial minorities received harsher treatment under the white-dominated criminal justice system.

Chapter 4 provides an assessment of the social instability that permeated Las Animas County, Colorado. An examination of the interaction of Hispanic, Italian, eastern European, Greek, black, and other white coal miners in company towns, including their struggle for union organization, reveals the presence of a regional culture of violence. Chapter 5 focuses on the development of Apache culture, white intrusion and takeover, and the clash of these two cultures in Gila County, Arizona. The discovery of silver and gold in the mountains surrounding Globe, Arizona, encouraged whites to move into this region. With the development of copper mining during the 1890s, the demand for labor quickly created an ethnically diverse population that remained unstable for two decades. Both white and Apache societies in Gila County also displayed a proclivity for a regional culture of violence, but Apache defendants paid a higher price than white defendants. Finally, chapter 6 provides an assessment of the implications of high lethal-violence levels.

Comparative methods will not be restricted to the three counties surveyed. Previous research has revealed that homicide indictment rates in eastern cities declined throughout the period under study. Therefore, a comparison of data from this study with those from a similar study of seven counties in California; Dickinson County, Kansas; and findings from Boston, New York City, and Philadelphia will be instructive. If homicide is a fair measure, and I think it is, the data offer definitive evidence that the American West was indeed more violent than the East.

Murder Most Foul

Comparative Homicide Data

Homicide has been a popular topic for social scientists for years, but until recently researchers have concentrated mainly on twentieth-century eastern urban centers. The best examples of methodology have been provided by sociologists, including H. C. Brearley, who in 1932 suggested that "the homicide problem has received relatively little study in the United States."[1] Using vital statistics and other data, Brearley concluded that homicide rates per 100,000 population increased from 5 to 8.5 from 1906 through 1929. Sociologist Marvin E. Wolfgang, in a 1958 study of homicide in Philadelphia (1948–52), used police records to develop a sophisticated model for statistical analyses.[2] Wolfgang notes that "on the local county level of inquiry, direct use of coroners' files may be possible," but he suggests that they "lack details of the offense and of investigation which police files possess."[3] Although Wolfgang provides an important framework for examining homicide, his study is narrow, covering a five-year period in one city without cross-cultural analysis. Nevertheless, he does ask important questions dealing with factors such as race, gender, time, and place.[4]

In 1979, Roger Lane's *Violent Death in the City* provided a historical model for the statistical examination of nineteenth-century homicide and suicide.[5] Lane views the urban setting—with well-organized police forces, courts, and local regimentation—as the best arena for investigating violent behavior. He claims that "the records of mortality are superior to those of criminality . . . in that virtually all violent deaths of adults were officially registered in some fashion."[6] Lane discarded both arrest records and coroner's inquests: the former because they were unreliable, and the latter because they "are available for only a few years." He claims that "only one satisfactory measure of homicide remains: the number of indictments prepared for the grand juries each year."[7] The weak link in his research, however, lies in his use of indictments as a measure of homicide occurrence. He agrees that the coroner's inquest verdicts would be a good source of recording homicide data, but because they were unavailable, he relies on indictments as an indicator of homicides rates. Using this methodology in studying the nineteenth-century American West would eliminate a significant number of homicides such as lynchings, interracial killings, and so forth.

Although a significant body of eastern urban and modern studies exist,[8] homicide as a form of violence remains virtually unexplored in the American West. This study, by developing and comparing ratios of actual homicides (by linking coroner's inquests with indictments to produce accused/indicted ratios),[9] discloses whether Native Americans, blacks, Asians, and Hispanics, as well as other whites, received equal justice. Any pattern of discrimination will be discovered. By comparing homicide data, including coroner's inquests, indictments, plea bargains, and sentences across both racial and regional lines, it is possible to document whether bias existed within the criminal justice system. Further, by establishing the relative levels of lethal violence in the American West and comparing this information with data from eastern urban centers during a similar time frame, any differences in the two regions' violence levels are revealed.

Homicides occurred frequently in the American West, and newspapers usually covered such crimes with banner headlines and detailed descriptions of the killing. For example, in Trinidad, Colorado, an August 1908 headline blared: "Despoiler of home riddled with 4 charges of buckshot."[10] In this particular case, Charles M. Moore's wife was about to "run off" with Abe Cohn. Mrs. Moore and Cohn, a young painter, had been carrying on a love affair for some time. Although unable to catch them in the act, Moore suspected something was going on and decided it was time to act. When Moore discovered that his wife had packed and removed a trunk full of clothes from the house, he immediately suspected that she intended to run off with Cohn. Moore picked up a shotgun, loaded it, filled his pocket with shotgun shells, and proceeded to the railroad depot. There he stood in the shadows and observed his wife with Cohn.

Table 2.1 Homicide Cases
by County, 1880–1920

County	N
Douglas	391
Las Animas	372
Gila	214
Total	977

Source: Coroner's inquests.

Moore walked quickly up to Cohn and gave him both barrels. The killer calmly reloaded his shotgun and fired two more rounds into the helpless victim lying on the ground. A reporter noted that "the dead man has the entire back of his head on the right side torn off and the left arm was broken near the shoulder."[11] The next day Moore showed no remorse for his crime, and the public sympathized with him. Two days after the murder, details revealed at the coroner's inquest created a sensation. Harry Williams, a friend of Cohn's, admitted that he had seen Mrs. Moore and Cohn driving together on several occasions.[12] Juries seldom convicted men or women for "protecting" their family, and the sympathetic jury found Moore not guilty.

The aggregate data for this study consist of 977 homicide cases recorded between 1880 and 1920 (table 2.1). Douglas County, with the largest population, contributed 391 cases, followed by Las Animas and Gila counties with 372 and 214, respectively. Variable data coded include names of the victim and perpetrator, crime location, date, time, day of week, sex, age, ethnic identity, occupation, weapon, alcohol use, relationship, cause, and coroner and indictment information.

Homicide in the American West tended to be a crime committed by a male under the influence of alcohol in a saloon or outside on the street, typically late at night. The homicide usually resulted from some minor disputes with an acquaintance, and more often than not was committed with a handgun. Evening hours proved the most dangerous, particularly on weekends. Dance halls and saloons provided a common meeting place for males in Omaha, Trinidad, Aguilar, Sopris, Globe, Payson, and Miami, and everyone seemed to carry a handgun.

In family disputes, victims often were killed in their own homes. Love trysts, gunfights, and police shootings add a further dimension to homicide in the

Table 2.2 Victims by Gender, 1880–1920

County	Female		Male	
	(N)	(%)	(N)	(%)
Douglas	75	19.5	310	80.5
Las Animas	44	12.5	308	87.5
Gila	41	19.7	167	80.3
Average		17.2		22.7

Source: Coroner's inquests.

Table 2.3 Perpetrators by Gender, 1880–1920

County	Female		Male	
	(N)	(%)	(N)	(%)
Douglas	26	6.8	356	93.2
Las Animas	4	1.0	360	99.0
Gila	6	2.9	202	97.1
Average		3.5		96.4

Source: Coroner's inquests.

American West. Finally, as a result of the homicide, the accused, if indicted, began a journey through the criminal justice system, which usually punished ethnic and racial minorities more severely than whites.

Gender

Males, as perpetrators and victims, dominated homicide in Douglas, Las Animas, and Gila counties. Women seldom committed homicides, but they fell victim to an average 17.2 percent of all homicides (table 2.2). Gender relationships between victim and accused reveal that many female victims were killed by their husbands, whereas few of the male victims were killed by their spouses. Most of the female victims knew their perpetrators (other than their spouses). Females were more likely to be killed by related family members and roommates. Strangers seldom killed females; when they did, the victims usually were prostitutes or targets of robbery. Female victims were killed in their own homes more often than in any other location.

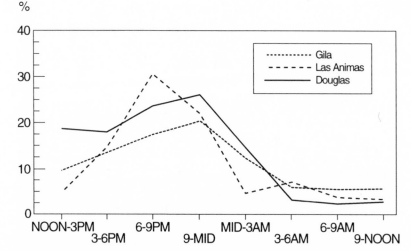

%

Fig. 2.1. Homicide by time of day in Douglas, Las Animas, and Gila counties, 1880–1920. *Source:* Coroner's inquests.

Males committed 96.4 percent of the homicides within the three counties (table 2.3). More than a third of the male victims were killed in saloons or on the streets in front of them. After spending the day laboring in a mine, meatpacking plant, or a ranch, men liked to spend their evenings drinking and gambling. Fights that started in a saloon often spilled out onto the street. Analysis of time, place, cause, and scenario will help to place homicide in the West in proper perspective.

Time

Homicides can occur at virtually any time or place, but in these three counties perpetrators often committed their crimes at night (fig. 2.1). The hours between 6 P.M. and 9 P.M. proved the most dangerous in Animas County, while in Douglas and Gila counties, the most deadly hours were between 9 P.M. and midnight. In Las Animas County, coal miners left work in late afternoon and flocked into the saloons in the various company towns. Heavy drinking began early, and consequently fights started earlier than in Omaha and Globe, where alcohol-related killings were more common later in the evening. After midnight, however, homicides were committed less often.

Homicide time patterns display a strong correlation with day of week, and with the saloons open on Sundays, weekends proved lethal. In Douglas and Las

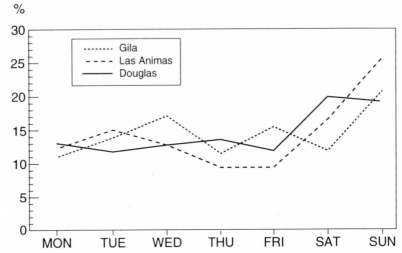

Fig. 2.2. Homicide by weekday in Douglas, Las Animas, and Gila counties, 1880–1920. *Source:* Coroner's inquests.

Animas counties, most homicides occurred on Saturday and Sunday (fig. 2.2). All three counties experienced high homicide rates on Sunday. Half of the homicides in each county occurred on weekends, again reflecting the tendency of men to congregate in saloons, pool parlors, dance halls, and brothels. After a few drinks an earlier grievance might surface, or an alleged insult or any of a variety of things could quickly trigger a violent confrontation.

Place

Homicide location varied somewhat, but in all three counties, many homicides occurred on the streets (table 2.4). The victim's home proved to be the second most common location for homicides, followed by saloons, the perpetrator's home, and other buildings. In Omaha, more than half of the homicides were committed in saloons or on streets.

In Las Animas County, more than half of the homicides were committed in saloons, in victim's homes, or on the streets. Saloons and alcohol-dispensing dance halls were the only recreational facilities in the company towns, and when fights broke out within saloons, the streets around them tended to be another flash point for homicides. Homicide patterns in Las Animas County were spread out among the coal camps and small towns along the Purgatoire River valley. Many of the homicides occurred in Trinidad, followed by Ludlow,

Table 2.4 Homicide Locations, 1880–1920

Location	Douglas (%)	Las Animas (%)	Gila (%)
Victim's home	25.8	18.4	24.4
Street	38.7	16.0	21.8
Saloon	13.2	18.4	7.4
Perp's home	6.4	3.4	—
Farm/ranch	0.8	4.7	1.0
County road	1.0	10.6	13.3
Reservation	—	—	20.7
Mine	—	20.2	1.5
Other building	10.7	6.8	4.7

Source: Coroner's inquests.

Delagua, Aguilar, and Segundo. A significant number of killings were committed in isolated areas. These statistics reflect the influence of Italian vendettas or feuds. Many of these cases remained unsolved. In some circumstances the county attorney could not gather enough evidence to prosecute.

Gila County offers another spatial perspective with 20.7 percent of its homicides occurring on the San Carlos Reservation. The number of saloon-related homicides is significantly lower. The Globe and Miami street killings include altercations that began in saloons and then spilled out into the streets for gunfights. However, the victim's home was the most likely place for a homicide to occur, followed by streets, the reservation, and county roads (see table 2.4).

Race and ethnicity help to account for the variety of homicide sites within the three counties. The impact of black culture provides an important variable for understanding violent crime in Douglas County. The high rate of homicide occurrence in the streets and saloons reflects the mixing of whites and blacks in downtown Omaha's red-light district, which, outside of the workplace, was virtually the only place where these two races intermingled on a regular basis. High interracial homicide rates for blacks reveal the outcome of such interaction. In Las Animas County, homicides were even more likely to occur in saloons than in either Douglas or Gila counties, reflecting the heavy drinking in company-town saloons by Italian, Greek, Bohemian, Austrian, Croatian, Serbian, and other recent European immigrants. Interracial and inter-ethnic homicides were relatively common in these coal-company towns, where Hispanics, Italians, and blacks were likely to select someone from another ethnic group as a victim. Once again, the interaction of differing racial or ethnic groups provided the opportunity for such killings to occur. Miners' strikes also contributed to the large number of killings (20 percent) that occurred on coal mine property. The large number of homicides on the San Carlos Reservation in Gila County also attests to the significant impact of race or ethnicity. Although there were interracial killings involving Apaches and white victims during the early period, by 1900 intraracial homicides became the rule.

Cause

Modern homicide detectives are well equipped to evaluate perpetrators' reasons for killing; however, because researchers lack access to physical evidence, witnesses' statements, interviews of defendants, and other information, it is not feasible to evaluate motives beyond a cursory discussion.[13] Quarrels (a dispute between two participants not married or related) were the most common immediate causal factor in homicides (table 2.5). Domestic disputes proved to be the second most common causal factor, followed by brawls, police shootings, and robberies. All three counties had significant numbers of police shootings. In Douglas County, robberies doubled the percentages found in the other two counties. Strike and vendetta causal factors existed only in Las Animas County and reflect coal mining strikes and the large number of Italian immigrants. Abortion-related deaths of women were not common but did occur.

In Douglas County, quarrels were the most common causal factor, followed by domestic disputes, robberies, brawls, and police shootings. Quarrels, sometimes interracial, occurred in saloons, dance halls, brothels, and on the streets of Omaha. Domestic disputes also were common and sometimes involved love triangles. This is reflected in twenty-six cases that included a homicide followed by a suicide. All of these cases involved male perpetrators. Robberies in Omaha sometimes included shoot-outs between police and robbers on the streets in front of jewelry stores and banks.

In Las Animas County, petty disputes that turned into violent quarrels were the most important causal factor. The list of grievances included too much foam on the beer, unpaid fifty-cent bets, pool games, bar tabs, and a myriad of other minor issues. Strike-related killings were significant in Las Animas County. The appearance of mining company guards, Baldwin-Felts detectives, Colorado National Guardsmen, and armed miners proved to be a deadly mix, especially in Ludlow, the most explosive example. Police shootings involving company-town marshals, deputy sheriffs, and police attempting to arrest citizens provided

Table 2.5 Homicide Causes, 1880–1920

Cause	Douglas (%)	Las Animas (%)	Gila (%)
Domestic	26.3	13.4	19.6
Quarrel	41.5	38.7	58.2
Brawl	8.4	8.1	5.8
Killed by police	4.2	7.1	8.9
Police killed	2.6	1.8	2.1
Robbery	10.0	4.0	4.2
Abortion	1.5	0.3	—
Vendetta/feud	—	6.5	—
Strike	—	17.5	—

Source: Coroner's inquests.

another deadly combination. Finally, vendettas reflected the influence of an Italian subculture in southeastern Colorado. Killings were committed to get even with another family that had committed a previous killing.

As in the other two counties, quarrels between unrelated persons were the most common antecedent for killings in Gila County, accounting for 58 percent. Again, they usually began over trivial matters in saloons and ended on the streets of Globe or Miami with shootouts between two armed men. Domestic disputes were common; twelve cases, all involving female victims, included homicide followed by suicide. Police shootings usually involved attempts to arrest citizens under the influence of alcohol.

The data for the three counties reveal various causal factors, but it is significant that race or ethnicity sometimes became an important variable. Whether it was a quarrel between a black and a white in an Omaha saloon, a vendetta in Las Animas County, or a dispute between an Apache and a white in Gila County, the results could be deadly.

Weapons

These three counties also offer an opportunity for weapons analysis, particularly the use of handguns. Until recently, there had been little research exploring weapon use during the commission of homicides in the West. In studying Philadelphia, Roger Lane discovered that 25 percent of the defendants used guns to commit homicides in Philadelphia between 1839 and 1901.[14] Unlike the

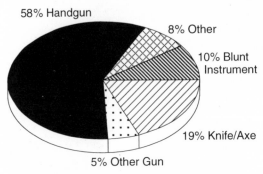

Fig. 2.3. Weapon use in Douglas County, 1880–1920. *Source:* Coroner's inquests.

residents of eastern counties, however, those in Douglas, Las Animas, and Gila counties often carried concealed weapons.

Cheap handguns were plentiful in the American West. Most weighed fifteen to sixteen ounces and had three-inch barrels that could easily be concealed in coat or pants pockets. Laws prohibited carrying concealed weapons, but few obeyed them.[15] The carrying of handguns ensured that violent physical confrontations would often be lethal. In the late nineteenth and early twentieth centuries, victims of assaults with knives, blunt instruments, and fists had a better chance of surviving than those shot with firearms.[16] By their very nature handguns, rifles, and shotguns were more lethal. This helps to explain the high homicide rate for Las Animas County. Instead of ending as an assault with a deadly weapon causing injuries that would probably heal, shootings usually concluded with a homicide, partly because doctors were not trained to deal with the trauma associated with such wounds.

Most defendants accused of homicide in Omaha had used handguns patterned on the Webley British Bulldog double-action revolver (patented in 1883), a model with an easily concealed two- or three-inch barrel. Smith and Wesson, Colt, and other American arms manufacturers copied this design and produced large quantities of these five-shot revolvers in several models, including .38 and .32 calibers.[17] In Omaha, those in search of quick solutions to quarrels could purchase guns almost anywhere.[18]

A breakdown of weapons used by residents of Omaha to commit homicides is remarkable. More than half chose handguns, compared to 5 percent who selected rifles or shotguns (fig. 2.3). Assailants used knives less frequently and

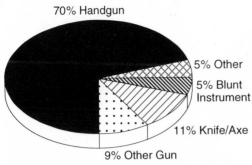

70% Handgun

5% Other

5% Blunt
Instrument

11% Knife/Axe

9% Other Gun

Fig. 2.4. Weapon use in Las Animas County, 1880–1920. *Source:* Coroner's inquests.

seldom chose blunt instruments. The high handgun-homicide rate may indicate the absence of gun-law enforcement in Omaha.[19] Similar weapons patterns were discovered in Las Animas County, where, again, most people who committed homicide used handguns (fig. 2.4).[20] A smaller number selected rifles, shotguns, knives, and blunt instruments. In a pattern that became all too familiar in towns like Trinidad, Segundo, Sopris, and Aguilar, men carried concealed handguns when visiting saloons, and apparently lawmen did not enforce concealed-weapons laws. Of the homicides in Gila County, Arizona, 82 percent were committed with guns, and more than half with handguns (fig. 2.5). Numerous cases involved two men shooting it out in the street.

Why did so many assailants in Douglas, Las Animas, and Gila counties choose to carry weapons? According to Philip D. Jordan, "First, men liked weapons, wanted weapons, enjoyed the power that weapons lent them, and insisted on having and using and carrying and handling them as they pleased." Second, many men "were disciples of a religion known as the 'higher law.'" Finally, sometimes weapons were required for self-defense.[21] Also, as noted above, cheap handguns were easy to acquire. "Suicide specials" manufactured by Iver Johnson, Harrington and Richardson, Remington, and Forehand and Wadsworth could be had for two or three dollars, and even a Colt or Smith and Wesson could be purchased for about twelve dollars.[22]

Weapons comparisons with recent studies of the twentieth century suggest that the Omaha, Trinidad, and Globe handgun-homicide rates were indeed very high. For example, Margaret Zahn's study of homicide in Philadelphia from 1969 to 1973 revealed that firearms were used 50 percent of the time in the

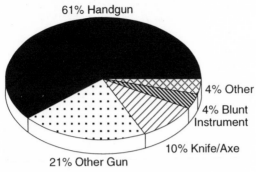

Fig. 2.5. Weapon use in Gila County, 1880–1920. *Source:* Coroner's inquests.

commission of homicides. However, the firearms-homicide rates in such cities as Houston, Miami, and Washington, D.C., jumped significantly after 1955, reaching 82 percent in Washington, D.C., by 1974.[23]

The congregating of well-armed men in saloons, dance halls, and pool halls in all three counties proved to be an important factor in homicides. Although handguns and knives could easily be carried concealed, the open carrying of revolvers seemed most common in Gila and Las Animas counties. Bartenders in all three counties wore handguns openly to "prevent" trouble, but in saloon altercations they only tended to increase the lethal nature of disputes. A discussion of a variety of homicide scenarios will help to place the use of weapons and abuse of alcohol in perspective.

Scenarios

SALOON FIGHTS

Alcohol was a common component of homicide in the American West. Whether it was in a saloon in a small coal mining town like Delagua in Las Animas County, a bar in Omaha, or a *tiswin,* or *tulapai,* party on the San Carlos Reservation, the consumption of alcohol could be deadly. In all three counties, 56 percent or more of the participants in homicides had been drinking (table 2.6), and communities maintained large numbers of saloons. At any given hour of the night, particularly on weekends, such bars were filled with coal miners, meatpacking employees, railroad workers, gamblers, merchants, and common laborers. The mixture of blacks, Hispanics, Apaches, Italians, Greeks, east Europeans, and other whites also made these drinking establishments hot spots for fights.

Table 2.6 Alcohol Use by Victim/Perpetrator,
1880–1920

	Douglas (%)	Las Animas (%)	Gila (%)
Perpetrator	75.4	60.2	71.4
Victim	65.2	56.3	63.9

Source: Coroner's inquests.

A common aspect of many saloon homicides is the minor nature of their origins. For example, on October 10, 1906, State Jones entered the Mandolin Saloon in Globe, Arizona, and demanded payment of a thirty-five-cent debt from Henry Davis. Both men began to argue loudly. Davis pulled a revolver and shot Jones to death on the spot.[24] In a similar case Samuel Jacobs and Manuel Hernández argued over a card game in a coal mining camp in Las Animas County. Within seconds Jacobs drew a revolver and killed his antagonist.[25]

With men carrying guns, and saloon arguments occurring over such minor issues, bartending could be dangerous. Bartenders usually prepared themselves for such possibilities and wore handguns in plain sight, but sometimes saloon keepers could not avoid shootings, and being prepared increased their chances of survival. During the forty years covered by this study, eighteen bartenders fell victim to shootings, but thirty-one killed customers in saloon altercations. All of the bartenders who killed customers in Gila County used handguns, and more than half of those in Douglas and Las Animas counties employed them also. Bartenders as victims usually died from wounds inflicted with handguns. Only one homicide case involved a bartender using a shotgun. The famous "shotgun behind the counter" film scenario apparently is a myth, or perhaps bartenders did not have a chance to use it.

In March 1908, one of the most intriguing cases involved Edward James, who entered a saloon in Bowen, Colorado, and demanded a beer. He told the bartender to "be quick about it." After being served, James complained that there was "too much foam on his beer," which started a quick, heated argument. Both drew revolvers, but bartender John Russik won, instantly killing James.[26] On December 1, 1895, in Globe, Arizona, Roderick McContach shot bartender William Gill after arguing about a bar bill.[27] Although he was indicted for murder, the charges were dropped. Three years later, in a similar Globe saloon incident, Charles Dye demanded a drink on credit. Bartender R. M. Anderson refused. Both men began to argue loudly, both pulled handguns, and, once again, the bartender won. A coroner's inquest exonerated Anderson.[28]

In July 1905, in the coal mining camp of Hastings, Colorado, Giovanni Raino and Garlano Falsetti argued loudly in a saloon and then rushed out the door into the street. Both drew weapons and fired. Both died on the spot.[29] Perpetrators of such killings could be vicious. In June 1916, William Sparks and Frank Thompson carried their dispute into the streets of Globe, where Sparks bested his adversary in a gunfight, returned to the bar for another drink, then walked back out into the street and fired two more shots into his victim, lying prone in the street.[30]

Two shootings that occurred in Aguilar and Trinidad less than two weeks apart remain somewhat mystifying. In both cases the men claimed to be doing the "Curly Bill" spin (spinning the gun with the trigger finger) when their guns "went off." Both victims were women, Lucita Martínez and Rose Myers. Conditions surrounding these cases were suspicious, and no one had observed the actual shootings. Nevertheless, authorities declined to file charges against the male assailants.[31]

On occasion, gunfights occurred on the streets between armed citizens who took offense from the behavior of others. For example, in January 1910, cowboy Jack Lane rode into Payson, Arizona, and began to drink at one of the saloons. A little after 3 P.M., well under the influence, Lane mounted his horse and began to ride up and down the street shooting his revolver. When Lane rode up to William C. Colcord, a local rancher, and made a threatening movement by waving his gun, Colcord quickly pulled his Colt .45 and shot Lane off his horse.[32] No charges were pressed against Colcord. There is every likelihood that the homicide could have been avoided; however, Colcord, a southerner, was practicing the time-honored concept of "no duty to retreat." If both participants were armed, it was legal for the person challenged to shoot the aggressor. Legal authorities in most western states would rule such action self-defense. In another interesting case involving "self-defense," Russell Lynn pulled a gun on James Abbott in a Trinidad saloon. After being called a coward for drawing a gun, Lynn replaced it in his pocket, only to be attacked and stabbed thirteen times by Abbott.[33] A jury found Abbott not guilty. In the eyes of the jurors, he was only defending himself. Numerous other gunfights occurred in which both men were "armed and dangerous."[34]

Love triangles and family fights were comparatively common in Douglas, Las Animas, and Gila counties. The combination of concealed weapons, alcohol, and broken love affairs could be lethal, as in the case of D. B. Munroe and John Handy. The men were drinking together in a Majestic, Colorado, saloon when they commenced to argue whether Mrs. Handy had changed her affections to Munroe. Mrs. Handy was also in the bar that night, and she and Munroe denied the charges. Mrs. Handy accused her husband of consorting with a black woman, a charge he did not deny. Not satisfied with the discussion, John Handy left the saloon, walked home, and secured a revolver. When he returned to the saloon, he confronted Munroe and shot him at close range, inflicting a mortal wound in the abdomen.[35] The sixty-year-old miner died the next day. An understanding jury found Handy not guilty. In a similar case, Bennett Burleson and David Bobb met on horseback near Earl, Colorado, where they began to argue violently. Mrs. Bobb had recently taken up residence with Burleson. The furious Bobb pulled a Winchester 30-30 rifle from a scabbard and shot Burleson dead.[36] A jury found the defendant not guilty. In 1909, another love triangle ended in tragedy when James Justice confronted Edward Butler in Butler's saloon in Trinidad. Justice accused Butler of breaking up his home. After a brief heated argument, Justice pulled a .32 caliber revolver and shot Butler while he stood behind the bar.[37] A jury found Justice not guilty.

Not all cases, however, ended in verdicts of not guilty. Another Las Animas homicide, in 1907, was perpetrated by Santiago Tafoya. He had suspected for some time that his ex-wife was consorting with Pete Griego, but he had been unable to discover them. One morning Tafoya, a coal miner, left for work but returned and went to his ex-wife's house a few hours later, armed with a revolver, and caught the couple in bed. Tafoya shot him as he tried to run out the door. The fact that Tafoya shot Griego five times, and that the woman was no longer his wife, may have influenced the jury. They found Tafoya guilty of murder in the first degree and recommended the death penalty.[38] Ten years later in Las Animas County, José A. Vigil and Reyetas Domíngues argued over a woman, and the angry Vigil went to a pawnshop to redeem his revolver. He then returned to the red-light district on Santa Fe Avenue, where he shot and killed Domíngues.[39] A jury found Vigil guilty.

Several cases involved pimps and prostitutes, particularly in Omaha. On the night of August 15, 1913, John Kane, a white man, visited the "black dives" at the Kuzlo Hotel, apparently seeking prostitutes. Whether the quarrel originated over payment or an insult, Louis Bess, a black, pulled a knife and severely slashed Kane, who bled to death.[40] A jury found Bess guilty of murder and sentenced him to life in prison. In another case, this one involving two blacks in the brothel area near North Fourteenth and California, Ole Jackson shot and killed Alfred Jones with a .38 caliber revolver. After some debate and a split vote, the inquest jury, which included blacks, found in favor of self-defense.[41]

Murder followed by suicide offers another category of homicides related to marital problems. There were twenty-six such cases (6.6 percent of all homicides) in Douglas County, followed by twelve (5.6 percent) in Gila County, and just three cases in Las Animas County.[42] Five Douglas County cases involved love triangles and included a double homicide prior to the suicide. There was one similar case in Gila County. Handguns were the preferred weapon in this category. All perpetrators who committed homicides followed by suicide were males. Six victims in these cases were males.

POLICE SHOOTINGS OF CITIZENS

Today police who shoot and kill citizens are seldom prosecuted and rarely convicted, and beatings of citizens by law enforcement officers, or charges of excessive force, sometimes result in investigations that are not satisfying to the victims. On the other hand, citizens who shoot and kill law enforcement officers can expect severe punishment from the criminal justice system. It is a peculiar dichotomy. By examining the treatment of police shootings within the criminal justice systems of Douglas, Las Animas, and Gila counties during the period 1880 to 1920, we may gain some insights on public perception of law enforcement.

Police shootings occurred in all three counties, with a total of seventy-seven cases (7.8 percent of all homicides). Most (fifty-five cases) involved law enforcement officers killing citizens; twenty-two cases resulted in the shooting of police by citizens. Las Animas County had the highest number of police shootings (twenty-nine) followed by Douglas (twenty-seven), and Gila (twenty-one).[43] Police shootings with citizens as victims usually resulted from law enforcement officers attempting to make arrests. The number of these incidents increased significantly after the 1890s, reaching a high point during the first decade of the twentieth century (fig. 2.6). Only Douglas County continued to show an increase in police shootings after 1910.

The development of modern law enforcement came gradually in the three counties. Virtually anyone could become a town marshal or qualify as a police officer or sheriff's deputy. Prospective law enforcement officers usually gained office through patronage. If you were related to or knew the sheriff or chief of

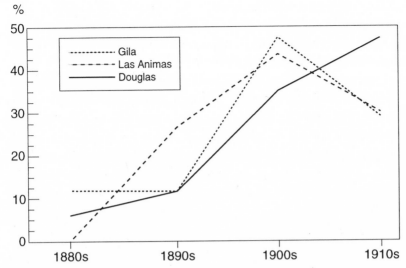

Fig. 2.6. Police shootings of citizens in Gila, Las Animas, and Douglas counties, 1880–1920. *Source:* Coroner's inquests.

police, it was easy to gain employment. It was common in Las Animas and Gila counties to hire men who not only knew how to use guns but were willing to use them. The development of private police in coal and copper mining towns only complicated things.[44] The Colorado Fuel and Iron Company relied on the Baldwin-Felts Detective Agency to hire gunmen to police their property. During the 1913–14 coal strike, Las Animas County Sheriff J. S. Grisham "deputized" all 348 of the guards at the coal mines, providing them with a cloak of authority both on and off company property. This may help explain the motivation behind the shooting of union organizer Gerald Lippiatt in downtown Trinidad by Baldwin-Felts guards Walter Belk and George Belcher. The implications of seven bullet wounds exacerbated problems between the coal miners and the Colorado Fuel and Iron Company.[45] These kinds of shootings also increased the general distrust of law enforcement.

A variety of factors helps to explain police shooting incidents. First, alcohol played an important role. A majority of the citizens killed by law enforcement were drinking prior to the incidents (94 percent, 86 percent, and 82 percent, respectively, for Las Animas, Gila, and Douglas counties). Many police officers also had been drinking before these shootings (24 percent, 36 percent, and 18 percent, respectively). Second, shootings normally occurred on streets during attempts by law enforcement officers to arrest citizens, usually for disturbing the peace. In most cases a lone officer had to make the arrest. The lawman some-times found himself confronted by several friends of the suspect, and in such instances the threat of being overpowered may have precipitated the use of lethal force. Third, the practice of carrying concealed weapons increased the danger for police officers, town marshals, and deputy sheriffs attempting to arrest suspects. Any furtive move by the suspect might have caused the officer to shoot first, under the assumption that he was about to be shot. The number of officers killed (twenty-two) indicates that it could be a deadly business. Finally, because of nepotism and patronage, law enforcement officers were sometimes employed for their connections, not qualifications. Many of the town marshals, coal company guards, police officers, and sheriff's deputies lacked experience.[46] Under the stressful conditions of attempting an arrest, this could result in poor judgment. The data indicate that this was common.

The typical police shooting occurred at night on a dark street or in a saloon, included alcohol as a factor, and involved an attempt by a law enforcement officer to arrest a male suspect for disturbing the peace. One such case occurred on December 12, 1902, when Trinidad policeman John Boyle received a call at 1:30 A.M. to stop a fight at the Gem Saloon. As he entered the front door, several of the participants, including Adolfo Griego, slipped out the back door. As Boyle stepped out the back door, Griego and another man tossed rocks at him. Boyle ordered them to halt, but even after he fired in the air, they continued throwing rocks. None of the rocks struck the officer, but, by now exasperated, Boyle fired at the suspects in the darkness, fatally wounding Griego.[47] No formal charges were pressed. A similar case four years later involved Constable Andy Mayes, who attempted to arrest Tom Dagoney on a street in Globe, Arizona. Under the influence of alcohol, Dagoney threatened to "whip" the marshal. During a scuffle Dagoney struck Constable Mayes with a rock. Mayes drew his revolver and shot Dagoney three times.[48] A coroner's inquest ruled that Mayes acted in self-defense.

Sometimes lawmen became involved in shootings in the streets that resem-bled "High Noon" gunfights. When Antonio Mendoza drew a revolver and fired upon Sheriff Edward P. Shanley in Globe, Arizona, in 1905, Shanley drew his revolver, shot, and mortally wounded his assailant.[49] Two years later, on October 31, 1907, John W. Nelson fired at Deputy Sheriff Oscar Felton on Broad Street in Globe. Though wounded in the leg, Felton drew his .38 revolver and killed Nelson.[50]

Police shootings were often unpredictable. On April 20, 1906, John James, under the influence of alcohol, pulled his gun and "terrorized" citizens on the main street of Starkville, Colorado. When Sheriff Deputy Charles P. Edgar ordered James to surrender his weapon, he refused to put down his gun and shouted, "Damn you, die!" After a second warning Deputy Edgar shot and killed James.[51] Six years later, after Edgar had become town marshal of Cokedale, he attempted to disarm Frank Vance in a saloon. Vance, an ex-marshal, threatened to shoot Edgar if he did not leave. The *Trinidad Chronicle-News* reported that "with his six-shooter in his hands Frank Vance, who has boasted that he has killed sixteen men in his life time, was last night shot to death in the barroom of the Carbon Club at Cokedale."[52] The coroner found three bullet wounds in Vance. In a similar case later that year, Officer Zeke Martin attempted to arrest C. H. Johnston in a Trinidad boardinghouse. Johnston had purchased a revolver earlier that day and had been threatening to shoot other boarders. Martin ordered him to put the gun down. When Johnston refused, Martin fired one fatal shot.[53] There were other similar "gunfight" scenarios,[54] but none of these officers were prosecuted.

In some cases, lawmen who killed citizens were prosecuted but found not guilty. On May 15, 1899, William Wooten visited Nicolli's Saloon in Hastings, Colorado, and began to drink heavily. Several hours later he pulled his handgun and threatened to shoot anyone who bothered him. Town Marshal Joseph Johnson entered the saloon and tried to "disarm" the suspect. During a scuffle Johnson shot and killed Wooten.[55] On November 7, 1908, Las Animas County Deputy Carlos Sandoval attended a wedding in San Miguel, Colorado. At the celebration some of the intoxicated guests began to fight, and members of the wedding party asked Deputy Sandoval to stop it. During the ensuing brawl, one or more men struck Sandoval in the face. When he pulled his revolver in an attempt to intimidate his adversaries, it discharged.[56] Three years later Marshal E. M. Cook attempted to arrest Pongre Culk on the main street of Delagua, Colorado. Culk and several others had been drinking in a saloon and were continuing their celebration on the street at about 3 A.M. As two company guards and Marshal Cook struggled to subdue Culk, Cook drew his revolver and fired one shot, fatally wounding Culk.[57] Although Las Animas County prosecutors indicted Johnson, Sandoval, and Cook, juries found them not guilty.

In Gila County, prosecutors indicted two sheriff's deputies and a sheriff for shootings. On April 19, 1909, Deputy Sheriff Robert J. Edwards attempted to arrest Nick Zucich for shooting his revolver in the streets of Globe. Zucich had been drinking in the Pioneer Saloon and emerged on the street at about 1 A.M. to celebrate by shooting his gun. In a struggle to disarm him, Deputy Edwards shot Zucich.[58] A jury found Deputy Edwards guilty of manslaughter, the only such verdict for a lawman in Gila County. Two years later Deputy Sheriff S. Y. Hawkins became involved in a dispute with Feliciano Bracamonte on the main street in Winkelman, Arizona. Bracamonte left a saloon shortly after midnight and argued with several of his companions. Hawkins ordered Bracamonte to "stop fooling around, or I will have to arrest you."[59] When Bracamonte continued to quarrel, Deputy Hawkins shot him at close range. An examination of the body revealed that Bracamonte had been unarmed. During the trial, Hawkins insisted that Bracamonte had threatened him and that he had believed the suspect was armed. The jury found him not guilty.[60] Later that same year Gila County Sheriff John Thompson and Harry Temple, a friend, visited a Globe saloon on Broad Street to celebrate Christmas a little early. After drinking for awhile, they began to quarrel with bartender Mike Juraskovich. During a scuffle, Thompson shot and killed the bartender.[61] Although a coroner's jury absolved Sheriff Thompson of guilt, some believed otherwise. On January 4, 1912, Thompson resigned his position at the request of the Gila County Board of Supervisors. Several months later, however, a jury found him not guilty.[62]

Two cases involving the shooting of Apaches deserve examination. On December 5, 1895, Gila County Sheriff Deputy Bill Voris visited the San Carlos Reservation to arrest several Apaches accused of butchering a steer from the Flying V Ranch. Voris organized a posse with two cowboys, and armed with John Doe warrants, they proceeded to the reservation to arrest the cattle thieves. They soon came upon a camp where Nan-tan-go-tagze and several other Apaches were sitting around a campfire roasting a steer. Finding his group outnumbered, Voris pulled his revolver and shot Nan-tan-go-tagze. The posse quickly fled.[63] The Gila County coroner did not bother to conduct an inquest, and the county attorney declined to prosecute Voris.

On the night of February 18, 1906, Arizona Ranger J. B. Holmes received a complaint that some Apaches were drinking and creating a disturbance at an Indian camp near Roosevelt. In the company of Fred Russell and Chuna Eskah, the Apache who complained of the disturbance, Holmes rode out to the camp. During a coroner's inquest, Russell testified that upon reaching the camp, Holmes said, "There he is" and shined a light on an Apache standing by a wagon with a rifle in his hands. The Apache was not aiming his weapon at them. Justice of the Peace J. C. Evans asked Russell what happened next. "Holmes made some remark 'Hi, there! With that gun!' and fired almost at the same time."[64] After examining the body, Dr. R. F. Palmer discovered "wounds of entrance five in number" in the victim's body. Matze, the victim of the shooting, had not been involved in the drinking argument at the Apache camp. All witnesses agreed that Holmes began shooting at the same time he shouted and that the victim did not make any threatening movement, but stood with his rifle cradled in his arms.[65] Despite this testimony, the coroner's jury cleared Holmes of any wrongdoing in the shooting.

In Douglas County, prosecutors indicted 47 percent of the police officers who killed citizens. On August 13, 1899, Officer Anton Inda arrested James Smith, a black entertainer, and Tom Lewis in front of Hamilton's saloon on Dodge and Ninth streets in Omaha. As they entered the jail hallway, Smith jerked free from the policeman and swung at him. Officer Inda struck Smith with a night stick. The physician who performed an autopsy determined that a four-inch puncture wound could have been made by "some such instrument as a meat skewer or a .22-calibre bullet."[66] No one heard a gunshot, and one policeman testified that Inda only hit Smith with his fists. After further probing, the examining physician discovered a bullet fragment in the wound.[67] A Douglas County prosecutor indicted Inda, but a jury found him not guilty.

In a similar Douglas County case, Officer Fred Moore followed George O'Neill and another man into Henry Keating's saloon on Seventeenth and Davenport at 5 A.M. on a Sunday morning. Moore asked one of the men what he was doing out at that time in the morning. At that point O'Neill said something to Officer Moore and a fight broke out. In the melee Officer Moore hit O'Neill with a billy club and pushed his head through a plate mirror that served as a screen at the end of the bar.[68] The victim had been drinking. Moore was indicted for murder but found not guilty.

Although prosecutors indicted seventeen lawmen (31 percent) for shooting citizens, juries in all three counties were reluctant to convict them. Gila County had the highest conviction rate, 33 percent, followed by Las Animas at 16.6 percent (fig. 2.7). Despite the indictment and prosecution of seven Omaha police officers for murder, juries did not find a single officer guilty. However, the shooting of police by citizens ended with very different results.

POLICE AS VICTIMS

Police shootings involving law enforcement officers as victims created a great deal of interest. Citizens killed twenty-two lawmen in the three counties between 1880 and 1920.

On March 27, 1889, William Dunton, Willis Means, and Sam Mills, all cowboys, rode into El Moro, Colorado. After drinking in the local saloon, they mounted their horses and raced up and down the street "shooting up the town." Town Marshal Harry C. Montague tried to disarm them. Dunton refused to

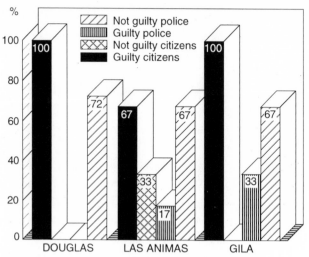

Fig. 2.7. Conviction rates for police and citizen gun homicides, 1880–1920. *Source:* Registers of criminal action.

surrender his revolver and after a brief argument shot the marshal.[69] Eventually charges against Dunton were dismissed.

Other cases, however, brought severe punishment. Shortly after midnight on November 21, 1895, Albert Noble became involved in a scuffle with Officer John Soloman behind the Colombian Hotel in Trinidad. Noble pulled a revolver and killed the officer.[70] Noble was indicted by the county prosecutor, found guilty of first-degree murder, and sentenced to death by hanging. The state carried out the execution on February 26, 1896. Frank Cantania shot Las Animas Deputy Sheriff Antonio Shelby to death in front of a saloon in Aguilar at 10:30 P.M. on April 6, 1908, for admonishing the defendant for his treatment of a ten-year-old boy.[71] The defendant had been drinking prior to the incident. A jury found him guilty of first-degree murder.

In Gila County some citizens apparently did not like sheriffs or their deputies. At least two, Edward P. Shanley and Charles B. Edwards, met death by gunfire at the hands of "persons unknown." Shanley died of a bullet wound to the head while feeding his horse. Some Globe citizens believed that Shanley may have committed suicide. However, the coroner's jury listed the incident as "killed by persons unknown," the common euphemism for such unsolved cases.[72] One or more persons ambushed Sheriff Deputy Edwards eleven miles north of Roosevelt. The perpetrators waited along the county road and used a shotgun.[73] Law enforcement officers failed to solve the case. On Christmas day 1882, a mob hanged Sheriff Deputy Thomas Kerr in Pioneer, Arizona, for shooting to death a local citizen in a saloon incident. As usual, the coroner listed the death as a hanging by "parties unknown."[74]

When captured, perpetrators of homicides against law enforcement officers in Gila County were dealt with harshly. Plennie E. Stokes shot and killed Officer Charles Woods in Miami, Arizona, on January 10, 1911. A Gila County jury found him guilty of first-degree murder, and a judge sentenced Stokes to death by hanging.[75]

Similar cases occurred in Las Animas County. On August 10, 1911, residents of Trinidad, Colorado, found William Walker, the town marshal, lying dead on a county road just outside of town. He had been attacked by two men, and it appeared that the motive might have been robbery. Despite a lengthy investigation the case remained unsolved.[76] Even when cases were solved, it did not necessarily mean that the defendant would be prosecuted. On the night of January 24, 1918, someone shot Deputy Sheriff George Penolas through a pool hall window. Las Animas County officials prosecuted four Greek coal miners for the crime; however, the charges were dismissed for lack of evidence.[77]

Omaha citizens shot and killed eleven police officers, the largest number in any of the counties examined. Ninety-one percent of these homicides occurred after 1900, reflecting the influence of the automobile, which gave criminals mobility. Seventy-three percent occurred on the streets, usually near saloons or brothels. On January 14, 1909, Hugh Jackson shot and killed Patrolman Lafayette A. Smith in front of a brothel on Ninth and Douglas streets. The officer's partner returned fire, killing Jackson.[78] Approximately a month later, John Masourides shot and killed Patrolman Edward Lowery near a brothel in South Omaha. After he arrested Masourides and a young female, Lowery failed to search Masourides for weapons. As they walked along a dark street, the perpetrator pulled a revolver and shot the officer. As he fell, dying, Lowery returned fire and seriously wounded his assailant.[79] This killing sparked riots against Greeks living in South Omaha. A jury found Masourides guilty of murder in the first degree, and the judge sentenced him to death, but the governor commuted the sentence to life.[80]

On February 10, 1915, after observing the suspicious activities of Juan Parral and another individual, Detective Tom Ring climbed up to watch them through a transom over the door of their hotel room. Apparently Parral heard the police officer, pulled a .44 caliber revolver, and shot Ring in the head. Then, as he lay helpless on the floor, Parral shot him one more time.[81] Possibly because of the peculiar circumstances of the shooting, a jury found Parral guilty of manslaughter. In another case a jury found Macario Romero guilty of first-degree murder, and the judge sentenced him to life in prison for the killing of patrolman Neil Cross. Citizens who killed policemen in Omaha normally used handguns. Only one, August Kastner, used a shotgun, and that case involved a robbery attempt at a saloon on Twenty-fourth and Decatur streets.

Legal authorities in all three counties were reluctant to indict either police or citizens accused of killing the other. County prosecutors indicted eight citizens (36 percent) for killing lawmen. However, the conviction rates were quite different from those involving police as perpetrators. Both Gila County and Douglas County had a 100 percent conviction rate, whereas Las Animas recorded a 66.6 percent conviction rate (see fig. 2.7). Apparently juries perceived the shooting of lawmen by citizens in an entirely different light from that of police shooting citizens.

RACIAL HOMICIDE SCENARIOS

Several homicides in the three counties reflect the hostile attitude of some whites toward racial minorities. For example, on October 3, 1899, John Bowers threatened Lee Ching in Globe. Witnesses heard Bowers shout, "I'll kill all the black s—s of b——s!"[82] Lee Ching shot his assailant with a .32 caliber revolver. The coroner's jury found that Lee Ching had acted in self-defense. On September 14, 1909, J. "Ribs" Henderson became involved in what he called "an argument" with a "drunken" Indian on a road near Roosevelt, Arizona. Henderson quickly pulled his rifle and shot Chil-chu-a-na, an Apache. Typical of such shootings, the coroner ruled the killing "justifiable."[83] In Bowen, Colorado, Frank Raymond, a white man, shot an unidentified black on April 28, 1902. After a coroner's inquest ruled the homicide "justifiable," the county attorney refused to file charges.[84] In another case, C. F. Lough Miller threatened Moses Inman, a black laborer, in Weston, Colorado. Miller shouted racial epithets and claimed, "I'm going out to kill that nigger."[85] Miller put a revolver in his pocket and "went out on the hunt for Moses Inman." A reporter stated that "the crime is one of the most brutal that has been committed in this county for many years."[86] Apparently the jury agreed; they found the defendant guilty. This, however, was an exception. In most cases involving whites killing racial minorities, juries found the perpetrators not guilty.

On March 9, 1916, James P. Epperson refused to eat at a table with Robert Tindall, a sixty-year-old black porter, at Cardenas Hotel in Trinidad. Epperson, a southerner, had recently arrived in Trinidad, where he began to work at the hotel. After a brief argument Epperson went to his room, armed himself with a

Colt .45 revolver, returned to the dining room, and shot Tindall to death.[87] A jury found the defendant not guilty. About a year later, Albert Smith accused James C. Rose, a black, of insulting his wife, causing her to leave him. Whether the insult was real or imagined is unknown. After making numerous threats, Smith waited in the dark to ambush Rose. As Rose pulled his wagon up to his home on a Trinidad street, Smith stepped out of the darkness and fired four shots into the unsuspecting victim.[88] It took the jury just ten minutes to find Smith not guilty.

Homicide Rates

Homicide rates provide the best measure of violence levels in the three western counties. Although Douglas County (essentially Omaha) homicide rates were higher than those of eastern cities such as Boston, New York, and Philadelphia, the rates increased significantly in each county as one moves westward. Douglas County homicide rates averaged 6 per 100,000 population for the forty-year period between 1880 and 1920, followed by Las Animas County with 34 per 100,000, and Gila County with 70 per 100,000. Because the Gila County homicide rates are so high compared to those of Douglas and Las Animas counties, a separate graph is used for each county, followed by a composite of Boston, New York, Philadelphia, and Douglas County to show the significant differences between eastern and western homicide rates in an urban setting. The Douglas County homicide rate was 2.6 per 100,000 in the early 1880s and increased to 9.7 between 1915 and 1919 (fig. 2.8). (The high homicide rate between 1905 and 1919 reflects the extremely high homicide rates for blacks in Omaha.)

Las Animas County homicide rates ranged from 21.4 per 100,000 in 1880 to a high of 70.5 per 100,000 during the Ludlow massacre era (fig. 2.9), significantly higher than those for Douglas County, and never dropped below 10 per 100,000. The homicide rates for the forty-year period were fairly consistent. Even by eliminating the Ludlow sample from the data, the rate for the period 1910 through 1914 was 38.5 per 100,000. Consequently, from 1900 through 1919 the average homicide rate in Las Animas County was 38 per 100,000.

The Gila County data provide the strongest evidence of a violent tradition in the West. The white homicide rate was 152 per 100,000 in 1880, and then dropped during the period 1885 through 1889, finally declining to a low of 42 per 100,000 between 1900 and 1905 (fig. 2.10). The Apache homicide rates were also dramatic, reaching a high of 178 per 100,000 between 1885 and

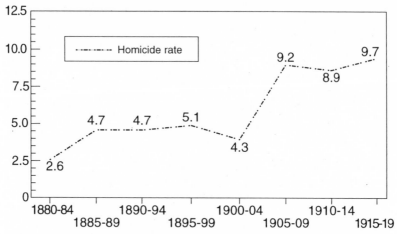

Fig. 2.8. Homicide rates (per 100,000 population) in Douglas County, 1880–1920. *Source:* Coroner's inquests.

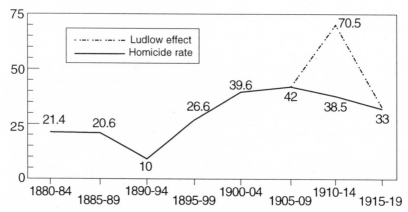

Fig. 2.9. Homicide rates (per 100,000 population) in Las Animas County, 1880–1920. The Ludlow massacre dramatically increased the number of homicides in 1913–14. *Source:* Coroner's inquests.

1889, reflecting the significant number of killings on or near the San Carlos Reservation. The rate declined to 89 per 100,000 by 1890. The average rates for the forty-year period are 65 and 75 for Apaches and whites, respectively. Gila County's combined homicide rates averaged 70 per 100,000, twice the average rate in Las Animas County (34 per 100,000), and twelve times higher than in Douglas County.

A comparison of Douglas County homicide statistics with those of Boston, New York, and Philadelphia indicates the significant difference between these

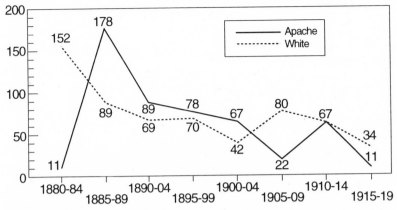

Fig. 2.10. Homicide rates (per 100,000 population) in Gila County, 1880–1920. *Source:* Coroner's inquests.

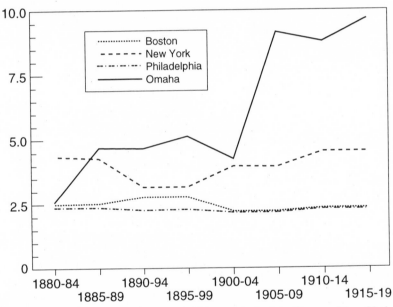

Fig. 2.11. Homicide rates (per 100,000 population) in Boston, New York, Philadelphia, and Omaha, 1880–1920. *Source:* Coroner's inquests.

cities and Omaha. The homicide rate for Omaha was 2.5 per 100,000 in 1880 but steadily climbed, reaching a high of 9.7 by 1920 (fig. 2.11). On the other hand, the rates for the other three cities throughout the four decades maintained a more even level.

However, a final comparison of black and white homicide rates in Douglas

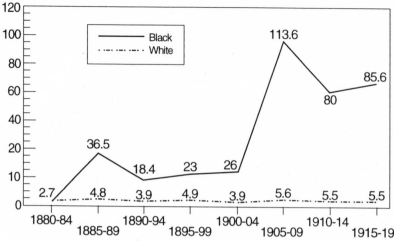

Fig. 2.12. Homicide rates (per 100,000 population) for blacks and whites in Douglas County, 1880–1920. *Source:* Coroner's inquests.

County shows the peril of making such blanket comparisons with eastern cities. If the two rates are separated, the difference between black and white rates appears dramatic (fig. 2.12). Because of the sheer number of homicides committed by whites, when combined, their low rates tend to minimize the black homicide rates. Any similar attempt to correlate Las Animas or Gila County with Boston, New York, and Philadelphia would decrease the rates for the three cities and therefore would not be a useful comparison. Nevertheless, the data prove the existence of high violence levels in the American West, at least in Douglas, Las Animas, and Gila counties.

Data Summary

Homicide data from Douglas, Las Animas, and Gila counties verify that high levels of violence existed during the period 1880–1920. A variety of factors including rapid population growth, economic change, high population mobility, ethnic diversity, racial hostility, the carrying of concealed weapons, and extensive alcohol consumption helps to explain this phenomena. Homicide in the counties remained a crime committed mainly by males (96.4 percent). Women seldom committed homicide, and although they were more likely to be victims, only about one in five victims was female. All forty cases of homicide followed by suicide were committed by men and involved female victims. Saloon fights, love triangles, gunfights, and police shootings were common scenarios for homicides. Homicide was normally a night crime, and perpetrators usually killed victims in saloons, on the streets, or in their homes. The weekend proved to be the most dangerous, with more than half of the homicides committed during these leisure hours. This, of course, reflects workers' tendencies to congregate in saloons and dance halls. Alcohol proved to be the most common ingredient in homicides in all three counties, with 56 percent or more of the participants drinking before the crime.

Saloon fights, gunfights, love triangles, and police shootings provided scenarios that sometimes appeared to be scripts from western movies. It seems incredible that two men would argue over "too much foam on the beer," but they did, and it cost one man his life. Bartenders faced danger every day, and most wore revolvers, with which they killed seventeen men in bar shootings. Despite being armed, eighteen barmen died at the hands of disgruntled customers. Arguments that began in bars often spilled out onto the streets, where two armed men confronted each other not at high noon, but late at night.

Love triangles and family fights were numerous and dangerous in all three counties (19.7 percent). Many of these homicides occurred after long visits to saloons, and since handguns were plentiful, they were the most common weapon employed in such killings. Newspapers gave heavy press coverage to love-triangle homicides, and juries, at least in Las Animas County, tended to side with the party who committed the crime unless it seemed overly vicious. Juries did convict some perpetrators, but there had to be aggravating circumstances, such as shooting the victim five or six times.

Police shootings proved to be the most surprising of all homicide scenarios. They were common in all three counties, and the prosecution of some police accused of shooting citizens indicates a different perception of law enforcement during that era. The significant number of police shootings also suggests a lack of professional standards among lawmen during the period 1880–1920. Virtually any male could become a deputy sheriff or town marshal, especially if he had connections with the sheriff or mayor. Most police killings of citizens occurred while police were trying to arrest them. Inexperience, disrespect for the law, and alcohol were common variables of incidents that ended in death, either for the citizen or the lawman. Most lawmen who killed citizens were acquitted; however, citizens indicted for killing policemen usually were convicted and given long prison sentences.

Homicide rates per 100,000 population within the three counties were high. The average rates for the forty-year period 1880–1920 were 6, 34, and 70 per 100,000 for Douglas, Las Animas, and Gila counties, respectively. These homicide rates, particularly for Las Animas and Gila counties, were dramatically higher than those of eastern cities, and even Douglas County rates towered above Boston, New York, and Philadelphia rates (see fig. 2.11). The only other study that documents similar homicide rates in the West is Roger McGrath's examination of violence in nineteenth-century California. He found homicide rates of 116 and 64 per 100,000, respectively, for Bodie and Aurora.[89] McGrath's study, however, covers limited time spans: 1877 to 1882 for Bodie, and 1861 to 1865 for Aurora. Both were boom towns of short duration, and because of their nature (gold camps full of young, single, well-armed men drinking in saloons), one would expect them to be deadly places.

But there is another aspect of homicide—the treatment of racial and ethnic minorities. The three case studies that follow will provide analyses of how the criminal justice systems in Douglas County, Las Animas County, and Gila County treated blacks, Hispanics, Italians, Apaches, and other whites. Each case study stands alone, and, as will be seen, each county treated defendants differently.

Seeds of Destruction

The Black Experience in Omaha, Nebraska

Few social histories examine the black experience in the American West, and virtually none of them offer useful data on the criminal justice system and its treatment of black defendants.[1] Although a good deal of scholarship has examined homicide among blacks in eastern cities and the South, there is a dearth of information on blacks in the American West. The movement by social historians into criminal history is very recent. Roger Lane's pioneering study *Roots of Violence in Black Philadelphia, 1860–1900* revealed high homicide rates for blacks.[2] Most of the other new studies of black homicide examine eastern and southern states.[3] The literature on violent behavior in the South that often forced blacks to migrate to the northern cities and into the American West is more fully developed.[4]

Using methods similar to Roger Lane's, but with significant modifications that include the extensive use of coroner's inquests and data analysis, this case study examines the black experience in Omaha, Nebraska. As will be seen, the explanation for the high homicide rates among blacks in Douglas County can be traced to the development of a subculture of violence[5] that southern blacks brought with them to Nebraska. It will be demonstrated that black defendants were treated differently than white defendants.

Douglas County, Nebraska

A typical example of the violent behavior in Omaha in the early twentieth century occurred in April 1903 at Garrity's Saloon at Tenth Street and Capitol Avenue, in the middle of the red-light district. On April 4, a newspaper headline announced: "Colored man pulls his revolver and quickly shoots down the ranchman from Colorado."[6] H. J. Walker, the victim, had arrived in Omaha from Ouray, Colorado, a few hours previous to the shooting and had been drinking heavily in several bars earlier in the day. After entering Garrity's Saloon that evening, Walker took a table and began telling stories about ranch life on the high plains. He was soon surrounded by "women with painted cheeks and scarlet dresses and rough men who laughed long and loudly at the coarse jests and uncouth stories he told." When Pat Jackson, a black entertainer hired to provide music, contributed a personal story about horses and cattle, the boisterous rancher made some racial remarks. According to one witness, "The cow puncher didn't like having him butt in that way and called the coon names."[7] Walker threatened to take Jackson outside and teach him some manners, but "Jackson wouldn't stand for that kind of talk and says, 'I guess you won't,' and with that he pulls out a gun and plugged the puncher." Jackson fired two shots in quick succession from his Smith and Wesson .38 revolver. His victim slumped to the floor, mortally wounded.[8] This homicide is particularly significant because of the interracial factor.

Newspaper coverage of the murder of H. J. Walker evokes the typical western movie scene, and it also reinforces a popular misconception that shoot-outs were representative of the West. The taking of another human being's life under such circumstances could hardly be considered heroic, yet novels and films often portray it in such terms. Historically, homicide, then and now, has been relegated to the sensationalism of tabloids, novels, movies, and television specials. It is misunderstood and, until recently, has been ignored by professional historians.

An examination of violent behavior in Omaha, Nebraska, may offer some insights on race, homicide, and justice during the period 1880–1920, when county officials indicted 280 people for homicide, 91 percent of them male (table 3.1). Omaha at that time was an urban mix that included racial and ethnic diversity. An evaluation of racial factors in Douglas County may help to form meaningful conclusions about historical homicide in an urban setting. To examine and explain the interrelationships of homicide, race, and justice, an analysis of statistical data collected from Douglas County district court records has been assembled. These data provide keys to understanding how homicide defendants were handled within the criminal justice system, particularly black defendants. Did blacks receive the same treatment as whites? Equally

Table 3.1 Homicide Indictments,
Douglas County, 1880–1920

	N	%
Other white	196	70.0
Black	67	24.0
Italian	9	3.2
Hispanic	6	2.1
Greek	2	0.7
Total	280	100

Source: Criminal appearance dockets.

important, did Omaha residents normally kill within their own racial group? By using comparative social-history techniques to answer these and other questions, a glimpse of violent crime and justice at the turn of the century will help place racial factors into proper perspective.

Black Migration

Omaha experienced significant population growth, particularly after 1880, when the railroads and stockyards provided the economic impetus. Both businesses offered employment opportunities for European immigrants and blacks. Ethnic groups proliferated within Omaha, where Bohemian, German, Irish, Danish, and Swedish neighborhoods developed in the 1880s and 1890s.[9] Blacks first began to enter Omaha in the late 1880s and also developed their own neighborhoods. Most were adjacent to the Union Pacific Railroad yards, but a few neighborhoods were farther south, next to the stockyards in South Omaha. Although the stockyards attracted many ethnic groups, the railroads provided the largest number of job opportunities for blacks recently arrived from the South and, to a lesser extent, the East. Many of them became porters, cooks, and common laborers.[10]

Black migration to Omaha increased dramatically during the 1880s, registering a 574 percent gain, increasing from 881 to 4,665 by 1890 (table 3.2). Despite this influx, there was little indication of racial unrest in Omaha.[11] By 1900 the number of blacks remained relatively stable at 4,014, rising gradually to 5,143 in 1910 (a 28 percent gain), before doubling to 10,315 by 1920. This population explosion during the World War I era brought with it signs of unrest within the

Table 3.2 Omaha Population, 1880–1920

	1880	1890	1900	1910	1920
White	30,518	143,847	124,428	144,355	181,046
Black	811	4,665	4,014	5,143	10,315

Source: U.S. Department of Commerce, Bureau of the Census.

white population as well as among blacks. Their rapid increase in numbers made blacks more visible to white citizens and, to some extent, more vulnerable to discrimination, something many had experienced in the South.

Census data confirm that, similar to northern cities such as Philadelphia, New York, and Chicago, Omaha received the majority of its black population from the South. A 20 percent random sample of the 1900 and 1910 manuscript census reveals that 79 and 77 percent, respectively, of the blacks in Omaha were born in southern states.[12] In 1900, 9.4 percent of the black population traced their heritage from "deep south" states, but in 1910 that number had increased to 22.9 percent. This pattern reflects changes occurring in that region during the first decade of the twentieth century, and the effect of push-pull factors operating in the South and the North to either drive out or lure in blacks.

Although historians have cited natural disasters such as droughts, floods, and boll weevil infestations as major migration motivations,[13] other explanations can be identified. For example, the nature of local southern law enforcement had an important impact. Many blacks viewed police power as repressive and unjust. Police brutality in Atlanta, Richmond, and other cities created unrest among southern urban blacks, who on occasion resisted. Atlanta, particularly, experienced violent reactions by blacks. In 1881, "a large group of Negroes had stoned a policeman and two of the blacks had resisted arrest with drawn guns."[14] Police who shot and killed alleged criminal suspects seldom suffered any penalty of law. There were a few cases of suspension or imprisonment, but they were rare.[15]

Lynchings were another push factor. "Black flight" increased after the beginning of the twentieth century, with 170,000 leaving the South in the first decade and an additional 450,000 during the next. In a recent study Stewart Tolnay and E. M. Beck discovered "a very striking relationship between migration and lynching in Georgia and South Carolina."[16] Sanctioned lethal violence against blacks in the form of lynching became commonplace in the South, where there were at least 2,409 victims between 1889 and 1918.[17] Some lynchings led to significant out-migration of blacks from Georgia and South Carolina. Similarly, the South had a high execution rate for blacks convicted of capital offenses. One researcher concluded that "a 'legal lynching' [execution] is little, if any, improvement over an extra-legal lynching."[18]

Overt violence against blacks forced many to leave the South to seek a safer environment in a variety of northern and western cities, including Omaha, but there were also positive factors influencing out-migration, including job opportunities and better living conditions. The absence of racial persecution also encouraged migration into Omaha. Usually the first blacks who ventured into urban cities were single or married men who maintained strong lines of communication with their relatives in the South. They often wrote letters describing life in the city and encouraging their families to move up north with them. As soon as married men earned enough money, they sent for their loved ones. The Union Pacific Railroad, Union Stock Yards Company, and the Cudahy, Armour, and Swift meat-packing companies offered job opportunities,[19] and equally important, Omaha did not have Jim Crow laws restricting blacks from housing or other accommodations. This, however, began to change by the first decade of the twentieth century, with rental "listings especially for blacks [that] implied a restricted market for that group."[20]

The economic growth that had encouraged the "Great Migration" of blacks to Omaha also provided opportunities for entrepreneurs who developed service-related industries such as saloons, gambling parlors, pool halls, and brothels. For example, the number of businesses "selling liquor by the drink" jumped more than 100 percent between 1905 and 1915.[21] This statistic is not surprising, since saloons served as the social gathering places for hundreds of workers employed by the stockyards and railroads. In some ways they were one of the few social settings where integration occurred. They also became centers for urban violence. A few drinks and an argument among patrons carrying concealed weapons could be deadly.

The Red-Light District

Omaha's red-light district developed in a core of city blocks that by 1900 extended from Davenport south three blocks to Douglas, and from Eighth Street west six blocks to Fourteenth Street. Over the next decade, prostitutes' cribs and houses became heavily concentrated within an even smaller core district. The northern and southern boundaries (Davenport and Douglas) remained the same, but they extended westward only three blocks, from Ninth

Omaha police patrol wagon (circa 1890s), used to pick up suspects arrested at saloons. (Courtesy of Nebraska State Historical Society, no. 054-99)

Street to Twelfth Street.[22] Although it is difficult to obtain reliable statistics, in 1900 at least 266 women were identified as working in Omaha's cribs or brothels. A decade later only 116 women (44 percent of the previous figure) were recorded as working in the identifiable red-light district. Black prostitutes numbered 18 and 26 percent, respectively, for the two decades, much higher than their proportion within the general population.[23]

Most of the blacks who had recently migrated into Omaha lived within and around the red-light district, and also north and west of that area.[24] East of the red-light district was the main railroad center and depot, the major employer of black men. Many of them moved through the red-light district daily on their way to work. Mixed in with the brothels were numerous saloons where workers could spend their leisure time. In 1891 Omaha boasted 285 saloons and liquor stores; a decade later there were 284 establishments that sold alcoholic beverages. By 1911, there were 293 businesses serving thousands of satisfied customers. (To be more specific, in 1911 there were fifty-eight saloons in the red-light district, and another sixty-four bars within three blocks.)[25] Saloon owners and bartenders, however, were not hospitable to all racial groups. Blacks sometimes found themselves unwelcome, as described in an August 1910 issue of the *Omaha Monitor,* a black weekly newspaper: "Today many of the saloons refuse to serve colored men, and others break glasses in the presence of colored men they have served. . . . In still other saloons signs are posted which read 'Negroes not Wanted.' "[26]

The highly concentrated and heavily traveled red-light district was a ghetto within a ghetto. Since crime usually flourished within such districts, it should be no surprise that residents within or around the area were labeled as criminal elements, or what Eric Monkkonen and others have called the "dangerous classes."[27] To some extent this was true—the area did entice and cater to the criminals who pimped, sold drugs, and committed violent crimes. However, there was a tendency to blame blacks for most crime—real or imagined. As newspaper editor H. J. Pinkett noted, "So eager are they [editors of Omaha's white newspapers] to find something degrading in Negro life that the history of the Negro of the city of Omaha is being written very largely from the records of the police court."[28] Although Pinkett admitted that blacks committed violent crimes, he viewed most cases as a "relative killing a relative" or a similar situation.[29] A decade later he conceded that blacks did commit crimes, "but that they are guilty of all the crimes alleged against them is undeniably false."[30] Pinkett pointed out that disreputable saloons were creating problems for neighboring black residents, and he ran several editorials calling for a clean-up of the "bootlegging and gambling joints" that were "rapidly multiplying in the northern section of Omaha, where many of our race reside."[31] He also complained about the availability on the streets of morphine, opium, and cocaine, which were creating havoc among the young people. "Laws against the sale of 'dope,' either by druggists or peddlers should be rigidly enforced."[32]

Discrimination

Prejudice and discrimination against blacks took a variety of forms in Omaha, including Jim Crow policies. For example, in March 1910 the Douglas County Grand Jury delivered a report on the condition of the county jail. "We . . . recommend that the cells be so arranged that white prisoners may be together and colored prisoners confined by themselves."[33] The angry editor of the *Monitor* stated that the grand jury had "committed an outrage upon the colored people" of Omaha and Nebraska. County officials proposed Jim Crow laws for the jail that paralleled similar legislation in the South. The editor condemned segregation in any form. "Certain agencies and individuals have been scheming, plotting, and working to bring about segregation . . . by which our people would be restricted to certain districts, both as to residence, business and civic privileges."[34]

Census data for 1900 and 1910 reveal the lack of upward mobility among blacks. In 1900, 54 percent of the male heads of households listed their occupation as domestic, while 31 percent indicated laborer. In 1910 the figures had not changed significantly, at 52 and 29 percent, respectively. In 1900, census enumerators listed 1.5 percent professional; in 1910 that figure dropped to 1.3 percent.[35] In other words, 85 and 81 percent of blacks held menial jobs for two decades.[36] The only change, gradual at that, was an increase in the number of merchants, from 3.8 to 5 percent, respectively. These were service-related businesses, mostly barber shops.

One barrier to black upward mobility was workplace discrimination. Some companies would not hire blacks. The editor of the *Omaha Monitor* called the attention of his reading public to open discrimination by the Omaha Electric Light and Power Company. Addressing the company president, the editor stated, "Among your army of employees you have not seen fit to give employment even of the most menial kind to a single member of the Colored race. NOT ONE."[37]

In August 1916 the Union Pacific Railroad replaced all of the black janitors with Japanese workers. Less than a month later the same company fired the "Colored 'Red Caps' who have been employed at the Union Depot."[38] According to the *Monitor*, apparently the new president of the Union Pacific disliked blacks. It does seem somewhat surprising that the company would fire all the porters, a job category that whites often would not accept.

In 1919 the *Monitor* featured an editorial that demanded black representation on the police force. The editor criticized the policy of the Omaha Police Department's intention to appoint "special officers for ten days to work exclusively among the colored people to round up loafers, the unemployed and undesirables in order that the city may be rid of such characters."[39] Recent black migrants from the South had seen too much of the hard hand of the law and its results among them. Some refused to accept it. To prevent confrontations and to smooth relations between the races, the editor recommended hiring blacks as police officers on a regular basis, and he proudly pointed to several black officers already serving well in that capacity.[40] Editor Pinkett and a group of African

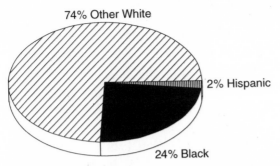

74% Other White

2% Hispanic

24% Black

Fig. 3.1. Homicide indictments by race/ethnicity in Douglas County, 1880–1920. *Source:* Criminal-appearance dockets.

American community leaders requested to see the mayor to discuss the permanent hiring of blacks in the police department in an effort to reduce tensions between the races and control crime in Omaha. Their experience in Omaha suggested that something needed to be done to lower the rate of violent crime.

Indeed, Omaha appeared to be a violent city, but particularly for blacks. During the period 1880–1920, county officials indicted 206 whites, 66 blacks, and 6 Hispanics for either murder or manslaughter (fig. 3.1).[41] A racial breakdown for Omaha's population indicates that blacks accounted for 2 percent in 1880, 3 percent in both 1890 and 1900, 3.5 percent in 1910, and just over 5 percent by 1920, yet 24 percent of those indicted for homicide between 1880 and 1920 were black. This significant disparity suggests a need to explore racial relationships in Omaha. The number of indictments in Douglas County by racial group per half-decade indicates that black defendants' rates rose sharply after 1900, while white rates reflect, at least to some degree, moderate population increases during the same period. On the other hand, there is no correlation between homicide indictments and population changes for blacks. For example, even though the black population remained relatively stable between 1890 and 1910, black homicide indictment rates jumped rapidly in the first decade of the twentieth century.

Although recent homicide studies have found that most murderers select victims from within their own racial group,[42] that was not the case for 32 percent of the black homicide defendants in Omaha, whose victims were white (table 3.3). In contrast, only 4 percent of the white murderers killed out of their racial group.[43] At first glance, the data suggest that the high interracial homicide

Table 3.3 Race of
Perpetrator / Victim, Omaha
Homicides, 1880–1920

	%
Black / black	52.3
Black / white	32.3
Black / unknown	15.4

Source: Douglas County district court
cases.

rates might explain high conviction rates for blacks. However, a few case histories will illustrate the implications of a typical Omaha interracial homicide scenario and its consequences.

Interracial Homicides

Interracial homicides involving black perpetrators and white victims can be divided into three basic categories: saloon-related fights, disputes involving women, and robberies. Alcohol was a common denominator, and saloon killings usually occurred in the evening. The homicides usually occurred after minor incidents, such as a jostle, verbal epithet, or some real or imagined damage to honor. A typical case began on February 15, 1888, when William Ferguson, a black born and raised in the South, entered a saloon and began to play pool. The pool-room attendant, who recognized Ferguson from a previous fight, asked him to leave. Ferguson refused. Quickly the two became involved in a fight, and Joe Holmes, a black pool attendant, beat and ejected Ferguson from the saloon. Within minutes Ferguson returned, sneaked in through the back door, and opened fire on Holmes. The pool attendant ducked as the bullet whizzed by, struck, and instantly killed Ole Olson, a white patron.[44] County authorities tried, convicted, and sentenced Ferguson, just eighteen years old, to life in prison for second-degree murder.[45]

In a similar case, William Fouse, a black, visited Levy's and the Midway Saloon in the 300 block of North Twelfth Street. He met James Bowles, a white soldier from the Sixteenth Infantry, in one of the saloons, and they began to walk back and forth between the two saloons, drinking and arguing. Bowles allegedly pulled a knife and struck Fouse, who quickly retaliated by grabbing a brick that he used to cave in his victim's head. A jury found him guilty of first-degree murder and sentenced him to death.[46] Another saloon killing occurred on October 18, 1913, after Tom Jones entered the Leoneo pool hall and saloon at 1006 Capitol and began to play pool and drink beer. When Jones began arguing with white owner Samuel Leoneo over a fifty-cent bet, tempers quickly flared. Jones pulled a revolver and fired, killing Leoneo instantly. He was convicted of murder and sentenced to death.[47]

The striking thing about these three cases is that they all involved drinking, they occurred in saloons, and they started with minor incidents that escalated into physical violence. In the first case an innocent bystander had the misfortune to be present in a saloon that acted as the only significant social gathering place for the interaction of the races in Omaha, and he lost his life because of a fight that did not concern him. In the second case, Fouse frequently drank heavily when visiting Omaha. Bowles, his victim, also became inebriated, and a petty argument turned to blows and death. The third case seems even more incomprehensible, ending in death over a fifty-cent bet, but petty disputes were a common denominator in many homicides that occurred in Omaha and throughout the American West. The habit of carrying concealed handguns only increased the tendency to use them, and with many armed men under the influence of alcohol, it is little wonder that altercations ended in death. These three cases were quite typical Omaha homicides.

Two interracial homicides involved women. One occurred on the night of July 27, 1905, in front of the Cambridge Hotel, at the corner of Thirteenth and Capitol streets. William Miles, a black, and Florence Flick, a white woman, had been living together for two years in the red-light district. Miles and Flick, a cocaine addict, were well known to the police. Apparently Harry McGechin won favor with Flick, who then moved in with him. When Miles and McGechin met in front of the hotel and began to argue, Miles pulled a knife and cut his victim's throat from ear to ear. McGechin died within a few minutes.[48] The other case occurred on the night of October 15, 1913, after an unidentified black took offense to remarks made about a woman he was escorting by three white men at Twenty-sixth and N streets. The three white companions, under the influence of alcohol, stopped the black woman and made some derogatory remarks. The unknown assailant, referred to in the press as "Lucky Brown," reacted quickly, drew a knife, and soon one white victim lay dying in the street. The police failed to apprehend the suspect.[49]

These two cases reflect the heightened degree of honor among blacks conditioned by living in the South. A careless comment, an unintended jostle on the street, or a gesture could bring a quick response. Both cases also suggest prostitution-related behavior. Since they lived in the red-light district, it is very possible that Miles had been keeping Flick as a prostitute. The second case also occurred in an area of South Omaha noted for prostitution. Pimps protected their territory. Anyone viewed as a threat was dealt with quickly.

One of the more interesting cases involved Juan Gonzales and James Silk, a black. On his forty-first birthday Gonzales began celebrating early. Toward the end of the day, much under the influence, Gonzales entered the Rooney Saloon, managed by Silk, and demanded a beer from the bartender at gunpoint. The bartender gave him two bottles of beer and then sprinted out the back door. Silk walked in and tried to wrestle the gun away from Gonzales. Failing to do this, and fearing for his own safety, Silk drew his revolver and shot Gonzales dead on the spot.[50] A coroner's inquest ruled it self-defense.[51] In another case involving a black victim and a white perpetrator, bartender Charles Austin demanded payment of twenty cents more for a drink delivered to Jacob Williams. The patron had no more money. Austin beat Williams severely about the head, kicked him when he was down, broke his leg, and then literally threw him into the street where he was run over by a streetcar.[52] No charges were filed against Austin.

Several homicide cases involved robbery. On May 14, 1906, Harrison Clark, Calvin Waln, and Clarence Gathright, all blacks, attempted to rob a streetcar conductor at the Albright Terminal. During the scuffle, Clark fired at Edward Flury with a revolver, and the conductor fell dead. Two days later a mob attempted to storm the county jail to lynch the prisoners. Police repulsed the mob.[53] A Douglas County jury found the three men guilty of murder in the first degree, sentenced two to life in prison, and recommended the death penalty for Clark. He was executed at the Nebraska State Penitentiary in Lincoln.[54] In a similar case, Governor Hall, Luther Hall, and William Collins, all carrying handguns, attempted to rob Nathan Shapiro's store on the night of August 27, 1919. During a struggle with Shapiro, Collins shot and killed the store owner with a .38 caliber revolver. Surprisingly, all three received short sentences.[55]

In the first case only Clark received the death penalty. This might seem surprising considering that the victim was white. In the second case the age of the three perpetrators (fourteen, fifteen, and seventeen) may help to explain why they received relatively light punishment for a homicide during a robbery, but another factor was that they had all plea-bargained guilty, as did Gathright in the previous case.

White Homicides

Intraracial homicides involving white perpetrators followed similar patterns, including being frequently precipitated by minor issues. For example, on July 6, 1880, William Garzolla began to quarrel with Louis Zerga in Nestal's Saloon at Thirteenth and Harney streets. Both had been drinking, and the dispute became very heated. Garzolla said, "I have killed a good many, and I can kill you."[56] He suddenly drew a Bulldog .44 caliber revolver and shot Zerga to death. Garzolla had purchased the gun the day before. In October 1880, a jury found him guilty of second-degree murder, and a judge sentenced him to twenty-five years in prison.[57] In a similar case in 1895, Omaha Councilman Cornelius DuBois fired his brother-in-law, Claude Hoover, partly because of his heavy drinking. Hoover visited the Douglas Street Pawnshop and purchased a Bulldog .38 five-shot revolver on Friday, December 13, 1895. It turned out to be an unlucky day for both men. Hoover walked up to DuBois and said, "I got you now," and fired two deadly shots into his victim.[58] A jury found Hoover guilty of first-degree murder, and the judge sentenced him to death by hanging.[59]

Bernard McGinn and Edward McKenna had been on unfriendly terms since an attack by McKenna's dog. At 7 P.M. on July 29, 1893, McGinn met McKenna on his way home from work at the corner of Twenty-fourth and Grand streets. Without saying a word, McGinn pulled a revolver and shot McKenna. The victim exclaimed, "Don't shoot!" and fell mortally wounded. "Within an hour over a hundred men" began to search the area for the perpetrator.[60] Two hours later McGinn surrendered to the police. A jury found McGinn guilty of first-degree murder, and the judge sentenced him to death.

Alcohol played an important role in some of these homicide scenarios. On August 22, 1900, four men sat drinking beer behind a blacksmith shop near Twenty-fourth Street and Cuming. When Edward Fee walked up and began to talk to them, the four men threatened to beat him up if he did not buy them some beer. Fee pulled a pint of liquor from his pocket, took a drink, and offered it to them. They refused and became abusive. Finally, Harry Flock began to beat Fee with his fists. After knocking him unconscious, the four men left. One of the men, John Watchner said, "I will go back and fix him."[61] Fee died from the wounds. A jury found both Flock and Watchner guilty of manslaughter.

When drunken revellers woke John O'Connor, an Irishman, from his sleep about midnight on July 1, 1907, he loaded a shotgun, opened his second-story bedroom window, and fired a round at Frank Caroker, killing him instantly. A jury found him guilty of manslaughter.[62] A decade later, long-time Serbian

This beer saloon on Thirteenth Street (1886) was a typical gathering place for Omaha railroad and meat-packing employees on their way home from work. (Courtesy of Nebraska State Historical Society, no. 054-100)

friends Djoko Czejen and Gyoke Sorati began to quarrel over who should purchase the next bucket of beer. After drinking all day, they were well under the influence. Suddenly Sorati pulled a knife and stabbed his friend to death.[63] A jury found Sorati not guilty.

Love triangles also proved to be hot newspaper items in Omaha. Van Goodell had become "madly jealous" over the affections of Edna Kenneth and had purchased a .38 caliber revolver just prior to his crime. After catching Edna with a young man on the street some time previously, he had viciously slashed the man with a knife while she escaped. On September 4, 1908, Goodell walked up to her on the street in front of her apartment at 314 North Fifteenth Street and fired three shots in quick succession, killing her instantly.[64] A jury found him guilty of first-degree murder.

Eloise Rudiger complained of being abused and beaten numerous times by Henry Reiser, "the Baron" of South Omaha. Apparently, Reiser met and "seduced" Mrs. Rudiger and then spurned her. The angry Eloise purchased an American Bulldog .38 revolver at Koutsky Brothers on Twenty-fourth Street on October 26, 1893. That same day she met "the Baron" on a nearby street corner, drew the revolver, and shot him three times.[65] When her husband soon appeared on the scene, she exclaimed, "I have killed him, killed him, and you should have done it."[66] Apparently the jury agreed; they found her not guilty.

Guns and Alcohol

Although a wide variety of weapons were available to perpetrators, handguns were the favorite, followed by knives. By the late 1880s cheap handguns could be purchased in any gun store or pawnshop. They were usually five-shot, double-action weapons with short barrels that could be concealed easily in any pocket. A discussion of several homicide cases offers an opportunity for further analysis of handgun use.

On numerous occasions in 1908, Jess Brown, a black dining-car waiter for the Union Pacific Railroad, fought with Carrie Carter, the black woman who lived with him. After several bitter quarrels she finally left him, but Brown quickly discovered her new residence and tried to convince her to come back. She refused. On February 8, 1909, apparently exasperated, Brown visited a neighborhood pawnshop, where he hocked his overcoat in exchange for a handgun and a box of shells. He loaded the weapon and walked to Carter's new residence at 1223 Capitol Avenue. After a brief argument in front of her house, Brown fired two shots. One, penetrating her chest cavity under the right arm, proved fatal.[67]

The fact that Jess Brown, in the dead of winter, could just walk into a pawnshop and trade his overcoat for a handgun and a box of shells is clear evidence of the ease of obtaining handguns in Omaha. The details of the case also reveal the single-mindedness and premeditation of this particular perpetrator.

Similar cases involved black perpetrators and victims. On May 12, 1906, Robert Johnson used a Russian Bulldog .32 caliber to kill his brother in a boardinghouse quarrel. Both had been drinking. George Johnson killed his wife with a similar .38 caliber revolver on August 24, 1910.[68]

Whites also selected cheap handguns to commit their crimes. For example, Claude H. Hoover fired two bullets from a .38 Bulldog in a deadly altercation at 418 South Thirteenth Street on December 13, 1895. Thomas Collins used a .38 Bulldog to kill Charles Groves at his saloon at Thirteenth and Dodge on December 10, 1899.[69] Numerous other cases also involved the use of cheap handguns.

Alcohol was a common component in Omaha's deadly confrontations. Saloons provided a social gathering place for the working classes of Omaha during the period under study.[70] Although the data on alcohol are sketchy, 26 percent of the homicides committed by blacks occurred in saloons. For the sixty-eight black homicide indictments in Omaha, at least 43 percent (and probably more) of the persons involved had been drinking, and at least one had used cocaine.[71] These cases also show another factor present in most homicides—victims and perpetrators usually knew each other.

Males dominated violent crime in Omaha. Ninety-two percent of the indicted whites and 89 percent of the indicted blacks were male. Although females were not prominently represented either as perpetrators or victims, there is a disparity in conviction rates between the two races for females. Courts convicted 50 percent of the black female defendants, whereas 9 percent of white females received guilty verdicts. Most female perpetrators had killed their husbands, just as female victims commonly were killed by their spouses.

The common habit among blacks of carrying weapons led to many lethal incidents. This trait may have originated in the South, where blacks had to contend with overt threats of violence from white citizens. What is surprising is that whites were less likely to be armed with handguns than blacks, by 18 percent. This may indicate the southern influence among blacks who had recently migrated. With so many men carrying handguns, the addition of alcohol turned minor squabbles into lethal shootings.

Indictment Data

Homicide verdicts for black defendants in Douglas County are revealing. Juries or judges convicted black defendants 85 percent of the time, found 6 percent not guilty, and dismissed 9 percent of the cases (fig. 3.2).[72] Whites experienced very different results. The criminal justice system convicted 34 percent of white defendants, while 38 percent were found not guilty, and 28 percent of the cases were dismissed. Juries found only four women guilty of murder or manslaughter (16 percent). Black females experienced a 60 percent conviction rate (three cases), while white females experienced a 5.5 percent conviction rate (one case). In some ways the not-guilty verdicts are most revealing. The white not-guilty verdict rate was six times that for blacks. When portrayed in graphic form, the comparison is quite striking. One might be inclined to assume that there was an inherent bias in the criminal justice system. To a certain extent that is true, but other factors help explain what happened during the judicial process.

Fig. 3.2. Homicide verdicts for whites and blacks in Douglas County, 1880–1920. (Two percent of the cases involving white defendants ended in hung juries.) *Source:* Criminal appearance dockets.

In a major study of violence in Philadelphia, Roger Lane suggests that "if blacks had a higher ratio of convictions to arrest than whites, this might indicate a greater likelihood of guilt or, alternatively, bias on the part of judges and juries."[73] Both factors offered by Lane are important in understanding the treatment of blacks in Omaha, and plea bargaining provides an important vehicle for assessing Lane's criteria and the general treatment of black defendants.

Historians disagree on the definition of plea bargaining. Lawrence M. Friedman asks, "Can we be sure we know plea bargaining when we see it? The answer for the most part is yes. Some cases have unambiguous signs—more notably a change in plea from *innocent to guilty of a lesser charge.*"[74] All of the black plea bargains (twenty-one cases) in Omaha involved a change of plea from not guilty to guilty. Mark H. Haller adds an observation that also applies to this study. In discussing two possible types of nineteenth-century plea bargains, he notes that "one stemmed from the fact that defendants were generally poor, sometimes foreign-born, and frequently unrepresented by an attorney. Their guilty pleas often reflected a railroading of the defendant by a variety of threats and promises that the defendant would be in no position to evaluate or resist."[75] This certainly was the case for black defendants in Omaha. For example, after heavy pressure applied by the police investigators, Luther Hall, Governor Hall, and William Collins all plea-bargained guilty. In the case of the 1906 streetcar

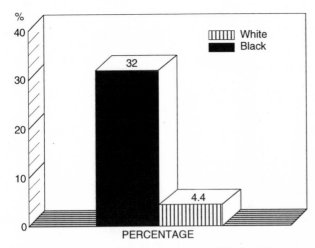

Fig. 3.3. Plea bargaining by whites and blacks in Douglas County, 1880–1920. *Source:* Criminal appearance dockets.

conductor robbery, Clarence Gathright also plea-bargained. Fear of the death penalty may have increased his desire to change his plea.[76]

Plea bargaining helps illuminate the high conviction rates for blacks. Thirty-two percent of black defendants plea-bargained during the judicial process (fig. 3.3).[77] Less than 5 percent of the white defendants chose that option. The fact that plea bargains by black defendants are almost perfectly split between white and black victims suggests that the race of the victim was not the main consideration for the plea bargain.

Any admission of guilt during a preliminary hearing heavily favored the county attorney. In one case there are indications that police and prosecutors used "third-degree" tactics to gain a confession.[78] Nebraska law did not require that indigents be provided with legal counsel until the trial stage. At that point, if the defendant lacked counsel, the court appointed an attorney. Few black defendants had the financial means to employ good legal counsel, and consequently, they received unequal treatment in the Douglas County criminal justice system.[79] On the other hand, the prosecutor used plea bargaining as a means to save time and money. Possibly because of the race or economic status of the defendants involved, apparently few lawyers who defended blacks questioned or challenged this practice.

Omaha homicide indictment rates per 100,000 population provide the most revealing contrast. These are not actual homicide rates, but only represent

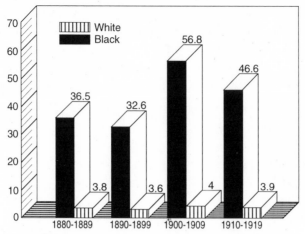

Fig. 3.4. Homicide indictment rates (per 100,000 population) in Douglas County, 1880–1920. *Source:* Criminal appearance dockets.

indictments. The high rates for blacks in Omaha are remarkable (fig. 3.4). The lowest homicide indictment rate for blacks was 32.6 indictments per 100,000 (1890–99); the highest rate, 56.8 per 100,000, was reached during the decade 1900–1909. White homicide indictment rates in Omaha averaged 3.8 per 100,000 population and never exceeded 4 (1900–1909).

Black homicide indictment rates consistently exceeded white rates by a factor of ten or more. Omaha, however, was not the only city that displayed such disparate figures. Roger Lane discovered that indictment rates among blacks in Philadelphia reached 11.4 per 100,000, five times the white rate (2.1), during the period 1890–1900. Another earlier study indicates that homicide rates for blacks continued to be high during the 1920s, with Nebraska urban rates reaching 68.9 per 100,000 in 1920 and 1925.[80] The Omaha rates have seldom been equalled except in certain cities during the present era.[81]

Homicide Locations

Analysis of the Douglas County data poses several important questions. Why, for example, did blacks kill outside their race so frequently? One factor could be the mixing of racial groups in Omaha's urban core. There are no studies that adequately document black movement within Omaha, but we do know that they settled mainly around the Union Pacific Railroad center near the Missouri River and, to a lesser extent, near the Union Stockyards in South Omaha.

Recent homicide studies indicate that perpetrators usually kill their victims in their own neighborhoods, and the location of homicides committed by blacks in Omaha clearly supports this premise. Blacks killed sixteen of the eighteen white victims, most near the railroad center. Only two white victims were killed near the stockyards. Black defendants also murdered nineteen black victims in the central business district, and nine black victims near the stockyards.

Blacks killed whites in the following locations: four in saloons, five on streets near them, two by the railroad center (robbery victims), and one on a street in South Omaha (also a robbery).[82] Whites and blacks normally mixed on a regular basis only in or near saloons in one largely black neighborhood that apparently was frequented by whites because of brothels and saloons.

The Southern Subculture of Violence

Is there any explanation for black homicide indictment rates that are ten times that of whites? Why were blacks more likely to turn to violence? Roger Lane believes that "the roots of black crime are threefold: a different social psychology resulting from blacks' exclusion from the dominant experience with factory, bureaucracy, and schooling; a heritage of economic and other insecurities; and a long and complex experience with criminal activity."[83]

In support of this thesis, black newspapers in Omaha often complained of segregation and job discrimination. As mentioned earlier, the *Omaha Enterprise* criticized a Douglas County grand jury's recommendation that the jail be segregated, and other editorials complained about Omaha companies that failed to hire blacks or, in some cases, fired them without redress.[84] Equally important, Omaha's residential segregation trapped blacks in an area where physical violence was deemed appropriate action by some individuals. With handguns readily available, it is little wonder that blacks carried and used them, whether in self-defense against white aggression—real or imagined—or to settle arguments.[85]

Other more elaborate and meaningful theories explain the high homicide indictment rates for black males. A majority of the blacks in Omaha migrated from the South, with 79 and 77 percent for the 1900 and 1910 census, respectively.[86] They came to Omaha not only looking for economic opportunity, but also to escape an oppressive system of tyranny enforced by white lynch law.

They brought with them a heritage of violence—in essence a "subculture of violence."[87] Two sociologists found that blacks born in the South who moved to the North had higher homicide rates that blacks born and raised in the North.[88] It is quite probable that blacks who migrated into Omaha brought with them this "subculture of violence" born of their experience in the South. Many of the young men involved in homicides may have witnessed or experienced violence at the hands of whites.

Sheldon Hackney applied the "subculture of violence" theory to the South and suggests that southerners tended to identify with certain forms of violence but rejected others. As did previous researchers, he discovered high homicide and low suicide rates among southerners. The region also displayed moderate property-crime rates. With a wry touch of humor, Hackney concluded that "high murder and low suicide rates constitute a distinctly southern pattern of violence, one that must rank . . . ahead of mint juleps in importance as a key to the meaning of being southern."[89]

Sociologist Raymond D. Gastil critiqued earlier studies of the subculture of violence and developed the idea of a "regional culture of violence" that might be applicable to the Omaha case. He claims that violent patterns can be identified across racial and ethnic lines in a specific region. In other words, the region in which they lived determined whether they would be violent, not their particular culture. Gastil criticized the subculture of violence concept, suggesting that his theory of a regional culture of violence is superior because it "will help to explain why subcultures of violence do not develop equally everywhere under apparently similar conditions."[90] Gastil used the term "southernness" to help identify the persistence of southern culture in transplanted members of that society who moved to other regions. They carried with them a cultural tradition that included a propensity to settle problems, especially those that concerned "honor," with force, which often could be lethal. Gastil notes that southerners "made up a large part of the original migration to the Far West and Rocky Mountain states."[91] He also established high correlations of southernness with blacks and high homicide rates. This supports Roger Lane's conclusions that blacks who had recently migrated from the South had the highest homicide rates.[92]

Exactly what in southern culture accounts for the high violence level? In *The Mind of the South*, Wilbur J. Cash suggests that high violence levels can be explained by exploring southern historical traditions. Honor in the South became a cult that had to be defended at all costs. Hackney agrees, and suggests that slavery and the plantation "reinforced the tendency toward violence."[93]

Edward L. Ayers also offers some important clues to the puzzle of southernness and why blacks might have accepted it as part of their culture. After the Civil War, southerners developed chain gangs as a method to clear jails and complete public works projects. Chain gangs provided two advantages; they reduced public revenue demands and controlled blacks. Prison population figures reveal that whereas few white southerners were incarcerated, black prison commitments skyrocketed.[94]

According to Ayers, the foundation of southernness lies in the attitudes of whites who dominated blacks. White southerners developed their own unwritten code of "ten commandments" of law. The first four dealt with the "protection" of women against "rape, adultery, seduction, or 'slander against chastity.' "[95] Physical violence by a male relative of the offended woman was the only acceptable response for any of these offenses. The fifth unwritten law was that "the survivor of a duel must be acquitted," and the sixth called for the acquittal of one who killed another in a "fair fight." Finally, any lie or "opprobrious epithets" were considered insults, and each one was "equal to a blow" or any other form of assault.[96] It was common to use physical force, often lethal, to settle any of these grievances. John Shelton Reed theorizes that southerners are more likely to be violent when "honor" is at stake, particularly in love triangles or family disputes. "Violence and the conditions that call for it," says Reed, "will be *learned* in childhood."[97]

Handguns and murder in Omaha also correspond to this southern-migration theory. Ayers found that it was common practice for southerners to carry handguns, and this created deadly situations. "As a rule one does not arm himself for the specific purpose of shooting another. He just puts a pistol in his pocket and struts out among his fellow men to be ready for emergencies, which he generally proceeds to make. A drink or two will put him in a humor for a row, and make him sensitive to insults."[98] Because of this readiness, Ayers concludes that "an acute sensitivity to insult and a propensity for violence—the manifestation of honor—came with each passing decade to be identified more and more with . . . poor urban blacks."[99] A small push or a derogatory remark quickly brought reaction. "A male is expected to defend the name and honor of his mother, the virtue of womanhood . . . and to accept no derogation about his race . . . or his masculinity."[100] Ayers believed that black migrants from the South who were isolated in ghettos continued to display these facets of southernness. In fact, they "generate an honor of their own."[101]

During the 1890s in Philadelphia, W. E. B. DuBois discovered "evidence of the appearance of a set of thieves of intelligence and cunning" within the black population—what he called the "real Negro criminal class."[102] He also found that of those who had been arrested, 54 percent had recently migrated from the South.[103] The southern connection of blacks in northern cities was apparent in Philadelphia. Many had a great disdain for white-imposed law. Blacks from the South viewed southern courts as "instruments of injustice and oppression and upon those convicted in them as martyrs and victims."[104]

Frustrated by being trapped within a ghetto controlled by an unjust system and carrying with them a "code of honor," Omaha's blacks often reacted by resorting to violence, sometimes with the slightest provocation. The results can be seen in the black homicide indictment rates that were ten times that of white defendants. In support of this hypothesis, the black population was fairly stable, yet the number of homicides increased dramatically during the period 1902–10. A decade or more of low-paying, demeaning work, segregated housing, racist behavior by saloon keepers and other white merchants, and racial mistrust created tremendous pressure on Omaha's black population. In conjunction with southernness exhibited by blacks, this may have caused an increase in the socialization of aggression, with black hostility then turning outward against both black and white victims.[105]

Another question also requires some response and further analysis. Do the conviction rates of black defendants who killed black victims differ from those whose victims were white? The conviction rates for cases with white and black victims were 91 and 79 percent, respectively.[106] Throw out the one dismissal for a case involving a white victim (the evidence was so flimsy that there probably should not have been an indictment), and the conviction rate for black defendants who killed whites is 100 percent. All three not-guilty verdicts and the other four dismissals of black defendants involved black victims. It made no difference whether the homicide involved a robbery; the victim needed only to be white to assure a conviction. To put this in perspective, we need to evaluate the treatment of white defendants who killed black victims. Of the seven cases involving white perpetrators and black victims, four of the white defendants were found not guilty, while the other three cases were dismissed. Clearly it was the race of the victim that counted most.[107] This analysis of the indictment data proves that black defendants did not receive equal justice within the Douglas County criminal justice system.

When assessing the criminal justice of this era, it is important to place it in the context of the conservative legal and political system that dominated the United States. European philosophers such as Auguste Comte and Herbert Spencer, American educator William Graham Sumner, and a conservative United States

Supreme Court dominated by Justice Stephen J. Field helped to shape the ideas of conservatives who gained an inordinate influence throughout society. This pervasive conservative thought that dominated the judicial system, congressional bodies, and the business community included a strong dose of racism—verbal and physical, covert and overt—that justified dispossessing Native Americans and violating their civil rights, as well as those of blacks, Hispanics, and Chinese. The United States Supreme Court set the tone with the Civil Rights Cases of 1883 and *Plessy v. Ferguson* in 1896. These two decisions wiped out equal protection for blacks and legalized Jim Crowism.[108] In assessing this era, one historian claimed, "What is noticeable is that American thought of the period 1880–1920 generally lacks any perception of the Negro as a human being with potentialities for improvement."[109] That was true of many whites in the American West, including Omaha, who felt the same about Native Americans, Hispanics, and Chinese.

The data support the contention that a subculture of violence existed among blacks in Douglas County. Although black homicide indictment rates were high for the forty-year period, the rates jump significantly in the two decades following 1900 (see fig. 3.4). Southern blacks brought their subculture of violence with them into Omaha, almost doubling their homicide indictment rate for 1900 to 1910. The low homicide indictment rates for whites also support the theory of a black subculture of violence. White rates held steady at approximately 4 per 100,000 the entire four decades (fig. 3.4). High levels of violence were subcultural, not regional.

Lynchings

Although homicide normally is a confrontation between two individuals, under certain circumstances homicide is committed by a group of a handful to hundreds, even thousands, of participants. Newspaper accounts of two lynchings in Omaha provide graphic depictions of such group killings.

Concurrent with legal abandonment, many groups, particularly in the South, subjected blacks to ruthless, often lethal forms of violence. Lynchings were common toward the end of the nineteenth century, and not confined to the South. Violent race riots occurred sporadically throughout the North, including those in Springfield, Ohio, in 1904; Springfield, Illinois, in 1908; East St. Louis, Illinois, in 1917; and Chicago in 1919.[110]

Omaha's predominately white population developed and harbored significant animosity toward blacks during the period 1880 to 1920, and occasionally people vented it in violent ways. Although lynch-mob violence has more commonly been associated with the Far or Mountain West, particularly California, Montana, Wyoming, and Arizona, thousands of Omaha residents participated in and witnessed two lynchings of blacks and two other attempted hangings.

On Friday evening, October 9, 1891, only a few hours after a legal execution had been carried out at the Douglas County jail, and possibly spurred into action by the spectacle of that event, a crowd of about a thousand people began to form around the courthouse. George Smith, a black who had been recently jailed and accused of sexually assaulting a young white girl, became the object of their intense interest. The crowd grew steadily as the night wore on, and eventually 15,000 people, including "hundreds of women," had gathered. As they milled around the courthouse with no apparent leadership except some men under the influence of alcohol, many of them discussed a report that had been broadcast throughout the city the day before and "published in the evening papers regarding the alleged death of little five-year-old Lizzie Yates, who was brutally assaulted by a burly negro."[111]

As the crowd grew, several agitators continuously taunted and yelled, "Bring out the nigger!" Then someone yelled, "Let's break the door." Sheriff John F. Boyd came out on the steps of the courthouse to address the crowd, but although he may have wanted to disperse them, his words only increased the taunts and yelling. Boyd pleaded, "Gentlemen and fellow citizens, as sheriff of Douglas County I command you to disperse." Unfortunately, he closed by saying, "If I had my way, and was not sheriff, I would furnish the rope to hang the wretch."[112] This last comment seemed to encourage the more aggressive members of the crowd, who began to increase their shouts of "Give us the nigger." At this point the crowd quickly turned into an unruly mob. A group of men brought up a utility pole and began to ram the door of the jail. City council representative Edward F. Morearty encouraged them by breaking out the jail windows with his cane. The mob became more emboldened with every passing minute. They quickly broke in the door and overwhelmed the jailers inside. One member of the mob took a position by the door and kept the people surrounding the courthouse informed about the proceedings within the jail. "They are working on the door." "The nigger is praying." Without warning, a large group of men suddenly burst explosively through the jail doors with a long rope tied around their victim's neck. A hundred men grabbed the rope and ran down the steps of the courthouse and into the street. Their victim "was dragged by the neck all the way and must have been nearly dead before he had been dragged 100 feet. The mob rushed upon him, kicking and jumping upon him as he was jerked down over the rough pavement, his clothing being almost entirely torn from his body, and the skin and flesh bruised and bleeding in a shocking manner."[113] Police officers struggled in vain to seize the prisoner. The reporter noted, "The officers had the good sense not to draw their clubs or revolvers. If they had there would have been terrible bloodshed."[114] George Smith, the victim, possibly with a last gasp, protested, "You are killing me! By God, I'm innocent!"[115] After dragging him in the street, the mob threw the rope over a streetcar line and quickly pulled him into the air. Some observers believed that Smith probably died before he was actually hanged.[116] "The people remained quiet for a time, hardly recognizing that it was really a lynching that they were witnessing. Then some men grew faint and began pushing their way out while others began jostling inward to get a closer look."[117]

It was an incredibly frightening scene. The reporter noted that the hanging brought satisfaction to the huge mob gathered around the corpse. "Then such a yell! It sounded like the chorus that arises from the camp of a band of Indians engaged in a war dance. . . . No tragedy ever to be enacted in the theatre just across the street will thrill an audience with horror as did that spectacle."[118] A reporter observed that "no serious accidents occurred" during the wild spectacle that engulfed the county courthouse.[119] After the hanging, several leading citizens spoke to the crowd. George O'Brien said, "Of course public sentiment will frown upon such action as this as long as there are laws. I don't think there is a married man or woman, a sister, brother, father or mother in the whole city of Omaha that will not commend your actions of tonight and say that you all did right."[120] When Coroner C. P. Harrigan arrived, he added his comments: "What is done is done, actions speak louder than words." Despite yells of protest to "Let him hang damn him, it was a good job," the undertakers quickly cut down the corpse and placed it in a box, and the "wagon drove away down Farnam street at a gallop."[121]

The true magnitude of the tragedy lies buried in another newspaper account of the lynching. George Smith, a family man with a wife and a three-year-old son, lived in a house at Tenth and Nicholas streets. The victim had no prior criminal record, was gainfully employed, and had other relatives, including his mother, a brother, and a sister, living nearby. Smith's surviving family and relatives were devastated by the dramatic events that had overwhelmed them. Three days later, "the wife of the dead man stated most positively to Police Judge Lee Helsley this morning that at the time the assault was committed, between 2 and 4 o'clock Wednesday afternoon he was at home helping her to wash."[122] One reporter visited the home of Smith's widow and orphan son to discuss the events, "but they were too much overcome by the sudden developments of last night to talk about the matter."[123] With a touch of irony, an *Omaha Daily Bee* reporter visited the home of Smith's alleged victim and found that she was recovering from the shock of her attack. She had not been killed.[124]

On March 16, 1906, another mob gathered at the courthouse to demand release to them of three black men accused of killing a streetcar conductor during a robbery attempt. Following the same pattern described above, the crowd began to grow, and "those under the influence of liquor were the natural leaders, as they made more noise." By midnight the crowd had turned into an unruly mob. The bolder ones began to batter the door with a huge utility pole and broke quickly into the outer office of the jail. "Just as the lock of the second door was broken several police officers and deputy sheriffs in the jail poured out and began raining heavy blows on the heads of the intruders."[125] The rest of the crowd rushed to get out, many bruised and bloody from their wounds. This seemed to cool the mob somewhat, but several yelled for some dynamite. Finally the mob began to disperse. Only "an occasional yell or a pistol shot" in the air broke the silence that seemed to fall over the gathering. "As quietly and as mysteriously as they had come these would-be avengers . . . made their exit and faded away into the darkest shadows of Omaha's highways and byways."[126]

A murder in August 1917 in the community of Florence, several miles north of Omaha, incited another lynching attempt. When news that a black accused of the crime had been captured, "the infuriated citizens of Florence, a mob of men and boys congregated with the avowed intention of getting the slayer and hanging him to the tallest tree in the city." On this occasion, however, the prisoner was quickly taken to Omaha, and the lack of opportunity may have prevented another lynching.[127]

The most infamous Omaha lynching of a black occurred at the end of World War I. This cataclysmic event suggests the depth and intensity of racial fear and hatred harbored within the city. Several months prior to the lynching, the *Omaha Daily Bee* conducted a concerted campaign labeling all blacks as criminals.[128] Black newspaperman H. J. Pinkett complained bitterly that other newspapers, most especially the *Bee,* vilified blacks. In an editorial Pinkett claimed that "within the past three months the daily papers have run stories of more than twenty cases of rape or attempted rape on white women by Negroes."[129] The following month, police arrested William Brown, a black male accused of assaulting a white woman. The *Omaha Daily Bee* ran two large inflammatory banner headlines on September 26 and 27, 1919: "Girl identifies assailant" and "Officers keep mob off Negro." Accompanying the headlines was a story that

Race rioters gathering in front of the Douglas County courthouse in Omaha, Nebraska, September 28, 1919. (Courtesy of Nebraska State Historical Society, no. M936-72)

indicated the police had arrested Brown and taken him to the victim's house. According to police, "when Agnes Lobeck was brought into the room where the Negro stood she cried hysterically and repeatedly said: 'That's the man; that's the man.' "[130] Word spread that Agnes's attacker had been identified and was still at the Lobeck home. A crowd of about 250 men and women quickly began to gather around the house. One man in the crowd threw a lasso around the suspect's head, but the police officers jerked it off. The police officers were virtually under siege until reinforcements arrived and quickly spirited the alleged attacker away to the city jail.[131]

The next day, Sunday, September 28, a crowd began to gather around the county courthouse and jail. By early evening 15,000 or more men, young boys, and women were shouting racial epithets, taunting the police, and demanding that Brown pay for his crime. Law enforcement officials made virtually the same mistakes that their predecessors had in 1891. For unknown reasons the chief ordered forty police officers, held in reserve for an emergency, to go home. Less than an hour later the mob taunts increased, and the more aggressive individuals began looting gun shops and pawnshops for guns and ammunition. Others brought up a utility pole and began to assault the courthouse doors. Minutes later they set the building on fire with gasoline, forcing the police and sheriff's deputies to retreat toward the roof. When the final assault occurred, the "policemen and county officials, who were scattered through the building, offered no resistance to the mob."[132] By the time the mob emerged from the courthouse with their victim, "he had been beaten unconscious and every vestige of clothing torn from his body." "String him up and let us fill his body full of bullets," shouted one man. Another man rushed up and fired a full clip of ammunition from a .45 Colt automatic into the victim as he lay helpless on the pavement. Someone shouted, "Wait until we get him dangling into the air before you do any more shooting."[133] "No sooner was Brown's body hoisted than the mob opened up on his body with rifles, shotguns, and revolvers." Within minutes the "body was virtually shot to pieces as it hung suspended. We are going to teach these fiends a lesson, shouted the mob. . . . Any nigger who does this thing again will know what is coming to him."[134]

A significant number of similarities between the events surrounding the 1891 and 1919 lynchings are quite striking. First, prior to both lynchings Omaha experienced a significant increase in black population that made these new residents more visible. Between 1880 and 1890 the black population increased dramatically from 811 to 4,665. Similarly, during the "Great Migration" the black population doubled from 5,143 in 1910 to 10,315 by 1920. This increased "visibility" probably helped to trigger racial hatred toward these new citizens.

Second, in both cases police took the alleged suspect to the victim's house for identification, which created unrest in the neighborhood and led to rumors that the suspect had been "positively" identified.[135] Once the alleged attacker had been "identified," rumors spread quickly and brought hostile reactions that led to the gathering of a large mob. With a white population that apparently had developed a deep-seated hatred of blacks, any minor incident involving racial issues turned into a volatile situation. There was no physical evidence in either case to connect the suspect with the victim.[136]

In both cases law enforcement authorities made no plans to assure that their prisoner could be held safely until the criminal justice system dealt with the suspect. In each lynching the leaders of the mob were either community leaders or members who reflected a middle-class perspective. These "leading" citizens

Members of the lynch mob gather around the burning body of William Brown near the Douglas County courthouse, September 29, 1919. (Courtesy of Nebraska State Historical Society, no. M936-72)

encouraged the mob with their physical acts and racial taunts. Large numbers of women participated in both lynchings, offering support and encouraging the mob to attack the jail and hang their intended black victim to "save their honor." In both cases, despite attempts to prosecute the leaders of the mobs, not a single person paid for the crime.

Conclusions

The rich statistical data available in Douglas County provide an opportunity to examine the interaction of blacks and whites who committed homicide. Although more whites were indicted for committing homicides (206 cases compared to 66 for blacks), blacks had a much higher representation (24 percent of the actual indictments) (see fig. 2.1). The evidence suggests that a subculture of violence existed within the black ghetto that developed in downtown Omaha. The rapid relocation of thousands of blacks, mostly from the South (79 and 77 percent, respectively, for the 1900 and 1910 censuses), included many individuals who had experienced or seen violence at the hands of whites. They brought with them an exaggerated sense of honor that would not tolerate a careless comment, a jostle on the street, or a derogatory gesture. Such behavior could bring a quick violent response.

This black subculture could be seen within the red-light district around a core of saloons and brothels concentrated between Douglas and Davenport from Eighth to Fourteenth streets, an area known for vice, crime, and alcohol. The large number of homicides within or near this area involving blacks reveals the effects of the subculture of violence. Whether the victims were white or black, the killings usually involved alcohol and handguns. Saloons were the only place where blacks and whites mixed on a social level, and in some cases there was discrimination against black customers. Saloons thus became the "hot points" for potentially violent racial interaction.

Many who visited saloons in the red-light district were armed. The availability of cheap handguns that could be purchased at pawnshops or gun stores in downtown Omaha and slipped into any pocket encouraged men to walk around "ready for action." They usually got it. Blacks, who had experienced violence in the South, carried handguns for "protection" against whites or anyone who might accost them. The combination of a gun in his pocket, a drink in his hand, and an exaggerated southern code of honor that required a man to stand up for his rights or to protect his woman often led to a deadly conclusion. The homicide statistics confirm this. Interracial killings involving white victims occurred mainly on black "turf" in and around the red-light district. They involved alcohol and usually took place within or near a saloon. White violence, however, sometimes reflected the mentality of the mob, reminiscent of the South. Lynchings and attempted hangings of blacks in Omaha suggest that whites harbored deep-seated animosity toward blacks.

It should not be surprising that the Douglas County criminal justice system, dominated by a white society, convicted blacks at a much higher rate than whites. Racism might not have been as openly blatant or as vicious in Omaha as it was in the South, but it did exist. Saloon keepers refused to serve blacks, landlords forced them to settle into limited downtown areas, covenants prevented them from buying homes, businessmen hired them only for the lowest paying jobs, some companies fired employees without just cause, and police officers singled out blacks for "special" treatment, including physical violence. This lack of job mobility coupled with racial discrimination became the seeds of their destruction. But, in the final analysis, what is terribly disturbing and frighteningly ironic is that blacks left the South and moved to Omaha to escape "injustice in the courts, [and] lynching."[137]

4

The Violent West

Social Instability in Las Animas County, Colorado

Western historians have been exploring the ethnic-minority experience in a variety of categories, but little attention has been given to their treatment within criminal justice systems in the American West. Las Animas County, Colorado, with its rich ethnic composition that included Hispanics, Italians, Greeks, Serbs, Czechs, blacks, and other whites, offers an opportunity to examine the treatment of ethnic-minority defendants accused of murder.

The role of Hispanics in the West has received a great deal of attention in the past three decades.[1] There have been fewer studies dealing with other ethnic groups in the region.[2] Sarah Deutsch provides the best new scholarship on Hispanics in her book *No Separate Refuge,* a discussion of gender, class, and cultural change in the Southwest.[3] Deutsch pays particular attention to changes in Hispanic culture and the role of women in the southern Colorado coal mine towns. Her study includes a discussion of the Colorado Fuel and Iron Company's attempts to dominate the region. Despite the ethnic mix that included more than twenty different ethnic groups in the tent camps during the 1913 strike, Deutsch notes that the labor struggle "was not between Anglos and Hispanics but between the company and strikers."[4]

This case study focuses on the treatment of Hispanic and Italian defendants in Las Animas County, Colorado, and reveals that high homicide indictment rates resulted from the development of a regional culture of violence.[5] The critical convergence of a variety of factors helps to explain this phenomenon. Coal mining, the coercive nature of company towns, rapid population growth, bitter coal mining strikes, heavy alcohol consumption, the propensity to carry concealed handguns, the mixing of widely divergent ethnic groups in sufficient numbers, and the tendency of the general population to accept high levels of violence all tended to create social instability. The effect of these factors is reflected in two very important ways: first, in very high homicide indictment rates, much higher than in eastern urban centers such as Boston, Philadelphia, and New York;[6] and second, in low homicide conviction rates. An examination of Las Animas County homicide indictment data and comparison with similar statistics from eastern and other western cities will reveal and help to explain this regional culture of violence.

On July 18, 1911, a headline in the *Trinidad Chronicle-News*—"Ranchman's slain body riddled by bullets of assassin"—announced yet another ambush killing.[7] Whoever committed the crime had waited along a lonely county road near Aguilar, in northern Las Animas County, and had shot Ignacio Disalvo in the back with a shotgun at close range. "Disatio [*sic*] was literally blown to pieces by the shots. The top of his head was blown off, both arms shattered and broken, one charge had struck him in the back, another in the legs, while a fifth charge was evidently fired as the victim lay dying, face upward, in the roadway."[8]

This particular case has all the markings of an Italian vendetta,[9] and it was not the only homicide with such indications. In fact, at least twenty-one such cases among the homicides committed in Las Animas County may have been vendetta related. These unusual cases point contemporary scholars to a largely unexplored area of western legal history[10] and offer an opportunity to explore ethnic homicides—in this case Italian vendettas or feuds and their consequences. In the first case study (Douglas County, Nebraska), the ethnic, racial, regional, and social variables were somewhat different, but it has been demonstrated that violence in the form of homicide was fairly common. In comparison, just how violent was Las Animas County, Colorado? From the data available, can we conclude that its residents developed a regional culture or a subculture of violence? And if so, what ethnic groups were part of it, and how can we explain the appearance of the Italian vendetta within the larger context of this theory? An examination of this region may provide further insights into violence levels in the American West.

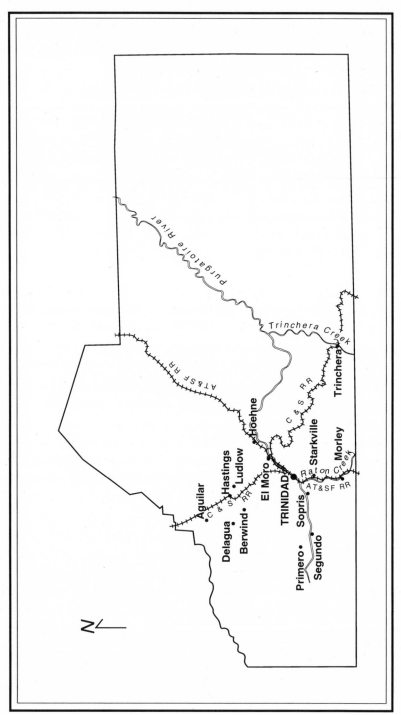

Las Animas County, Colorado

Table 4.1 Homicide Indictments,
Las Animas County, 1880–1920

	N	%
Other white	105	37
Hispanic	90	32
Italian	74	26
Black	11	4
Greek	2	1
Total	282[a]	100

Source: Registers of criminal action.
[a] This total does not include the 124
homicide indictments for the period
August 1913–14 following the Ludlow
massacre.

This case study relies on statistical data collected from the Las Animas County *Registers of Criminal Action.*[11] In a pattern similar to Douglas County, Nebraska, homicide in Las Animas County tended to be a male crime (96 percent of all homicide indictments involved men). Only 4 percent of the indictments were of women, who were also less likely to be convicted of murder (36 percent). The homicide indictment data for this rural county (table 4.1) reflect the ethnic variety of nineteenth-century society as a whole: 37 percent of those indicted were other whites,[12] followed by Hispanics[13] and Italians (32 and 26 percent, respectively). The significant number of Italian and Hispanic defendants provides an opportunity to examine their treatment within the Las Animas County criminal justice system.

Trinidad

Trinidad, Colorado, is situated in the narrow valley of the Purgatoire River on a mile-high plateau in southeastern Colorado, about twenty miles north of the New Mexico border. Hispanics from New Mexico established a permanent settlement there around 1860.[14] Within a decade whites also began to settle along the Purgatoire River (often called "the Picketwire"). Coal mining, cattle and sheep ranching, and the Atchison, Topeka and Santa Fe Railroad (built through Trinidad in 1878) provided employment. By the 1880s Trinidad had gained a reputation for being a wild, "wide open" town with numerous saloons and gambling parlors that attracted a wide variety of misfits. Gamblers, cowboys, ranchers, and some notorious characters visited the town, including Pat Garrett, Joe Antrim, Frank Loving, Charles Goodnight, Billy the Kid, Wyatt Earp, and Bat Masterson. After one shooting in 1882, newspapers labeled the town "Turbulent Trinidad."[15] To deal with this lawlessness, officials invited Bat Masterson and his brother to serve as marshals, but the Mastersons apparently contributed little to taming the town. In 1883 Bat ran for reelection as marshal of Trinidad and lost. He quickly left town, never to return.[16]

Located strategically in an ideal valley for a railroad route, Trinidad became the county seat and played a vital role in regional politics. Within two decades its population quadrupuled, growing from a sleepy town of 2,226 in 1880 to a dynamic economic center with a bustling population of 10,000 by 1910. The railroad and the development of coal mining provided the impetus for this rapid growth, which also impacted smaller mining towns such as Aguilar, Cokedale, Primero, Segundo, Sopris, Starkville, and Forbes.

Ethnic Migration

Hispanics first settled in the Purgatoire Valley by late 1859. In 1861, Felipe Baca and Hilario Madrid led a group of New Mexican settlers from Mora County into the Purgatoire Valley. The Madrid, Vigil, and Valdéz families decided to settle farther west. The small towns along "the Picketwire" still bear their names.[17] The 1900 census revealed that 10,222 Coloradans claimed heritage from New Mexico; most lived in Las Animas County.[18] A significant number of whites from eastern regions also began to move into the Purgatoire Valley, and by the 1880s they were challenging Hispanic hegemony in Las Animas County.

After a series of incidents, the two groups became involved in "the battle of Trinidad" on December 25, 1867. A fight broke out between the two ethnic groups during a celebration, and as a result one Hispanic was killed. After the accused was jailed, his friends broke into his cell and released him. Sheriff Gutierrez formed a posse and attempted to recapture the accused and his friends, who barricaded themselves in an adobe house. Four days later federal troops arrived and placed Trinidad under martial law.[19]

Although Hispanics soon became a minority, they still could muster enough votes to influence various political offices. Members of the Vigil, Barela, and Tafoya families served in a wide variety of administrative capacities, as judges, sheriffs, and other local officials.[20]

The first contingent of blacks, recruited by the Colorado Fuel and Iron Company to work as strikebreakers, arrived from Chattanooga, Tennessee, in 1884. As elsewhere in the United States, blacks in Colorado faced discrimination and segregation in company housing and within the mines. Some company-town managers refused to hire blacks.[21] Although never very numerous, blacks were represented in several of the Las Animas County mining communities as well as in Trinidad.

With the intensification of coal production, company officials began to hire agents to recruit emigrants from eastern European countries and Greece and Italy. Italians first entered Las Animas County in the 1880s. The first wave of Italian emigrants was from northern Italy, but by 1890 the southern portion, including Sicily, became the main region of out-migration. Italians from the rural areas of southern Italy predominated in the immigration movement to America that jumped from slightly more than a half million during the period 1891–1900 to more than two million during the first decade of the twentieth century.[22] The reasons for this are mainly related to agriculture and include insufficient rainfall, poor topsoil, and deforestation, particularly in southern Italy.[23] Population growth in Italy increased faster than food production during the last three decades of the nineteenth century. Already living on the margins of society, many Italians of the *contadino* class were on the verge of starvation. Some of these poorer agricultural workers began to sign up with *padrones* as common laborers to relocate in the United States.[24] However, only a small minority of Italians emigrated in this manner; most raised enough money to gain passage on their own.

Other factors also pressured Italians to leave their homeland for a new start. Volcanic eruptions, floods, pestilence, and other disasters created hardships that increased immigration to the Western Hemisphere.[25] Although Brazil and Argentina received large numbers of Italian emigrants, the United States soon became their main destination, particularly between 1896 and 1914. Job opportunities were the main attraction, and Italian emigrants created a network of communication between their new homes and their relatives in Italy. Industrialization in the United States assured employment and higher wages. Although most Italian emigrants moved into the cities, a significant group ended up in the coal mining towns of West Virginia and Colorado. Many sent money home to pay transportation expenses for their relatives.[26]

Some of these new emigrants from southern Italy were recruited by the coal companies to work in the mines of Huerfano and Las Animas counties in southern Colorado. By 1900 the Las Animas County census listed at least 1,625 residents who had been born in Italy, and a decade later 5,289 residents were identified as Italian.[27] Coal company operators often hired Italian, Greek, and eastern European emigrants to break strikes. Consequently, tensions between Italians and other whites and Hispanics surfaced early and continued to create problems, particularly during labor disputes. For example, in the early 1890s mobs lynched Italians in Gunnison and Denver. The Gunnison victims had killed a contractor during a job dispute. The day after the suspect was captured, a mob took him from the sheriff and hanged him. In 1895 six Italians implicated in the death of an American saloon keeper were killed by a mob of miners in the southern Colorado coal fields, and less than a decade later a mob hanged four Italians in Walsenburg, Huerfano County, about forty miles north of Trinidad.[28] These violent outbreaks indicate the hostility and ethnic prejudice harbored by those who controlled the power structure in southern Colorado counties.

Although less numerous, Greeks also immigrated to Las Animas County. Greece suffered from agricultural problems similar to those in Italy, and after the "complete failure of the currant crop" on the Peloponnesian peninsula in the 1880s, Greek farm laborers began to relocate in large numbers.[29] By the 1890s thousands of Greeks joined Italians in an exodus from the Mediterranean region. During the first decade of the twentieth century 167,579 Greeks immigrated to the United States. Throughout this period, many of them migrated to the intermountain West, with Idaho, Montana, Wyoming, Nevada, Utah, and Colorado their final destinations.[30] Although not particularly numerous in Las Animas County, Greek workers played an important role in labor organization in the coal mines.[31] During the 1913 coal miners' strike Louis Tikas served as an organizer for the United Mine Workers, and in 1914 he acted as director of the Ludlow tent camp.[32]

Coal companies increased their recruiting, especially after 1900, and hundreds of Italians and Greeks arrived in response to the need for strikebreakers during the 1903 strike. Company policy of replacing one ethnic group with another was part of "a conscious strategy" to divide mine workers and to hinder union organization.[33] By 1913 twenty-one different European ethnic groups, as well as Asians, Hispanics, and blacks, could be found living in company towns and laboring in the Las Animas County coal mines.[34]

Company Towns

The numerous towns that quickly developed in Las Animas County often had Hispanic names such as Aguilar, Vigil, Primero, Segundo, El Moro, and Valdéz. Some predated the coal mining boom, but others were created when John D.

Rockefeller's Colorado Fuel and Iron Company purchased thousands of acres in the county. Company towns were also established by the Victor-American Fuel Company. As soon as a company gained rights to the land, it quickly established control over the towns that were central to its mining operations. The coal companies restructured the Hispanic villages, and company towns were developed on a grid pattern with no central plaza or square.[35] These towns displayed none of the casual and warm ambience of traditional Hispanic villages. Company managers evicted most of the inhabitants, now labeled squatters, and developed company towns operated by mining officials, controlled by company guards, and backed by county political and legal power. Within a decade the Colorado Fuel and Iron Company virtually controlled Las Animas County politics by dominating its courts, the county sheriff, and the coroner's office.[36]

From Matewan, West Virginia, to Ludlow, Colorado, the coal mining industry gained a reputation for rough handling of labor, and the company town is a good example of its methods. The company towns throughout Las Animas County were created to provide housing for workers close to the coal mines and to develop a mechanism to control labor. The company towns of Berwind, Forbes, Delagua, Hastings, and Tabasco dotted the rugged canyons of northern Las Animas County. With the exception of Hastings (constructed by the Victor-American Fuel Company in 1893), all of these company towns were established after 1900, the main boom period of the coal mining industry in Colorado. A similar pattern occurred in southern Las Animas County with the development of Primero, Segundo, Valdéz, Sopris, Cokedale, Starkville, and Morley. Only Morley, Sopris, and Starkville predated 1900, and Colorado Fuel and Iron established Primero and Segundo in 1902.[37]

Anyone approaching one of these towns quickly realized that it belonged to the company. "Private Property—Keep Out" signs and a gate impressed all visitors. "Armed guards, employed by the coal company and deputized by the sheriff of the county, watched over the gates and kept order in the camp."[38] The first camps suffered from poor construction, inadequate sanitary conditions, poor water quality, and crowded living quarters. In many ways company towns resembled twentieth-century migrant-worker camps constructed throughout the Midwest, Florida, Texas, and California to house Hispanic agricultural workers.

In 1901 Colorado Fuel and Iron organized a "sociological department" to improve housing and living conditions in the camps, but despite a decade of work, town life had improved little by 1913. Eugene S. Gaddis, superintendent

Table 4.2 Company-Town
Ethnic Composition, 1913

	%
Other white	26.0
Italian	25.5
Hispanic	21.0
East European	13.0
Greek	5.6
Other	4.9
Black	4.0

Source: Eugene S. Gaddis, "Gaddis
Exhibit," in *Industrial Relations: Final
Report and Testimony*, vol. 8, (Washing-
ton, D.C.: U.S. GPO, 1916), 8905–6.

of the Department of Sociology, visited virtually every camp in the coal mining
district and found as many as "eight persons" crowded into one small room
designed to house only one or two. He further complained that "many of the
miners' families are living in hovels, box-car shacks, and adobe sheds that are
not fit for the habitation of human beings."[39] Conditions at some of the camps
were distressing. Gaddis reported that at one coal camp a "cesspool within a few
feet of the company store" had been allowed to overflow across the road for
more than a year without any attempts to alleviate the unhealthy conditions.
Seepage water from the mines had been allowed to contaminate the water
supply of three camps. In 1912–13, company-town physicians reported 151
cases of typhoid. Gaddis concluded that medical treatment for the camps in Las
Animas County was inadequate.[40] One author suggests that "the company had
unlimited resources with which to improve conditions, but chose not to do so."[41]
It appears that management was determined to increase profits while maintaining control of labor.

The company towns varied in size from 362 in Forbes to 1,441 in Sopris. The
ethnically diverse population within each camp usually included a mix of Italians, Hispanics, Greeks, east Europeans, and in a few of the camps, blacks.
Company policy, reflecting national social trends, segregated blacks and Hispanics, usually relegating them to the least appealing housing, reserving the
better structures for white workers.[42] Italians were the largest ethnic group,

followed by Hispanics (table 4.2). Among the eastern Europeans were four different groups: Bohemians, Austrians, Hungarians, and Slavs. The isolation of the company towns prevented effective union organizing and created a strong worker dependency by forcing laborers to purchase groceries and other goods from company stores.

COMPANY STORES

The Colorado Fuel and Iron Company established a chain of ten company stores throughout Las Animas County both as a money-making venture and to restrict outside influences.[43] The company-store concept positively and negatively affected mine workers. Living in the isolated canyons of Las Animas County with inadequate transportation, workers depended on the company store for food and various supplies. Most of the stores offered a wide variety of goods including bulk food items such as flour, sugar, coffee, vegetables, and fruit, as well as canned goods. Men could buy tobacco, pipes, and clothes, and their wives could order dresses and other items, including furniture. Since the company store usually contained the U.S. Post Office, it often became a gathering place where workers smoked and exchanged small talk or gossip while their wives shopped. In many ways it was their only contact with the outside world.

Company stores had significant flaws, however, that created hostility among the workers. The song parody "I owe my soul to the company store" had basis in fact.[44] The Colorado Fuel and Iron Company paid its workers in scrip redeemable only at the company store. Although Colorado passed laws to end this practice, they were largely ignored. Before the worker received his scrip, the company deducted charges for housing, medical dues, power and water, oil lamps, powder, caps, and fuses. These charges could total more than sixty dollars, or about 50 percent of the average worker's monthly pay.[45] Workers could obtain cash only by selling their scrip to brokers at discounted rates of from 15 to 25 percent.[46]

To prevent cash conversion and increase profits, company officials pressured workers to buy only from the company store, and many workers believed that they would be fired if they did not comply. The isolation of most company towns made it almost impossible to shop elsewhere. On occasion there might be an independent merchant outside the camp limits, but since the company owned most of the surrounding land, it was a rarity. Mine workers also complained of high prices. The company's demand that the stores be profitable motivated managers to mark up all their products. In his company history, H. Lee

Scamehorn admits that "profits had been excessive for a number of years," with earnings averaging 12.6 percent between 1918 and 1923.[47] These factors eventually contributed to union organizing.

COMPANY SALOONS

Virtually every company town boasted a company-owned saloon that provided a social gathering place for all coal miners, regardless of ethnic background. Hispanics, Italians, Greeks, and east Europeans lived and worked together in towns such as Berwind, Segundo, Primero, Forbes, and Ludlow, and they usually drank together in the company saloons. Saloons were not confined to the company towns, however. In 1907, Trinidad, the commercial and political seat of county government, supported thirty-seven saloons, and less than a decade later it still maintained thirty-five drinking spots. Aguilar, another non-company town, with a population of 1,400, supported ten saloons. These liquor

Saloons like this one in Douglas, Colorado, (circa 1890s) proved to be hot spots for violence involving coal miners, liquor, and handguns. (Courtesy of Colorado Historical Society, no. F43379)

Table 4.3 Company-Town Populations and
Saloons, Las Animas County, 1913

Company town	Population	Saloons
Berwind	650	2
Delagua	1,024	2
El Moro	579	3
Engle	668	5
Hastings	753	3
Segundo	1,000	24
Sopris	1,000	18
Starkville	1,400	12
Weston	646	5

Source: Eugene S. Gaddis, "Gaddis Exhibit," in
Industrial Relations: Final Report and Testimony, vol. 8,
(Washington, D.C.: U.S. GPO, 1916), 8915–17;
Trinidad City and Las Animas County Directory, 1907 (Salt
Lake City: n.p., 1907), 284–87; and *Trinidad City and
Las Animas County Directory, 1915–1916* (Salt Lake
City: n.p., 1916), 315–17.

emporiums provided the social center for virtually all communities in Las Animas County, but the saloons under company jurisdiction proved to be particularly disreputable.

Eugene Gaddis, the Department of Sociology superintendent for the Colorado Fuel and Iron Company, complained bitterly about the saloons in or near
company towns. In 1908 he counted eighty-two saloons on property owned by
John D. Rockefeller, and he perceived them to be the single most disruptive
aspect of company-town life.[48] Every company town maintained at least one
saloon. In 1913 Sopris (population 1,000) supported eighteen, and other company towns had similar numbers (table 4.3). Segundo (population 1,000) had
twenty-four saloons in 1913, or one saloon per forty-two inhabitants.[49]

The number of saloons was not all that concerned Gaddis; the disreputable
nature of some of these establishments created a good deal of controversy. Yet,
as he complained, the saloon offered the "only one place of public resort."
Because of the miserable living conditions in company towns, miners needed
some sort of diversion, and because there were no other recreational facilities,
the saloons became the social focus for men. Gaddis bitterly complained that
"there are many of our men living in shacks and dugouts almost without light or

heat and where there is no place for them to spend their spare time except at the saloon."[50] He recommended developing a "social settlement house" or some recreational facility that served soft drinks to allow the miners to enjoy their leisure hours without having to visit saloons. He noted that "a number of Italians play a ball game in the camp, and the losers of the game buy a bucket of beer."[51]

Other observers provided similar documentation: "You see that bucket? When we come out of the mine we used to go to the saloon, 10¢ fill 'em up. See, everybody go there when coming out of the mine, they stop in the saloon on the way home, for 10¢, fill up your bucket and take it home and you drink."[52] Frank Wojtylka of Cokedale reminisced about life in the company town: "You'd find a lot of guys at the saloon there. . . . They'd be all over the porch stretched out drunk."[53] Miners spent as much as 30 percent of their wages in the saloons and gambling halls in the company towns. Scamehorn agreed that "saloons, gambling halls, and houses of prostitution robbed employees of their earnings."[54] Bartenders violated liquor laws by serving minors, opening their bars illegally on Sundays, and staying open after state-mandated closing times. Gaddis found youngsters "not more than 16 years drinking liquor" in some of these saloons.[55]

Saloons provided not only the focal point for social gatherings, but also the mix of alcohol, guns, and ethnic groups that often led to violence. In Las Animas County, homicides were frequently committed by perpetrators under the influence, and with mining communities supporting at least eighty-four saloons in 1907 and eighty-one in 1915, it should not be surprising that these diverse communities experienced significant violence.

COMPANY POLICE

The Colorado Fuel and Iron Company provided its own law enforcement within company towns by appointing town marshals. These company guards or marshals also received deputy sheriff status. This practice is evidence of the political persuasion of the Las Animas County sheriff and the close relationship with company administrators and county officials.[56] Armed guards or town marshals controlled access to the company towns and watched closely for union organizers. Barron Beshoar observed that "intruders and malcontents were ferreted out by an intricate espionage system and treated by heavily-armed guards to the kangaroo, the coal district term for a professional beating. Along with the kangaroo went the dread sentence of 'Down the cañon.' And to go 'down the cañon' meant blacklisting and starvation—or exile."[57] Scamehorn naively claims that "marshals also handled disturbances, and they discouraged

Trinidad police officers, January 25, 1897. (Courtesy of Colorado Historical Society, no. F43351)

crimes and unwanted disturbances. Acts of violence were rare in the compact communities."[58] He could not have been more mistaken. Beshoar notes that "men could get as drunk as they pleased in the company saloon . . . and brawl with fists or knives without undue interference from the camp marshal or his deputies."[59] He might have added guns to his list of weapons, as verified in the homicide data.

Company police operated more to keep unwanted people out than to control behavior within the company towns. During periods of labor unrest the company brought in "professional" police contracted from the Baldwin-Felts agency. The agency provided what it called "operatives," or "labor spies," to infiltrate the coal camps and find out which workers supported unionization attempts.[60] These individuals were noted for using violence to break up strikes, and the use of weapons in such altercations was common.

Local individuals and Baldwin-Felts operatives selected as town marshals had little, if any, experience in police work. Usually they were chosen for their ability to use weapons. Under such conditions it is not surprising that company police were involved in nine homicides between 1906 and 1915.[61] These figures do not include strike-related shootings, but only those relating to "enforcement" of camp rules.

The repetitive nature of the typical shooting scenario is quite exceptional—virtually all police-related homicides involved guns and alcohol. Seven of the victims (77.7 percent) had been drinking prior to the shootings (the condition of two is unknown). All seven shootings occurred either within or just outside of saloons. At least three of the marshals also had been drinking; the condition of four is unknown.[62] Alcohol clearly played an important role in the behavior patterns of both coal miners and company police. Apparently coal mine operators, county authorities, and miners alike accepted this high level of violence with little, if any, complaint. And during union-organizing attempts and strikes, violence levels increased.

The 1903 Coal Miners' Strike

Colorado miners attempted to organize unions as early as 1878, and strikes occurred periodically after 1880. Leadville miners called a strike in 1880, and Cripple Creek witnessed violent confrontations in 1894. In both cases mine owners, in conjunction with county officials, used violent tactics to subvert unionization.[63] These early disputes were often bitter and usually turned violent. By 1903 the coal mine operators and the miners had become enemies, and having police powers in the hands of the mine owners created an extremely dangerous situation.[64] Colorado was shaken by labor unrest for more than two decades, and two strikes in southeastern Colorado in 1903–4 and 1913–14 provide context for the violent lifestyle of Las Animas County. In both strikes, governors used the Colorado National Guard to aid the company's fight against unionizing attempts.

In 1903 miners struck facilities in Cripple Creek and Telluride, and work stoppages spread rapidly south into Huerfano and Las Animas counties. These strikes forced Colorado citizens to "choose up sides either with the capitalists or with the workers: there was no middle ground."[65] Company operators in Las Animas County quickly hired large numbers of "special deputies" and strikebreakers to end the strike. When this failed, they turned to the state government for help. In an all-too-familiar pattern, the governor cooperated with the coal companies to thwart union-organizing attempts. On March 23, 1904, at the urging of the coal company operators, Governor James Peabody ordered the Colorado National Guard into Las Animas County to "suppress a presumed state of rebellion among coal miners."[66] Mine operators and National Guardsmen employed strong-arm tactics to break the strikers' spirits. Guardsmen hauled "fifty-two men to the state line and warned them never to return."[67] The strike ended with at least thirteen killings, but it was only a prelude to the most important Las Animas County coal miners' strike of 1913–14, discussed below.

Death in the Mines

Life appears to have been cheap in Trinidad and the surrounding mining towns. Mine accidents occurred regularly, injuring and killing thousands. An explosion at the Primero mine on January 31, 1910, killed seventy-five men.[68] Another explosion that year at Delagua killed twenty-three Hispanic miners. On June 19, 1912, twelve men trapped in a mine by an explosion suffocated. During the period 1910–13, at least 618 men lost their lives in mining accidents.[69] On April 27, 1917, an explosion rocked the Hastings mine near Ludlow. "The Hastings explosion was Colorado's worst mine disaster. One hundred twenty-one miners lost their lives in a gas explosion touched off by the mine inspector! Twenty-one matches and an open safety lamp were found next to the inspector's body."[70] This particular disaster indicates both the lack of, and the failure to enforce, safety regulations, a problem for the coal mining industry not only in Colorado, but throughout the United States, yet the coal companies neither received nor accepted blame for accidents. As one observer noted, "Not a single coroner's jury in Huerfano or Las Animas County has for many, many years passed the slightest criticism upon a mine owner, no matter how terrible and shocking was the carelessness which caused explosions in which hundreds of lives were snuffed out."[71]

The daily danger involved in coal mining, the insensitivity of coal mine operators, and the collusion between the companies and county officials may have created a tendency for Las Animas County residents to accept high levels of violence. Although explosions were spectacular, the daily exposure to dangerous machinery and unsafe working situations conditioned miners to accept the unexpected. Coroner's inquests list numerous accidents, many deadly, that became an everyday occurrence in the southeastern Colorado coal mining camps. Thus, even ignoring homicides, Las Animas County was a dangerous place, but the carrying of concealed weapons meant that confrontations in company-town saloons were often lethal.

In Las Animas County, handgun homicides were commonplace in the various mining towns, where 68 percent of the defendants had used handguns. Many men walked around with concealed weapons, and this usually led to

The Victor-American Fuel Company coal mining camp at Hastings, Colorado, site of the worst coal mine explosion in Colorado in 1917. The explosion left 120 miners dead. (Courtesy of Colorado Historical Society, no. 84-193279)

trouble. For example, on Sunday, February 9, 1902, a shooting occurred at about 8 P.M. in Bowen. Tamilado Trujillo had been drinking heavily and started arguing with James Shaw, a mining engineer. Lewis Chambers interceded and pushed Trujillo backward. Both Trujillo and Chambers drew revolvers and fired at close range. Trujillo died within minutes of multiple gunshot wounds. Prosecutors refused to indict Chambers.[72] In February 1903, Joseph Mathews and William Pickett, two coal miners, began a quarrel in Moran's Saloon in Rugby. Both drew revolvers and began shooting. Pickett fell to the floor fatally wounded.[73] That April, Aldridge Clifton got into a shoot-out with Tillman Thomas in a saloon in Bowen and lost.[74] On January 13, 1908, Walter P. Hendricks shot David Lowry to death after being fired upon with a shotgun. A jury found Hendricks not guilty. Late one evening the following September, Casmiro Casares and Gus DiGregorio began to quarrel in a saloon in Morley. Soon they emerged onto the street, drew revolvers, and began firing at each other. Casares fell mortally wounded.[75] A jury found DiGregorio not guilty of murder. Numerous other cases also indicate that both protagonists were armed.[76]

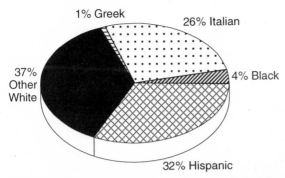

Fig. 4.1. Homicide indictments by race/ethnicity, Las Animas County, 1880–1920. *Source:* Registers of criminal action.

Indictment Data

During the period under study Las Animas County officials filed 282 homicide indictments.[77] Then, as today, homicide usually resulted from violent activity instigated by men; they made up 96 percent of those accused. These crimes often occurred in saloons between people who knew each other. Miners tended to congregate in the saloons after working hours, and alcohol had a way of loosening inhibitions and leading to trouble.[78] Whites composed the largest group of indictments, followed by Hispanics, Italians, blacks, and Greeks (fig. 4.1).

Surprisingly, the conviction rates for the three largest ethnic groups (white, Hispanic, and Italian) show little variance. Guilty-verdict rates were virtually even, with white, Hispanic, and Italian rates of 30, 31, and 26 percent, respectively (fig. 4.2). Italians had the highest not-guilty rate (38 percent), while Hispanics had the highest dismissal rate (42 percent). Considering previous research dealing with ethnic minorities in other regions of the West, these figures are quite remarkable, especially for Italian defendants.[79] The Hispanic totals might be explained by their large representation within the total population in Trinidad. The data strongly suggest that juries were fair in their treatment of ethnic defendants. The high dismissal rates (fig. 4.2) may indicate the inability to find witnesses who would testify, particularly in Italian vendetta cases. Hispanics had a higher dismissal rate, however, of 42 percent. With homicides often taking place in saloons, it is also possible that witnesses would testify for a defendant rather than against him, since they realized that anyone could get involved in fights, and so many carried handguns and were inclined to use them.

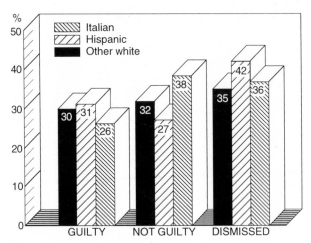

Fig. 4.2. Homicide verdicts by race / ethnicity, Las Animas County, 1880–1920. *Source:* Registers of criminal action.

Table 4.4 Inter-ethnic Homicides, Las Animas County, 1880–1920

Ethnicity of Perpetrator	N	% of total
Other white	14	32
Italian	22	30.5
Hispanic	18	22
Black	2	18

Source: Registers of criminal action.

The conviction rates are even more remarkable when compared with inter-ethnic killings. Italians, Hispanics, blacks, and other whites all killed outside of their ethnic group at a high rate (table 4.4). It is, however, important to add that the relatively high inter-ethnic homicide rates among all groups reflect opportunities created by the social mixing of these ethnic groups in saloons and other gathering places, and the development of a regional culture of violence. Trial verdicts for inter-ethnic killings in Arizona, California, and Nebraska during a similar time period were quite different.[80]

An examination of Las Animas County conviction rates involving inter-ethnic killings reveals a significant decline in convictions (from 27 to 15 percent) for Hispanics accused of killing individuals from other ethnic groups. On the

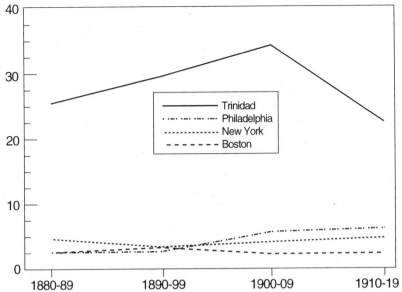

Fig. 4.3. Homicide indictment rates (per 100,000 population) in Las Animas County, Philadelphia, New York, and Boston. *Source:* Registers of criminal action; Roger Lane, *Violent Death in the City: Suicide, Accident, and Murder in Nineteenth Century Philadelphia* (Cambridge: Harvard University Press, 1979), pp. 60 and 71; Roger Lane, "On the Social Meaning of Homicide Trends in America," pp. 66–68, and Eric H. Monkkonen, "Diverging Homicide Rates: England and the United States, 1850–1875," pp. 85–87, in *Violence in America: The History of Crime,* edited by Ted Robert Gurr (Newbury Park, Calif.: Sage Publications, 1989; and Theodore N. Ferdinand, "The Criminal Patterns of Boston Since 1849," *American Journal of Sociology* 63 (July 1967): 84–99.

other hand, Italian defendants had a 21 percent increase in dismissals. White defendants experienced a slight increase in both conviction and dismissal rates. Once again, juries were not inclined to convict defendants unless the circumstances were exceptional. Certainly fights in saloons were not considered heinous, just unfortunate. Some jurors must have looked at the defendant and reasoned, "There, but for the grace of God, go I." Their verdict? Not guilty.

The homicide indictment rates per 100,000 population (fig. 4.3) for Las Animas County are dramatically higher than those in Philadelphia, New York, and Boston for similar periods.[81] Homicide indictment rates in Las Animas County began with a rate of 26 per 100,000 in 1880–89, increased to 35 by the period 1900–1909, then dropped slightly to 28.6 during the last decade.[82] Conditions were quite different in eastern cities, where Philadelphia homicide indictment rates per 100,000 population averaged 2.5 during 1881–1901; New York City homicide rates (not indictments) stayed between 3 and 4 for the same period; and Boston homicide rates hovered between 2 and 3.[83] A similar comparison of indictment data in seven California counties revealed rates per 100,000 averaging 25 in Calaveras and Tuolumne counties, and around 11 in the other five counties for the period 1880–1900.[84] Homicide indictment rates in Las Animas and Douglas counties indicate a much higher level of violence in the West. Analysis of several case studies might be helpful in explaining why.

ITALIAN HOMICIDES

A brief discussion of the concept of vendetta might provide some insights on the social dynamics of this phenomenon that appeared in Las Animas County. Although many Americans are familiar with the Hatfield and McCoy feuds in West Virginia and Kentucky, probably few are aware of vendettas, particularly those that occurred in the United States. The vendetta, with a long historical tradition in the Mediterranean region, is commonly defined as "a feud in which the relatives of a murdered or wronged person seek vengeance on the murderer or wrongdoer or on members of that person's family."[85] During the nineteenth century, Italy, Sardinia, Sicily, Corsica, Greece, Montenegro (located in present-day Serbia), Jordan, Israel, and other nearby regions suffered from numerous homicides related to vendettas or feuds. For example, throughout the first half of the nineteenth century Corsica's homicide rate averaged 37 per 100,000 and reached its apogee in 1848 with a rate of 91.[86] The homicide rates, however, are not as important as the social dynamics of the vendetta or feud. After carefully tracing and examining feuds in nineteenth-century Corsica, Stephen Wilson concluded that definite social-dynamic patterns could be identified. "Feuds went through distinct phases: a phase of escalation very often, then a period of active and violent conflicts, followed by reconciliation, quiescence, and then renewed violence, often after a lapse of many years."[87]

Feuds began for various reasons that often involved honor, especially among young males. If someone damaged your honor, it was essential to humiliate your enemy and in turn sully his honor. Wilson identifies two important aspects of honor among young men. First, it "demanded that men be armed," and second, "the challenge and the insult were crucial elements in male quarrels." Insults included verbal comments, jokes, gestures, and shouts. Sexual references were common, particularly "the notion of being cuckolded," an outrageous comment sure to cause a reaction and possibly a violent attack that might begin a feud. Men's honor "was intimately associated with that of women" through marriage or blood ties.[88]

Vendettas or feuds could begin quite innocently with a comment or gesture that often escalated into violent, explosive confrontations. An individual might be insulted and do nothing about it, but later, after brooding over the insult for days, maybe even weeks or months, the victim would lie in wait with a shotgun and slay the perpetrator of the affront. Ambush became a fairly common method of taking retribution during a vendetta. After a killing occurred, the members of the victim's family usually met and decided upon a course of retribution against the guilty party. In some societies it was imperative that "a vengeance killing take place on the exact spot where the previous victim met his death" and that "the killer who is killed in vengeance . . . [be] killed by a son of his victim."[89] Theoretically, after the family of the first victim retaliated with a killing, the feud was even and could be stopped. In many cases, however, the second killing included a grievous insult such as mutilation of the corpse. This concept of a "pay back in greater measure than was received" quickly escalated the feud. Although cutting off the head was rare, it did occur, and mutilation of sexual organs or cutting out the heart of vendetta victims was common in some societies.[90]

Vendettas were conducted along bloodlines; that is, families or clans tended to rally around the victim or perpetrator of these social killings. Refusal of a marriage proposal between two clans could often explode into a vendetta. Although men predominated in the practice of vendettas, on occasion women were drawn into these feuds both as victims and perpetrators. For example, if a woman refused a marriage proposal, she could become the first victim, sometimes by her own family, for the dishonor brought to them.[91] Rival suitors of the same woman also created fights that could lead to feuds. If a killing occurred, whatever the reasons, the blood relatives of the victim were required to avenge the death. If a father was killed, a son had to take action against the perpetrator's family. Although it was common to attack the killer, any close blood relative was fair game. Therefore the family of the perpetrator usually took precautions that might include barricading their home. If no blood was shed within three days, the family home would be safe, but any blood member of the clan or family could be attacked at any time away from the house.[92]

The attack often came in a well-planned ambush such as that involving Ignacio Disalvo the night of July 17, 1911, on a lonely county road near Aguilar in the northern part of Las Animas County. Two or more persons used two shotguns and a .32 caliber revolver to gain their revenge. Sheriff's deputies investigated the crime scene, discovered "where the weeds had been flattened out," and theorized that two men had waited in ambush.[93] The sheriff arrested Dominic Pistone, a former business partner of the victim, charging him with murder. A young boy had seen a man "carrying a shotgun" go into the Pistone residence soon after the crime had been committed. Other evidence included shoe prints that matched the shoes worn by Pistone, and the accused admitted owning a twelve-gauge shotgun. However, authorities noticed that several sixteen-gauge shotgun shell casings had been found at the scene of the crime, and the coroner discovered a .32 caliber bullet in the victim's body. Locked in jail, "Pistone [was] apparently unperturbed over the suspicions that have [been] directed toward him."[94] This lack of concern was a common trait displayed by individuals involved in vendetta killings in the Mediterranean region. They believed that their killings were "sanctified" by their moral or social code. They had only fulfilled an obligation to their clan or family—nothing more, nothing less. Although indicted, Pistone had little to fear from the Las Animas County criminal justice system. Charges of murder were dismissed. There were, however, other considerations that, after several years, he may have forgotten. Seven years later, almost on the exact day, Antonio Lapreto killed Pistone in Aguilar to resolve the feud.[95]

In a similar case in 1899 the county attorney indicted Guiseppe Maniscala for the murder of Bartolo Sylvestri. Charges against Maniscala were eventually dropped. Seven years later Vincenzo Provenzo shot Maniscala in his own home. Charges against Provenzo were also dropped, and as might be expected in such vendetta cases, a little more than seven years later "persons unknown" with shotguns ambushed and assassinated Provenzo on a country road between Hastings and Aguilar.[96]

Testimony at the coroner's inquest helps to explain the difficulty in finding Provenzo's killer. Provenzo left his home on horseback to visit Hastings. Apparently someone had been closely watching his every move. On his return trip someone waiting in ambush stepped out of the bushes, fired a shotgun blast into his face and upper torso at point-blank range, and literally blew Provenzo off his horse. Then his assailant(s) walked up and fired several shots into the victim as he lay helpless on the road. J. T. Bradley, the coroner, found a shotgun wad in the victim's mouth. Provenzo had been killed with a Peters twelve-gauge shell with I-5 buckshot.[97] The perpetrator did not even bother to pick up the shell casings, suggesting that there was nothing to fear from authorities. Friends of Provenzo noted that he always carried a pistol on his person. The exchange between Coroner J. T. Bradley and Louie Buono reveals the reluctance to implicate

Table 4.5 Vendetta Homicides, Las
Animas County, 1880–1920

	N	% of total
Guilty	3	14
Not guilty	2	9
Dismissed	6	28
Unindicted	10	48

Source: Coroner's inquests.

anyone. "Q: Do you know why . . . he carried a pistol all the time? A: Because he was afraid, he wanted to protect himself. Q: Who was he afraid of? A: I don't know."[98] In a similar exchange with Domenico Lucci, the coroner asked, "Do you know who it was that killed Vincenzo Provenzo? A: No sir, I don't know. Q: Do you know if he has any enemies? A: Not any."[99] The coroner's efforts proved fruitless. No one would provide information on possible suspects.

The ambush, a common feature of vendettas, and the reluctance of witnesses to testify in court complicated the Las Animas County criminal justice system's attempts to deal with these killings. This is reflected in the feud statistics. Of the twenty-one homicides that display some vendetta characteristics, 14 percent were found guilty, and 9 percent not guilty; 28 percent were dismissed and 48 percent never reached the indictment stage (table 4.5).

Of course, not all Italian homicides involved vendettas. As suggested earlier, all ethnic groups became involved in inter-ethnic killings (see table 4.4). Italians killed thirty-one individuals (24 percent) from another ethnic group. Juries convicted 38 percent of the Italian defendants who had killed white victims (thirteen), and they reached similar verdicts in 22 percent of the Hispanic victim cases. On the other hand, juries found only 7.6 percent of the Italian defendants not guilty in cases involving white victims, and 55.6 percent of those Italian cases involving Hispanic victims. Prosecutors, however, dismissed 53 percent of the Italian defendants who had killed white victims, and 22 percent of those cases involving Hispanic victims. Juries did not seem to show any particular bias against Italian defendants except those whose victims were white, and considering the jury composition, that should not be surprising.

WHITE HOMICIDES

Trinidad had its share of sensational homicides, including the death of a leading Trinidad citizen in 1905. "The most awful tragedy that has ever occurred in the city of Trinidad was the killing of John H. Fox, ex-county treasurer . . . this afternoon at one-forty-five, the murderer being Joe Johnson, an ex-deputy sheriff."[100] Johnson entered the post office, walked up behind Fox, drew his revolver, shouted, "You son of a bitch!" and shot him as he stood reading a newspaper.[101] A crowd quickly gathered and began to shout, "Hang him!" "Lynch him!" Despite the appearance of the sheriff, his deputies, and the Trinidad police force, all armed with rifles and shotguns, the crowd continued to grow and refused to disperse as ordered. The sheriff "informed the mob that the first man who stepped his foot upon the steps approaching the court house or jail would be given a dose of lead."[102] Apparently they believed him and began to disperse. To be safe, the sheriff and five deputies transported their prisoner to Pueblo by train that night. A jury found Johnson guilty of first-degree murder, and the judge sentenced him to death.

Another celebrated case occurred on Sunday, March 10, 1918, and involved incest. W. Tom Barneycastle had been carrying on an incestuous relationship with his daughter Lizzie that had begun six years earlier in Oklahoma. In 1914 Lizzie gave birth to Aaron from this relationship, and the family agreed to keep the matter secret by claiming that the child belonged to Lizzie's sister.[103] Later Lizzie married Laymond D. Williams. A displeased Tom wrote, "Now she struck a sucker that was crasey [sic] and has left me."[104] To gain revenge for Lizzie's leaving him, Tom, his wife, and twelve-year-old daughter Sallie plotted to kill Laymond Williams. The two women, disguised as male farm workers, approached the Williams ranch near Dalrose on Sunday night and shot him to death. The sordid love affair ended in tragedy for the whole family. A jury found all three Barneycastles guilty. Tom, who planned the killing, served only four years in prison before he escaped October 6, 1922.[105]

Most homicides, however, were less dramatic and usually involved petty grievances. In 1906 Arthur Larmiseaux, fourteen years old, and two young friends were out hunting near Hastings, Colorado. Jakimo Parlapiano, a sheep herder, tried to chase the boys away from his flock. In anger, he finally turned his dog on Larmiseaux and his friends. Larmiseaux shot Parlapiano with a .22 caliber rifle. At the coroner's inquest Larmiseaux claimed that Parlapiano threatened him with a revolver. Authorities found no weapon on the victim.[106] The jury found Larmiseaux guilty of manslaughter. In another case, two longtime friends, John Dietz and Arthur Wall, quarrelled on various occasions and finally Dietz decided to take action. He waited on a dark street in Delagua and attacked Wall with a club, killing him. A jury found him guilty of first-degree murder.[107]

Sometimes while under the influence of alcohol, people do stupid things, as in the case of David Stumbo and his friend Tuck Lee. The two had been drinking on a Saturday and decided to attend a dance. As they rode in a buggy to the dance hall, Stumbo spied a bottle along the side of the road and ordered his friend to stop. Stumbo began shooting at the bottle and shot his friend. A jury found him guilty of manslaughter.[108]

HISPANIC HOMICIDES

Alcohol was a common ingredient in killings, and homicides committed by Hispanics were no exception. In one such case, Juan Montoya returned home late in the afternoon, after drinking in a Segundo saloon all day, and began quarrelling with his wife. Finally he smashed her in the head with a club. (This case is unusual because he was sixty-seven, and his wife was seventy. Usually younger men committed homicides against their peers.) A jury found him guilty of second-degree murder.[109]

The brothels and saloons on Trinidad's "west end" were especially dangerous. On March 5, 1902, police discovered the body of Lily Talamantes lying in a pool of blood. She had been killed with a knife and axe. Although evidence suggested that her live-in boyfriend, Cruz Talamantez, may have committed the crime, the prosecutor refused to file charges.[110]

Some seemed to "get away" with murder, but on occasion they made mistakes. For example, in 1916 a district attorney indicted José Avelino Vigil for the murder of Elias Moya in a wild shoot-out at a saloon in St. Thomas, Colorado, that left one dead and three wounded. A jury found him not guilty.[111] On September 8, 1917, Vigil entered a brothel and fatally shot Reylitas Dominges, "an inmate of a resort at 303 Santa Fe Avenue."[112] He had been drinking before both shootings. This time a jury convicted him of murder in the first degree. Judge A. C. McChesney sentenced him to life in prison.[113]

Some Hispanic homicide cases involved jilted lovers and love triangles. Manuel Gallegos and Jetruditas Duran lived together for some time in Hastings, Colorado. When Duran left him, Gallegos became angry. He tried to convince her to return, but she refused. Gallegos visited a saloon, drank, and began to brood over his misfortunes. Later that night, Christmas Eve, he went to see Duran. After arguing with her, he pulled a .45 revolver and shot her. A jury found him not guilty.[114] In another case, Solomon Villegas suspected his wife had been seeing another man. On the night of October 14, 1908, Villegas retired to bed early. His wife told him she was going out to do some errands, but he demanded that she remain in bed. Within a few minutes Villegas heard a scratching noise at the screen. His wife claimed it was only mice. Villegas reached under his pillow, cocked a .44 caliber revolver, approached the back door, and shot José Mondragon, who had just entered the door.[115] In this case the jury probably viewed the crime as "just desserts." The victim had "violated" the home of the defendant as well as his wife. Juries seldom convicted a defendant who had killed another man in bed with his wife.

Hispanics killed outside their ethnic group at a rate of 22 percent. Guilty verdicts for Hispanic defendants were 31 and 20 percent for cases involving white and Italian victims, respectively. At 37 percent, guilty verdicts were higher for cases involving Hispanic victims. Not-guilty verdicts averaged 15 and 20 percent for the two groups, and more than 54 percent of cases involving Hispanic and Italian victims were dismissed. Prosecutors refused to pursue, and juries declined to convict, many defendants involved in homicides.

The Ludlow Massacre

"It was on the field of Ludlow where the blood of strikers, their wives and children, was shed by a subsidized soldiery."[116] The Ludlow massacre and the virtual civil war it started in Las Animas County provide the most vivid, dramatic, and explosive example of group violence. Although Ludlow no longer exists, the events that took place there on April 20, 1914, loom large in labor history as an example of the utter disregard of miners' rights by the coal mining companies. An examination of the events leading up to and following the Ludlow massacre reveal that in one year in Las Animas County, fifty-nine people fell victim to the war waged between the coal companies and the coal miners. How does one explain these killings?

Throughout the first three decades of the twentieth century, mining company management held the upper hand in disputes with labor, and when they met labor resistance, owners could always count on local and state authorities to tip the balance of power in their favor. This pattern is quite apparent in the coal miners' strike against the Colorado Fuel and Iron Company in Las Animas County during 1913–14. Armed men and violence often accompanied strikes, but there is a critical distinction to be made about the dynamics of a strike. One observer noted "the very presence of the police or troops at a struck plant carried with it the implication that the strikers were lawbreakers. It signified that strikers were the enemies of public order, for quite obviously the police had not been summoned to protect them, but company property *from* them."[117] Provocation by either side could create a situation that might quickly escalate into major violence.

Expecting a strike, company officials took the initiative. In 1913 the Colorado Fuel and Iron Company once again contracted with the Baldwin-Felts detective agency, noted for providing professional strikebreakers, to deal with laborers' attempts to organize. The coal company, with the aid of Baldwin-Felts operatives, employed approximately 348 men to deal with a United Mine Workers attempt to unionize Las Animas County miners. To sanctify the company's actions, Las Animas County Sheriff J. S. Grisham placed them on a special deputy list.[118] This empowered these "deputies" to operate within county jurisdiction as well as on company property.

On August 16, 1913, a few weeks before the miners' strike, George Belcher and Walter Belk, Baldwin-Felts agents, shot and killed union organizer Gerald Lippiatt on Commercial Street in the business district of Trinidad, Colorado. A coroner's inquest revealed that the victim suffered seven bullet wounds, all from revolvers. Three months later one or more miners shot and killed Belcher at the corner of Main and Commercial.[119]

A variety of factors helps to place these and the other fifty-seven killings into context. Enmity toward the company ran deep among the coal miners, and over the course of a decade, miners in southern Colorado had developed a long list of grievances against the Colorado Fuel and Iron Company. First, the miners complained about the oppressive nature of the company towns and company stores. The company controlled virtually every aspect of life within the company town. The company paid the town marshal's salary, hired numerous guards to protect property, employed spies to monitor any union-organizing attempts, and prevented union officials from entering company property. Anyone who joined a union was quickly fired.

Second, mining accidents occurred with remarkable frequency, and the company failed to provide adequate safety measures to reduce fatal accidents. Collusion between the Colorado Fuel and Iron Company and the Las Animas County coroner increased hostility between the miners and the mine operators. For virtually all of the deaths within the mines, County Coroner Burney B. Sipe absolved the coal company of any liability.[120] This collaboration permeated practically every aspect of local government. In Las Animas County the Colorado Fuel and Iron Company essentially controlled the judges, the sheriff, and, through the sheriff, the selection of individuals for any jury dealing with labor-management issues.[121]

The strained relationship between management and labor provided another important causal factor. Rockefeller, who owned Colorado Fuel and Iron, opposed any form of unionization and vowed to prevent it at any cost—a typical attitude of this era. He gave specific orders to his managers to block any unionizing attempts in Las Animas and Huerfano counties. During the 1913–14 strike, when questioned by members of the House Committee on Mines and Mining about his company's activities in Colorado, Rockefeller made it clear that he was prepared to use any means to thwart collective bargaining. In a telling exchange Chairman Foster asked Rockefeller, "You are willing to let these killings take place rather than to go there and do something to settle conditions? A.—There is just one thing that can be done to settle this strike . . . that the camps shall be open camps, that we expect to stand by the officers at any cost. Q.—And you will do that if that costs all your property and kills all your employees? A.—It is a great principle. Q.—And you would do that rather than recognize the right of men to collective bargaining? A.—No, sir—rather than allow outside people to come in and interfere with employees who are thoroughly satisfied with their labor conditions."[122]

Coal mining operators had a long history of staunch, almost fanatical opposition to unions, which usually led to violence. Company officials refused to deal with unions and felt that their demands were not legitimate. After examining the 1913–14 strike, Eugene O. Porter concluded that "in the final analysis, the strike was an inescapable conflict between uncontrolled property rights and human rights. . . . And the blame must rest squarely upon the shoulders of the operators. By their domination of public officials, by their violations of all laws, and by their shutting off of every normal and legitimate means of redressing grievances, they had made a social explosion inevitable."[123]

Prior to the strike, which began in September 1913, Colorado Governor Elias Ammons asked Deputy Labor Commissioner Edwin V. Brake to investigate conditions in Las Animas County to see if a strike could be prevented. "Brake reported that the companies had filled the region with armed guards and detectives." Commissioner Brake believed that the only way to avoid bloodshed would be "to disarm every man in the mining fields."[124] The Colorado Fuel and Iron Company began to import Baldwin-Felts operatives as strikebreakers and guards several months prior to the strike.[125] The company also began to ship in thousands of weapons to arm these men. Discovering the influx of strikebreakers and weapons, the United Mine Worker organizers also began to arm themselves. Exactly how many weapons were purchased by the two opposing sides is unknown, but the number must have been considerable. For example, after President Woodrow Wilson sent federal troops into the strike zone, the secretary of war issued a proclamation calling for the disarming of miners, mine guards, and other coal mining officials, including the sheriffs and police.

Baldwin-Felts detectives pose in the "armored death car" fitted with a machine gun, which was used by Colorado Fuel and Iron security in an early attack on Forbes and Ludlow miners' tent camps in 1913. (Courtesy of Colorado Historical Society, no. F6692)

Within seven days Major W. A. Holbrook's men had collected 3,000 guns, and a conservative estimate would place around 9,000 or more guns in the hands of the two adversarial groups.[126] The "Death Special," an armor-plated automobile with a mounted machine gun developed by the Baldwin-Felts agency in a Colorado Fuel and Iron Company shop, added a new dimension to the company's arsenal.[127] It suggested that the company would use any means to break the strike. Under such conditions, violence seemed inevitable.

The Lippiatt and Belcher assassinations, possibly more than any other events, dramatically polarized the two groups. After five homicides in October 1913, Governor Ammons ordered in the Colorado National Guard. From the beginning, General John Chase, commander of the National Guard, sided with the company. To assure loyalty, the company quartered and supplied the National Guard. With additional aid of the Las Animas County sheriff and other county officials, the company was able to bring in strikebreakers to operate the coal mines. However, as the strike continued into 1914, some guardsmen asked permission to return home to their jobs and families. Consequently, the composition of the militia began to change dramatically, with company guards, mining employees, and Baldwin-Felts operatives rapidly replacing the regular guardsmen. The units quartered at Ludlow reflected this radical change, and this development helps to explain the Ludlow massacre.[128]

Ten strikers, company guards, and mine employees were killed in 1913, including the five in October. The introduction of the National Guard seemed to calm the situation, and only one more homicide, in March 1914, can be attributed to the strike. The changing character of the guard, however, set the stage for the events of April 20, 1914.

In the early morning hours of that fateful day the Colorado National Guard, on the signal of three bomb explosions, began to pour machine-gun and rifle fire into the Ludlow tent camp. Exactly why they started shooting is unclear, but the results were tragic. After twelve hours of almost continuous firing, the shooting finally stopped. The Ludlow tent camp had been burned to the ground, and the bodies of Louis Tikas, four other strikers, and a young boy lay within the camp. One guardsman also had been killed during the shooting. Later, a curious telephone lineman sifted through the ruins, lifted up some rubble, and discovered the bodies of two women and eleven children in a small pit dug into the ground. The first day after the shootings, the National Guard barred the Las Animas County coroner from entering the camp to examine the dead. Eventually the coroner investigated the killings and found that the guardsmen had deliberately set the camp on fire, killing the women and children.[129]

John R. Lawson and other United Mine Worker organizers tried to prevent violence but were unsuccessful. Enraged by the massacre, approximately two thousand armed miners launched attacks on several mine properties in Las Animas County. The offensive came at Forbes, Delagua, and Tabasco, coal camps near Ludlow. A virtual state of war engulfed Las Animas County. On April 22, 1914, ten people were cut down by gunfire; on April 29, another thirteen were killed. By the end of April, forty-eight people had lost their lives to gunfire from the two opposing groups. The final death toll of the bitter dispute included fourteen women and children, eighteen miners and union organizers, twenty mine guards, six other company employees, and one National Guardsman (table 4.6).

Caught by surprise and besieged by coal company and miner supporters, Governor Ammons failed to act. On April 25, five hundred women marched on the Denver capitol building demanding action. After a temporary truce failed, Governor Ammons, under tremendous pressure from the demonstrating women, finally requested federal troops to restore order.[130] The federal troops' arrival brought an end to the shooting, and subsequent investigations brought

Table 4.6 Coal Strike Victims, Las
Animas County, 1913–1914

	N	%
Company guards	20	33.9
Miners	16	27.1
Women/children	14	23.7
Company employees	6	10.2
Union organizers	2	3.4
Guardsman	1	1.7
Total	59	100

Source: Coroner's inquests.

John D. Rockefeller, Jr., and the Colorado Fuel and Iron Company under national scrutiny.

A Las Animas County grand jury convened in Trinidad, Colorado, in August 1914 to investigate and indict those persons accused of committing crimes during the strike. The jury could hardly be labeled impartial. Three members were closely tied to the Colorado Fuel and Iron Company, and three others were either currently, or had been, sheriff's deputies.[131] The grand jury issued a series of multiple indictments, charging at least 332 miners with murder.[132] The jury failed to charge a single sheriff's deputy and indicted only two company guards accused of committing homicides.

Eventually the Las Animas County prosecutor dismissed all of the pending indictments against the coal miners except those for John R. Lawson and Luis Zancannelli, both union organizers. Lawson was charged with killing John Nimmo, and Zancannelli with the shooting death of George W. Belcher.[133] These two cases provide further evidence of the collusion between Colorado Fuel and Iron and Las Animas County officials. Both men were convicted of first-degree murder, and both appealed to the Colorado Supreme Court.

In *Lawson v. the People* the court noted that Lawson had petitioned for a change of judges for his case. To get around this maneuver the attorney general entered a *nolle prosequi* (a refusal to prosecute). Later he filed a new indictment, and when the defendant again requested a change, the court ruled that Lawson could not request a change to another judge. Consequently, Judge A. W. McHendrie, earlier removed, heard the case. The Colorado Supreme Court ruled that "the [original] indictment was by a grand jury. When the *nolle prosequi* was entered, that case was at an end. Any other conclusion might, in certain cases, defeat the object which the statute seeks to accomplish, if the defendant is entitled to but one change of judges."[134] The Colorado Supreme Court reversed the conviction.

The Zancannelli case is even more remarkable. Convicted of killing Belcher and sentenced to life in prison, Zancannelli also appealed to the Colorado Supreme Court. In this particular case the attorney general did not participate in the prosecution, and he filed "a confession of error." In a joint opinion the court noted that "the nature of the case, however, is such that we think a good purpose will be served by briefly stating the facts and commenting upon the same."[135] The coal mining companies provided the services of Jesse G. Northcutt to aid in the prosecution. Counsel for the defense filed papers to remove Judge A. W. McHendrie from the trial for reasons of prejudice. After the governor appointed Judge Hillyer to replace McHendrie, the defense attempted to remove him but failed. The case was tried before Judge Hillyer, but a jury could not agree and was discharged. In a second trial a jury found Zancannelli guilty. During this trial "several of the proposed jurors stated, upon examination by the prosecution, that they had formed, expressed, and then held, opinions concerning the guilt or innocence of the defendant; that such opinions and impressions were based upon hearsay rumors, conversation with other persons, newspaper articles, etc.; but that notwithstanding such opinions they could give the defendant a fair impartial trial."[136]

When the defense counsel examined these prospective jurors, they were asked, "Can you start out on the trial of this case giving the defendant the benefit of the legal rule that a defendant must be presumed to be innocent until he is proven to be guilty?"[137] The prosecution objected to this question and others, and Judge Hillyer sustained each one. For example, the defense counsel asked, "Have you any bias or prejudice touching the striking coal miners, either for or against them? Have you taken an active part on either side of the recent coal strike? Have you favored or advocated forcible deportation of the striking miners in this country? Have you read any of the literature sent out by the coal mining companies touching the Zancannelli case? Did you act as a deputy sheriff to go out in the armored cars the Colorado Fuel and Iron Company had?"[138] The defense counsel asked one prospective juror, "Do you know how the sheriff came to summon you, a man who had been in these battles, as a juror in this case?"[139] For every one of these questions (and twelve similar ones), the court sustained the prosecutor's objection.

In another example, the court refused to allow the defense to ask one juror, "Do you believe in the doctrine of the presumption of innocence of the defen-

Members of the Red Cross at Ludlow, Colorado, after the attack by the National Guard, April 20, 1914. Today only a United Mine Workers monument identifies the site of the massacre, which left twenty-one dead, including eleven women and children. (Courtesy of Colorado Historical Society, no. F17732)

dant?"[140] While sitting on the Zancannelli jury, a man named Burkhart bet with a Trinidad barber that the jury would find the defendant guilty. Prior to the trial Burkhart suggested that if he became a juror, "there would be either a hung jury, or a hung Dago."[141] After hearing that Burkhart was accepted as a juror, the barber refused to bet. Burkhart met the barber on a Trinidad street and said, "Now, I bet you four to one on the results of the Zancannelli trial."[142] Defense counsel tried to discharge Burkhart but failed. After describing the questioning of Burkhart by defense counsel, the Colorado Supreme Court noted:

> To appreciate the full force and effect of the disclosures above, it is essential to bear in mind that juror Burkhart had, upon his *voir dire*, said that he had certain business relations with the coal companies said to be interested in the prosecution, and that such relations might embarrass him in rendering a verdict, and if it appeared that such companies were desirous of prosecuting the case, or in some way engaged or assisting therein, it might tend to bias or prejudice him, and that he did not feel, because of his business relations with the companies, that he should be required to serve as a juror, and that the court would not permit him to answer the following

question propounded by defendant: "Is it not true that you would dislike to decide a case contrary to what they thought it ought to be decided?" or to answer the question: "Can you personally as a juror at the outset of the trial, give to the defendant the benefit of that rule of law" that he shall be presumed to be innocent until the evidence establishes his guilt?[143]

The justices ordered the judgment reversed.[144] It was, however, a hollow victory for the coal miners of Las Animas County.

The most violent strike in Colorado history ended quietly with the Colorado Fuel and Iron Company remaining in control of the southern Colorado coal mines and refusing to recognize the union. As in other industries throughout the United States, union organizers in Colorado would have to wait two decades before companies would accept the concept of collective bargaining. A discussion between union organizers Edward Doyle and John R. Lawson at a dedication of the Ludlow memorial on April 20, 1917, perhaps best symbolizes the uncertain danger of coal mine life in southern Colorado. " 'See those shadows, Ed,' Lawson said. 'Those same shadows were here three years ago today. They stabbed at the colony. They foretold the tragedy of that day. It was a tragedy the like of which we won't see again,' Doyle said. 'Death is gone from these hills now. Death is always present in the coal districts, Ed. It will strike many times, perhaps in a different way and in different circumstances, but it will always be present.' "[145]

Las Animas County as a Regional Culture of Violence

Can we conclude from this discussion of homicide in southern Colorado that a regional culture of violence existed in Las Animas County from 1880 to 1920? In 1971 Gordon D. Gastil critiqued Marvin E. Wolfgang's subculture of violence thesis and developed his own theory of a regional culture of violence in order to explain the impact of southernness, which did not really fit Wolfgang's model. Four years later Gastil revised his own theory, suggesting that "lethal violence"—meaning homicide—provided a better comparison than the "broader definition" of violence used by Wolfgang and Franco Ferracuti.[146] Gastil notes that lethal violence has a high reporting rate with accompanying statistics available for analyses, and he suggests that his regional culture of violence "would likely . . . be characterized by (1) more extreme subcultures of violence and/or larger percentage of the population involved in violence (with less limitation by class, age, or race); (2) lethal violence as a more important subtheme in the general culture of the region; and (3) weapons and knowledge of their use as an important part of the culture."[147]

Several distinct subcultural groups can be identified in Las Animas County, including Italian, Hispanic, Greek, and a variety of east Europeans such as Bohemians, Austrians, and Serbs. Twenty-one vendetta cases (28 percent of all Italian homicides) verify that Italians transported their cultural heritage, including the feud, to southeastern Colorado (see table 4.5). They exhibited this behavior in the form of homicides committed in isolated areas, some occurring seven years after the "wrongs" committed by their victims. Pistone, Lapreto, Maniscala, and Provenzo did not view their behavior as homicide; they were just "getting even."

Lethal violence was an important subtheme within Las Animas County society, as exhibited by shootings in saloons, on the streets, and on isolated county roads. Homicides involving police, Baldwin-Felts operatives, deputy sheriffs, National Guardsmen, miners, sheep herders, cattlemen, and others as perpetrators and victims constitute strong evidence that a regional culture of violence existed in southeastern Colorado. Equally important was the existence of a strong gun-based culture in Las Animas County, evidenced by a fourteen-year-old youth shooting a sheep herder with a .22 caliber rifle, a town marshal killing a miner in an arrest attempt, men conducting shoot-outs in the streets, two Baldwin-Felts operatives killing a union organizer in downtown Trinidad, and the National Guard firing thousands of rifle and machine-gun bullets into a tent camp. The influence of gun culture in Las Animas County was pervasive and deadly. Carried concealed or openly, guns seemed to be everywhere and in many cases proved to be the "equalizer" of western lore.

Gastil also suggests that a variety of factors helps to explain why certain regions tended to develop a culture of violence. For example, "disorganized conditions such as those found on the frontier" have been associated with high homicide rates, and in recently settled regions, high mobility and relative anonymity tended "to attract people with criminal tendencies" who may have taken advantage of the unstable conditions.[148] The region around Trinidad was one of the last "frontiers" in Colorado. It remained a small Hispanic town until the development of coal mining along the Purgatoire River. Between 1890 and 1920 Las Animas County was an unstable society with a mix of Italian, Greek, Hispanic, Bohemian, Serb, black, and other ethnic groups. Members of this society in transition may have been more inclined to carry concealed weapons.

Gastil also found that juries in the South were not as likely to convict individuals for homicide as they were in the North. "Jury members were more likely to accept the reasons given as justifying the killing."[149] Further, he observed that "if they convicted the murderer, they feared retaliation by his relatives." This certainly might have been the case with the Italian vendetta cases in Las Animas County and may help explain the high dismissal rate and not-guilty verdicts (see table 4.5). Gastil also noted that "the murder might have been committed for reasons they [the jurors] directly or indirectly approved."[150] The data confirm that juries were reluctant to convict defendants for committing homicides. With guilty verdicts averaging 29 percent for white, Hispanic, and Italian defendants (see fig. 4.2), juries seemed to be saying that violent death was acceptable. Because of the large number of homicides committed within company-town saloons, this suggestion of "approval" may have been a crucial factor for jurors.

High homicide indictment rates for all ethnic groups in Las Animas County support the regional culture of violence thesis. In contrast to cases in Douglas County, ethnicity—not race—was the crucial variable. Homicide was not confined to any single ethnic group; Hispanics, Italians, east Europeans, other whites, and blacks all committed homicides at high rates.

Conclusions

Several social, economic, and cultural factors provide corroboration that violence was indeed a regional cultural phenomenon that had serious implications for members of Las Animas County's isolated society. First, located in a region somewhat removed from the main arteries of transportation, Las Animas County developed in isolation from the rest of Colorado. Although two railroads passed through the area, they brought relatively little social contact or change. In 1880, after two decades of growth, Trinidad remained a sleepy town of 2,226 before doubling in each of the next two decades. Prior to the coal mining boom, the region surrounding the Purgatoire Valley supported a pastoral economy with cattle and sheep grazing on this mile-high plateau.

It is possible that the Texas cattlemen left their imprint on Las Animas County.[151] Evidence suggests that the people who eventually moved into the Purgatoire Valley either arrived heavily armed or soon purchased handguns for protection or for other purposes. As Bat Masterson observed, "Always remember that a six-shooter is made to kill the other fellow with and for no other reason on earth."[152] In isolated Trinidad, carrying a handgun became commonplace, and it was almost always worn concealed.

The development of the coal mining industry and rapid population growth increased social instability. Prior to the coal mining era, Las Animas County had a mix of Hispanics and whites, but that changed quickly during the first decade of the twentieth century. Italians, Greeks, Bohemians, Croatians, Serbians, Austrians, Poles, blacks, and more Hispanics, especially from Mexico, quickly swelled the ranks of coal miners, increasing the population of Las Animas County from 21,842 in 1900 to 33,643 a decade later. They all lived in close proximity within the company towns, and there was a good deal of hostility and mistrust among these various ethnic groups.

The development of company towns created more problems for society in Las Animas County. Company officials operated these towns in complete isolation from outside forces by erecting fences around the property and employing marshals to police the area. In most small towns, marshals and other officials were elected by the town's population, but that was not the case in company towns. There were no democratic elections. The company manager became the "mayor" and ran the town as he saw fit by employing "special" deputized town marshals (who were given powers similar to those of county deputies) to police and keep out any unwanted visitors. Managers also hired company spies to prevent union organizers from entering company towns to recruit members. Company marshals seemed more interested in keeping union organizers out than in policing the saloons on company property. In effect, this method of operating the company towns created a "siege" mentality among the miners.

The bitter nature of coal mining strikes produced a social climate that seemed to condone violent behavior. By hiring "special" deputies and Baldwin-Felts operatives, the Colorado Fuel and Iron Company virtually assured that any strike would result in violence. In 1913 the company, with the aid of the Baldwin-Felts agency, hired several hundred strikebreakers who were "deputized" by the Las Animas County sheriff. This gave them authority to operate outside of company property as well as within the mine boundary. Baldwin-Felts agents brought with them a long tradition of using violent means to gain their ends, including machine-gunning coal mine tent colonies in West Virginia. This is not to suggest that the miners did not bear some of the blame for violence during strikes. But by hiring these "goons," the companies condoned and encouraged the high level of violence that soon engulfed Las Animas County. When the Ludlow massacre occurred on April 20, 1914, open warfare ensued in mining camps throughout the area.

The tendency by the general population to accept high levels of violence further suggests that a regional culture of violence existed in Las Animas County. This is apparent in the attitudes of grand juries and prosecutors. Although they were more likely to indict ethnic minorities accused of committing homicides than to indict more-substantial members of society charged with the same offense, juries were not inclined to convict, regardless of ethnic origin. Whether the homicide occurred in a small company town or in Trinidad, the juries applied a "liberal" interpretation of justice to virtually all men accused of homicides committed in saloons. High homicide rates in mining towns like Aguilar, Delagua, Segundo, Berwind, and Trinidad reflect the forces of instability that also occurred in Sonora, Angels Camp, Stockton, and Sacramento, California. Indeed, one can conclude that Las Animas County was violent.

Red versus White

The Apache Experience in Gila County, Arizona

Western legal historians have barely begun to examine the treatment of Native Americans by criminal justice systems in the American West. Sidney Harring's groundbreaking study of Crow Dog's case is an excellent beginning for understanding the legal framework and is one of the few examples of scholarship based on the Native American view of legal issues in the West.[1] Most of the scholarship on Native Americans and the law has focused on tribal rights; however, a few recent studies have examined the legal rights of Native Americans, including those in cases of homicide.[2] Many writers have characterized Apaches in Arizona as the most homicidal group of Native Americans in the West, but is that really true? Equally important, what kind of treatment did Apache defendants accused of homicide receive in the Gila County criminal justice system? This case study will focus on Apache defendants and compare their treatment with that of white defendants.

On December 28, 1889, the Globe, Arizona, newspaper ran this headline: "Expiated his crime Nah-deiz-az, the murderer of Lieut. Mott, hanged." The accompanying editorial noted: "The first legal execution in Gila county took place in the jail yard of Globe on Friday morning Dec. 27th, in the presence of an assemblage of citizens invited to witness the lugubrious event. No criminal ever merited death more than Nah-deiz-az."[3] During the nineteenth century, Arizona newspapers frequently expressed this type of sentiment. In numerous cases white editors portrayed Apaches as villains—real or imagined—who deserved to be destroyed.[4] This editorial, however, reflected more than just a desire for white vengeance and retribution against Apache murder suspects. It points contemporary scholars to a largely unexplored area of western legal history: the treatment accorded Native American defendants involved in homicides during the late nineteenth century. It was an era when most whites had intense hatred of Arizona Apaches, and, unfortunately, nineteenth-century Arizona territorial authorities failed to provide methods for incorporating Native Americans into a foreign and culturally distinct legal structure.

Analyses of historical data will illuminate two standards of justice: one for Apache defendants and another for white defendants. Within the Arizona territorial criminal justice system, Apache defendants received inferior legal representation and experienced intense plea-bargaining coercion. Therefore, their conviction rates were higher than those for whites, and they were more likely to receive longer sentences. In light of the intense racial prejudice, it should not be surprising that Apache defendants in interracial homicide cases were treated so harshly.

Previous historical scholarship has demonstrated that murderers normally selected their victims from within their own racial or ethnic groups.[5] Between 1880 and 1890, however, the clash of white and Apache cultures in Arizona was accompanied by interracial killings. Nineteenth-century homicide studies of western states or territories are few, and, more significantly, interpretive data on crime in Arizona are virtually nonexistent. With a few exceptions, social historians have largely ignored the problems that Native Americans encountered during their attempts to adapt to American society.[6] The lack of materials cannot explain this, because there are excellent sources for effectively analyzing crime in nineteenth-century Arizona Territory.[7]

Gila County was selected due to its location, historical significance, availability of data, and because it displays a representative cross-section of ethnic population in Arizona during the period under study. Since Gila County contains a portion of the San Carlos Reservation, it provides a sample of Western Apache defendants. Forty-eight percent of these defendants were arrested in one decade, 1885–95. Thereafter the number of homicides committed by Apaches dropped dramatically.

It is the thesis of this case study that a regional culture of violence similar to

Gila County, Arizona

Table 5.1 Homicide Indictments,
Gila County, 1880–1920

	N	%
Other white	63	46
Native American	48	35
Hispanic	12	9
Black	8	6
Italian	4	3
Asians	2	1
Total	137	100

Source: Registers of criminal action.

that of Las Animas County, Colorado, existed in Gila County. Interracial kill-ings and the high frequency of gun use by homicide defendants support this contention. Due to a deep-seated hatred that seemed to have no limits, both groups killed members of the other group during the last two decades of the nineteenth century. Further, it is believed that because the white culture domi-nated the criminal justice system, Apache defendants paid a higher price for "justice."

Statistical data collected from the Gila County *Registers of Criminal Action* have been analyzed to determine how Apache defendants were treated within the criminal justice system. As in Douglas and Las Animas counties, males domi-nated homicide indictments in Gila County (95.6 percent). Also significant is the fact that the only females convicted of murder were two Apaches and one black. During the period 1880 to 1920, prosecutors indicted 137 people for homicide (table 5.1). Individual cases will be explored to explain interracial homicides.[8]

Early History of Gila County

Gila County is in central Arizona, surrounded by Maricopa, Yavapai, Navajo, Graham, and Pinal counties. In 1881 the Arizona Territorial Legislature cre-ated Gila County from portions of Maricopa and Pinal counties. Globe, the county seat, is in a small valley (elevation 3,541 feet) between the Apache Mountains to the north and the Pinal Mountains to the south. Pinal Creek runs parallel to Broad Street, the main thoroughfare.

The mountains surrounding Globe contained significant deposits of silver. In 1873 miners began to develop the Silver King and Stonewall Jackson mines. Globe residents became excited when miners discovered a 1,500-pound silver nugget in the Stonewall Jackson mine. Miners cut the nugget into "pieces with chisels so it could be removed from the mine."[9] However, copper proved to be the most important and enduring commercial metal in Gila County, and the industry provided the economic impetus for rapid growth. Unlike Omaha, Nebraska, and Trinidad, Colorado, Globe did not lie on a natural route for a railroad, but the Arizona Eastern Railroad arrived in 1898 and became a major factor in the growth of Globe's copper mining industry in the early twentieth century.[10]

Gila County is a region of small valleys situated within high block-faulted mountains: the Sierra Ancha, Apache, Mazatzal, and Pinal ranges. The communities of Payson and Gisela, eighty miles north of Globe, are in the Tonto Basin (south of the Mogollon Rim) and are watered by the East Verde River. Roosevelt is about thirty miles north of Globe and Miami. The mountains and valleys throughout Gila County supported cattle ranching and some farming.

East of Globe, a portion of the San Carlos Indian Reservation (including the city of San Carlos) lies within the county's boundaries and legal jurisdiction.

Gila County courthouse, Globe, Arizona, 1907. (Courtesy of Arizona Historical Society / Tucson, no. 61093)

Table 5.2 Gila County Population, 1880–1920

	1880	1890	1900	1910	1920
Globe City	704	803	1,495	7,083	7,044
Miami	—	—	—	1,390	6,689
Hayden	—	—	—	582	2,508
Payson	—	—	—	225	386
Roosevelt	—	—	—	707	570
Warrior	—	—	—	432	—
Winkelman	—	—	—	484	995
Pine	—	—	—	168	136
Others	—	—	—	2,244	—
Globe/other	—	—	—	—	2,109
Miami precincts	—	—	—	—	4,095
Fort Apache	—	—	709	740	595
San Carlos	—	—	—	1,383	248
Total	1,582[a]	2,021	4,973	16,348	25,678
% change	—	—	146%	228%	57%

Source: U.S. Department of Commerce, Bureau of Census.

[a] This population estimate for 1882–83 does not include the Apaches on the San Carlos Reservation (Hubert Bancroft, *The History of New Mexico and Arizona* [San Francisco: A. L. Bancroft, 1889], 626).

Apaches living on and off the reservation had a significant impact on the non-Indian citizens of Globe. Although whites viewed Apaches with suspicion and disdain, Apaches were an important source of labor for the copper mines.

Within two decades Globe grew from a small town of 803 in 1890 to a bustling mining city of 7,083 in 1910 (table 5.2). Social instability accompanied this critical convergence of ethnic groups and industrialization. Miners flocked to Globe, and later Miami, in search of work. The population of early Globe was a rich ethnic mix of Hispanics (9 percent), Apaches (1.3 percent), blacks (1.8 percent), Italians (4.8 percent), Asians (2 percent), and other whites (80.7 percent).

Copper Mining

Old Dominion Mining and Smelting, Inspiration Copper (a subsidiary of Anaconda Company), and Miami Copper were the main mining companies in Gila County. Old Dominion built its first smelter in 1885 and developed the main shaft five miles north of Globe. In the 1890s Lewissohn Brothers of New York gained control of this company and quickly introduced new technology, purchased new machinery, and increased the production capacity. By 1897 Old Dominion employed three hundred men,[11] and the company continued to be Globe's major economic resource for more than fifty years.[12]

In contrast to Globe, which was established by a combination of mining and ranching interests, Miami developed specifically as a copper mining town. Inspiration Copper Company was the first to develop open-pit mining in Gila County. Although it left unsightly tailings and debris, open-pit mining was a quicker and cheaper method of exploiting the copper ore. The demand for labor to work in the open-pit operations brought about the creation of Miami—an instant city.[13] The development of Inspiration Copper Company and Miami Copper Company in Miami, eight miles west, challenged the copper hegemony of Globe. Although it remained the county seat, Globe lost a lot of business to upstart Miami, including the *Arizona Silver Belt* newspaper.

Silver and copper mining provided employment for a diverse population. Silver mining boomed until the bust in 1893. With the coming of the railroad in 1898, copper replaced silver as the major economic force in Gila County. Most of the early copper mines in and around Globe were shaft mines.[14] After finding a large copper deposit in the Pinal Mountains, the discoverer called it "The Globe." By January 1897, the Hoosier shaft reached 280 feet into the ground. The Black Warrior Company sunk a shaft 175 feet and was sinking other shafts at 6½ feet a day. In 1898 one shaft reached the 1,200-foot level, where miners discovered a 65-foot-thick ore body.[15] Other mines, such as the Joyce, Continental, and Badger, achieved similar results.[16]

Copper mining required capital for profitable development, which led to buyouts by larger corporations. Eventually Phelps Dodge purchased Old Dominion, and Anaconda took over and developed Inspiration Consolidated.[17] These corporations introduced large amounts of capital to make copper mining and smelting profitable on a major scale. Between 1904 and 1907 company officials invested two million dollars in Old Dominion, a successful venture that paid fourteen million dollars to shareholders by 1920. The development of Inspiration Consolidated with the use of open-pit mining in Miami had similar results: stockholders received thirty million dollars by 1920.[18]

The railroad's arrival in 1898 provided transportation for shipping copper to industrial centers in the East and for importing new workers, many of whom were immigrants recruited by company officials. Dangerous working conditions created some unrest among the miners,[19] and by the late nineteenth century, copper miners conducted strikes to improve conditions in the hazardous underground mine shafts and to gain wage increases.

Substandard working conditions within the Gila County copper mines led to labor disputes and the involvement of white labor organizers in developing unions to improve workers' standard of living. In 1896 copper miners at the Old Dominion mine in Globe formed the first local of the Western Federation of Miners to protest wage cuts and the hiring of Mexicans. Old Dominion management closed the mine, but the union survived. Company officials called Globe the "center of labor agitation in the Territory."[20] When union leaders demanded a wage increase in 1909, once again Old Dominion officials closed the mines in protest and refused to reopen until union organizers left company property. Major strikes at other mines in Clifton-Morenci, Ray, Ajo, and Bisbee during the years 1915, 1916, and 1917 were met with telling blows. Strong-arm tactics, including the arrest and deportation of more than a thousand strikers, virtually destroyed the Arizona union movement.[21]

During the early twentieth century, in response to periodic labor shortages, mining officials recruited Hispanic laborers and Apaches from the San Carlos Reservation. In 1902 the all-white union organization in Globe protested the hiring of Apache labor. Company representatives preferred Apaches because they worked for less money, but their numbers were limited. Unscrupulous contractors promised work and collected fees from the Apache laborers' paychecks.[22] Union leaders disliked and discriminated against Hispanics and Apaches alike in the copper mines of Gila County.

Apache wage labor originated with the federal government's recruiting of Indian scouts and police in the 1880s. Local ranchers also required labor to dig irrigation ditches, construct buildings, and herd cattle. In 1898 the development of the Gila Valley, Globe and Northern Railroad across the San Carlos Reservation was the first large-scale project offering wage work for Apaches, and they "supplied at least 50 percent of the labor employed in building the line from Bylas to Globe."[23] Soon they became an important labor force in Globe. Indian Agent George D. Corson reported that Apaches "are industrious, and early seek work on the railroad, among the white farmers, at the mines, and . . . they have established a reputation as good workers."[24] Within a decade of the end of the Apache wars, the Apaches began to visit and work in Globe in large numbers. This increased the ethnic diversity of Globe and may have increased racial tensions. The diverse population of Gila County was a volatile mix, and homicide became common between 1880 and 1920.

While discussing the Globe trial of eight Apaches charged with murder, Edward Arhelger stated, "All were promptly found guilty, which I think myself was wrong, but the sentiment was such that a good Indian was a dead Indian."[25] How does one explain Indian hating by whites in Arizona? Were the Apaches the "red devils" depicted by numerous newspaper accounts, or have we been mislead by the white settlers and miners who were trying to "exterminate" them? Two decades ago C. L. Sonnichsen, in an essay on novelists' portrayals of Apaches, suggested that "the old concepts about the white man's role as a bringer of enlightenment to the Southwestern savage are still with us, but a large segment of the population, including many thoughtful and humane people, has come to believe that the white men were the real savages and that the Apaches were basically gentle creatures driven to vengeful violence by the brutalities of their conquerors."[26] After discussing novelists' tendencies to view Apaches as demons, Sonnichsen concludes, "It appears, however, that many otherwise sensible people will continue to believe, like the citizens of Tucson at the time of the Camp Grant massacre, that all Apaches are evil personified and deserve to be wiped out."[27]

In the historical literature on Native Americans, the Iroquois and the Apaches have earned the reputation for being the most violent. Jesuit missionaries spent an inordinate amount of time recounting the treatment of war captives held by both Iroquois and Apache warriors. For example, after four pages describing the torture of Fathers Jean de Brebeuf and Gabriel Lalement in extensive detail, the Jesuit narrator concludes, "Before their death, both their hearts were torn out . . . and those Barbarians inhumanly feasted thereon, drinking their blood."[28] In a similar passage Father Ignaz Pfefferkorn describes the results of an Apache attack in Sonora, Mexico: "In the fury of the onslaught they kill everyone in sight, and their cruelty is so great that they will inflict wound after wound, just as though their lust for blood were insatiable. I have buried victims whose bodies were unrecognizable, so gashed were they from head to foot by lances."[29] In both of these commentaries there is no attempt to explain either Iroquois or Apache customs or the context of these events. The narrators were more concerned with illuminating the barbaric treatment of whites, who were the focus of the violence. In each case a series of events preceded the actual tortures and killings, but neither author chose to reveal their significance.

Hatred of Apaches has had a long history in the Southwest, dating from

Spanish intrusion into what is now New Mexico and Arizona during the seventeenth century. One can find abundant anecdotes that portray the Apaches as "ruthless savages." Father Pfefferkorn described their habits in very unflattering terms: "They eat the meat not raw, but half roasted, and they have excellent teeth for this purpose. Such a diet is supposed to give them a very unpleasant odor."[30] Pfefferkorn also noted that when the Apaches returned to their camp with captives, "women and children fall upon the unfortunates like furies."[31] Samuel Cozzens claimed that "I soon found myself among a lot of the dirtiest, filthiest, most degraded-looking set of creatures that I ever saw in the guise of humanity."[32] Cozzens maintained that "the expression on the faces of all was cruel and brutal, a look of cunning pervading each countenance."[33] Another chronicler suggests that "for such demons there can be only one treatment— extermination—and the authorities on both sides of the border have at last arrived at this conclusion."[34] "The terrible tales of Apache barbarity would be simply incredible were they not well authenticated. After killing their victim they nearly always crushed the face and head with rocks and otherwise mutilated the body, and then shot it full of arrows. Those unfortunate captives who fell into their hands were horribly tortured. Sometimes they would be fastened to a tree and left a target for the arrows of the squaws."[35] "The doomed wretch would be frequently hung by the heels to a limb while a slow fire was built under his head. When wagon-trains were captured the victims were often tied to the wheels and literally cremated while the red devils would dance and yell in fiendish glee around their shrieking captives."[36]

In 1858, "the conductor on the stage from Tucson reported that just beyond the mouth of the cañon they had found the remnants of two wagons, with the dead and mutilated bodies of Frazier and his son tied to the wheels and partially burned."[37] While traveling near Apache Pass in 1862, Joseph Walker found three white men "hanging by their ankles . . . their hands tied behind them and their heads hung to within a foot of the ground and a little fire had been built directly under each head. They were dead and the skin and their hair was burned off of their skulls, giving them a ghastly appearance as they swung there perfectly naked."[38] When about forty Apaches approached Walker's camp, one of the prospectors claimed, "These naked, barbarous wretches sneak out of their holes as insidiously as so many rats, and are not entitled to a consideration more dignified than that which is accorded to the rats and mice about the city livery stable . . . the rifle and six-shooter were the proper implements with which to make such treaties."[39] Despite such threats, Walker prevented any attack on the Apaches by his men. Daniel Conner, a miner traveling with Walker, claimed that "it was a rigid rule all over the country to shoot these savages on sight."[40]

Arizona newspapers carried on a campaign of vilification against the Apaches. The Prescott *Arizona Miner* led the assault on the Apaches in early Arizona Territory. An editorial in 1864 suggested, "We see no other remedy— than to exterminate nearly if not the whole race of savages . . . and the sooner this is accomplished the better for the whole country."[41] Another editorial claimed that "if an Indian scalps an American soldier, outrages and then burns at the stake an American woman, or brains an American baby, [the government will] give him some beads and a new scalping knife, and let him go. . . . The Indian race has served its day and generation, and will eventually be studied upon earth as an extinct species of man. . . . They ought soon to be extermi-nated."[42] Bil Gilbert, commenting on numerous accounts "of bloodthirsty sav-ages massacring peaceful whites" appearing in the Prescott newspaper, finds it hard to believe that "the great majority of the victims were single women and children. Cumulatively the *Miner* reports suggest that northern Arizona was inhabited by thousands of Apache males and at least as many white women— mostly blond virgins—and infants."[43] The author notes that there were proba-bly fewer than 500 Apaches living in the region and that "hunting them down became something of a blood sport" among the white settlers in Prescott.[44]

At the end of the nineteenth century, ethnologist Elie Reclus painted a portrait of the Apaches as sinister beings who are "terrible to man and to every other animal." Apaches were described as "ugly and unpleasing, with an impassive physiognomy" and with eyes that "are slightly oblique . . . but the glassy glare in them suggests the eyes of the coyote."[45] In a discussion of dining etiquette, Reclus claimed that "greed and anguish so whet their teeth that they do not always wait until the prey is dead. Flinging themselves upon it, they devour it still alive, some cutting and carving, others tearing off the limbs and mangling them by main force, without more care for the suffering of their victim."[46] Later, when their hunger subsided, the Apaches would cook the remains of the carcass and "the entrails are looked upon as tit-bits, and bestowed as a special honour." Accord-ing to Reclus, "the distance seems trifling between raw-meat eaters and canni-bals, and the Apaches are accused of anthropophagy also."[47] He also wrote that the Apaches "glory in rapine, murder, and massacre" and are "treacherous and cunning," and that "these savages take a delight in making their prisoners undergo abominable torments."[48] "These wretched Red-skins . . . are obliged to do and suffer in their own person, to flay the martyr or roast the delinquent over a slow fire themselves."[49] Reclus concluded that "these horse-stealers and sheep-stealers will never be forgiven until they are exterminated down to the very last man. . . . the Apaches, the wolf tribe, will share the fate of the wolves. The wolf will perish."[50]

Soldiers in Arizona viewed some of the results of Apache attacks. Thomas Cruse came across "the bodies of the two men, stripped, marked with ghastly wounds. . . . It was grisly! I dreamed of it for weeks afterwards."[51] Cruse noted that "many settlers really favored the simple solution of just killing off all Apaches, those under guard as well as those on the warpath."[52] John Cremony also exhibited an ethnocentric point of view, suggesting that "from earliest infancy they [Apaches] are instructed to regard every other race as natural enemies. Their suspicions and savage distrust are aroused and cultivated before they ever come in contact with other people. . . . To rob or kill a Mexican, is considered a most honorable achievement; but to commit successful outrage upon an American, entitles the perpetrator to the highest consideration."[53]

As did other white observers, Cremony dwelled upon the fate of captives: "Their philosophy and treatment of the captive is entirely different. In such a case their savage and blood-thirsty natures experience a real pleasure in tormenting their victim. Every expression of pain or agony is hailed with delight, and the one whose inventive genius can devise the most excruciating kind of death is deemed worthy of honor."[54] Discussing the Apache treatment accorded captured Mexicans, Cremony wrote that "soon as their savage enemies had obtained control of their arms, each man was seized, bound to the wheel of a wagon, head downward, about eighteen inches from the ground, a fire made under them, and their brains roasted from their heads. . . . As I was the first to pass through Cooke's Cañon after this affair, the full horror of the torture was rendered terribly distinct. The bursted heads, the agonized contortions of the facial muscles among the dead, and the terrible destiny certain to attend the living of that ill-fated party, were horribly depicted on my mind."[55] According to D. C. Cole, "the Chiricahua treated Mexicans in a rough way when they were captured, but they didn't treat Americans like that."[56]

In 1871, Arizona residents sent a memorial to the U.S. Congress listing the "outrages perpetrated" by Apaches during the two preceding years. They complained that Apaches had murdered 178 whites in Arizona Territory. Juan Elias of Tucson claimed that "the Apache Indians are more hostile and successful now than ever before, on account of the superior arms and ammunition that they have."[57] The words "hostile" and "murder" appear throughout the thirty-two page document, but surprisingly enough, only eight men are said to have suffered mutilation: "the bodies of the men were badly mutilated and one of them burned"; "they were *scalped*, one partially burned, and another with his eyes gouged out"; and finally, the "murdered men" "were all mutilated in a horrible manner."[58] It is not known whether this was typical, but it does suggest that Apaches, assuming that they did commit all of these crimes, only occasionally mutilated or burned their victims' bodies.

But what of the Apache viewpoint? In 1866 a *New York Times* editorial discussing the problems faced by Apaches in Arizona Territory concluded: "The Apaches print no newspapers, and have no means of communicating to the world a knowledge of the outrages committed upon *them*. But it is on record, as the experience of all those most familiar with Indian affairs, that the aggressors in nearly all quarrels, and the beginners of nearly all outrages, are the whites— rarely indeed the Indians."[59] General George Crook knew first-hand the problems faced by Apaches in Arizona Territory. In a report sent to the Adjutant General's Office in 1883, Crook wrote that "public sentiment in frontier communities does not consider the malicious killing of an Indian, murder, nor the most unblushing plundering, theft."[60] Crook claimed that Arizona newspapers "disseminate[d] all sorts of exaggerations and falsehoods about" Apaches, "while the Indian's side of the case is rarely ever heard."[61] There is no doubt that Apaches committed raids and depredations against Spanish, Mexicans, and whites in Arizona, but there are reasonable explanations for their behavior.

Since their arrival in Arizona, Apaches had always raided the Hopis, Navajos, and Pimas. It was a natural way of life for them. The appearance of the Spaniards with their horses in the seventeenth century only increased their appetite for raiding. Apaches viewed all whites, whether Spanish, Mexican, or Anglo-American, as outsiders encroaching on their territorial claims to Arizona and Mexico. From the beginning, Spanish, Mexican, and American officials refused to accept the legitimate claims of Native Americans to the land they inhabited. Apache resistance to these intruders seems only natural; however, all three European-based cultures perceived this defiance to be an act motivated by a culture dominated by barbarism. The Spanish were unable to stop Apache raids against haciendas in Sonora, Chihuahua, and Durango and in present-day New Mexico and Arizona. Beginning in the 1830s, the Mexican government offered bounties for Apache scalps, which encouraged some Anglo-Americans and others along the border to kill not only Apaches but also other Indians and, on occasions, Mexicans for their scalps.[62] According to Morris Opler, the Mexicans "started it first—before the Chiricahua. They used to take scalps, including the ears, and sometimes they took the whole head."[63] Opler's informants claimed that "the Chiricahua do not take the scalps of all the fallen enemies; but they take just one scalp, that of the man they believe to be the leader."[64] Scalping was a cruel policy that not only failed to end the raids but also increased the hatred of the Apaches. It may help to explain the more numerous examples of captive torture in Mexico than in Arizona.

After the Mexican War, a series of incidents involved whites attacking Apaches. The Bascom affair in 1861, involving Cochise and Lieutenant George M. Bascom, left six whites and six Apaches dead. Because of this incident, Cochise, who typified a long line of Apache military leaders such as Mangas Coloradas, Juh, Victorio, Chato, Nana, Geronimo, Lozen, and Ulzana, became an imposing enemy of the Americans in Arizona. With such strong-willed leadership these Apaches were not easily subdued. Three years later, King Woolsey, a white miner, massacred a group of Apaches. Woolsey "had an undying hatred for Indians" and "while prospecting in the Bradshaw Mountains, he mixed pinole with strychnine and saw to it that some savages obtained the lethal concoction with disastrous results."[65] Richard Perry claims that "only after revenge and hatred came to dominate the conflict did they [Apaches] begin mutilating the dead and removing scalps, a practice that had been repugnant to them. Even so, they rarely kept scalps."[66] J. P. Dunn, Jr., also believes that Apaches adopted "the practice of mutilating the dead, which was formerly contrary to their customs."[67] When U.S. troops killed Mangas Coloradas trying to escape, as Apache comrades watched, soldiers decapitated and "boiled Mangas Coloradas' severed head in a cauldron to prepare the skull for scientific study."[68] Several years later, in 1871, the Camp Grant massacre engendered a great deal of hatred of whites by the Apaches. Forty Anglo-American and Hispanic men from Tucson, accompanied by a hundred Papagos, attacked the Apache camp at Fort Grant and murdered eighty-five Apaches, mostly women and children.[69] The Papagos, long-time enemies of the Apaches, led the massacre at Camp Grant. Although the perpetrators were charged with murder, a jury found them not guilty. "Arizonians simply would not convict a man for killing an Indian, even though the Indian might be a child."[70] These events detailing white treatment of Apaches in Arizona help to explain the nature of the enmity between these two divergent cultures.

One could provide examples *ad infinitum* of violent behavior by both Apaches and whites, but what were the cumulative results of "Apache warfare"? Can we come up with a body count? In a recent essay discussing inter-ethnic warfare in Arizona, Henry F. Dobyns provides some useful statistics that help to place the treatment of Apaches and whites into perspective. Dobyns "tabulated 6,443 persons slain during inter-ethnic conflicts in Arizona's wars of conquest between 1680 and 1890. Some 89.4 percent of them, 5,759 individuals, were Native Americans."[71] He claims that Apache tribes suffered the worst losses, with 2,246 dead, or 34.9 percent of the total number killed; whites accounted for 684 dead during the period surveyed, or 10.6 percent. In other words, the kill ratio was more than three Apaches for every white, which suggests that the Apaches paid a much higher price in defense of their land than the whites who aggressively dispossessed them during this era.

What explains these white attitudes toward Apaches in the Arizona Territory during the late nineteenth century? By 1860 most white settlers arriving in Arizona already had a "shared memory" of Indians being violent.[72] The 1862 Sioux uprising in Minnesota may have reinforced this common view of Indians as savages. Stories of Apaches torturing Mexican captives increased the apprehension of white miners and settlers. Newspaper accounts of Sioux atrocities in Minnesota mixed with older images of Indians as a "murder-loving race" whose "ruling passions" were "ambition, revenge, envy, and jealousy" made it easy to see Apaches as the new personification of the devil. Francis Parkman wrote that "the Indian is hewn out of rock. You can rarely change the form without destruction of the substance. . . . He will not learn the arts of civilization, and he and his forest must perish together."[73]

Robert Shulman claims that "from Parkman's day to our own, in the American myth of violence only the enemy is seen as really violent."[74] The "inhuman savagery" of the Apache required "retaliatory strikes" against them, even to their final extermination, or at the very least their removal. "As a murderer of women, children, and soldiers, the Indian [read Apache] is a criminal to be executed ruthlessly."[75] Parkman coined the phrase "Pontiac's conspiracy," and with little stretch of the imagination, it could easily become Cochise's, Mangas Coloradas's, or Geronimo's "conspiracy." Most Arizona pioneers would have concurred with Parkman's assessment that "the doom of the [Indian] race was sealed, and no human power could avert it."[76]

Whereas whites were portrayed as "defenders" of their farms, ranches, and mines, Apaches were said to exhibit a violence that was irrational, uncontrolled, and ferocious beyond belief. Their attacks came with the savage war cry that struck terror into the poor defenseless settlers. Apaches "murdered" and "butchered" defenseless white women, helpless children, and industrious male settlers and miners, while on the other hand, whites "killed" ruthless, cunning Indians. Clearly, whites perceived their struggle with Indians as a battle between civilization and barbarism. It was necessary to destroy the Apaches to save civilization.

Under such illusions, whites killed Apache men, women, and children with no qualms or guilt. One does not have to read Parkman to come to this conclusion; the Arizona newspapers were full of talk about genocide and its rewards for white settlers. In the final analysis, whites believed the Apaches must go.

The Nah-deiz-az case is evidence of the enmity for Apaches held by white citizens of Arizona. As a Globe newspaper editor noted, "There is, however, a Tonto Apache . . . who owing to his melancholy situation, no longer mocks the silent corridors [of the jail] with shouts of mirth or music's echoing strain. Death borders upon our birth, but he perhaps never realized the fact until twelve good and true men pronounced his doom for the murder of Lieut. Seward Mott."[77] After spending weeks in the "squalid cell," on December 27, 1889, Sheriff Jerry Ryan and deputies escorted the calm Nah-deiz-az to the gallows on a cloudy, somber day. According to observers standing close to the platform, when Sheriff Ryan said goodbye to the condemned before springing the trap, Nah-deiz-az replied, "Good-bye hell!"[78] Deputy Sheriff D. A. Reynolds "with one blow of the axe, severed the rope which held the weight suspended, and Nah-deiz-az shot upward to the top of the gallows frame and the recoil left the body suspended in the air. A twitching of his fingers, a slight contraction of the limbs and tremor of the body, and all was over."[79] Actually it was not quite that clean an execution. When the weight dropped, pulling his body up, "there was a swishing sound as Nah-deiz-az's body was jerked aloft to the gallow's top. A miscalculation of slack in the hanging rope permitted the body to go too high . . . it crashed into the crossbar atop the scaffold, badly crushing the skull. There was a gasp of horror from among the spectators. Ryan stood as if frozen."[80]

Newspapers provide numerous examples of extreme expressions of hatred for Apaches who killed white citizens. In a bitter tone, the editor of the Flagstaff *Arizona Champion* suggested, "If there are any good Indians outside of graveyards, they do not live in Arizona."[81] This outpouring of venom typified white hatred for Apaches in Arizona. With the wars just subsiding, a period of intense racial animosity permeated white society. In November 1889, the Florence *Arizona Weekly Enterprise* ran the following editorial under the banner headline "Murderers all!"

> The recent Apache outbreak gives the country another opportunity to learn that lesson in common sense with regard to its treatment of the Indians which it seems so slow to comprehend. Why should not the Indian be treated like any other resident? When he kills why should he not be hanged? As it is, he is almost coaxed

to commit outrages . . . so he starts out from his reservation, robs right and left, kills all the men, women and children he can find and leaves behind him a sickening trail of torture and mutilation.

It is safe to say that should a few bands of Apaches be taken from the war path and suspended by their necks, where the other Indians on the reservation could get a good, fair look at them, there would be no more Apache outbreaks, and Arizona . . . would have no more trouble. . . . It is time the American people stopped patting red murderers on the back.[82]

Contrary to the editorial, the crime had occurred two years previous, involved two victims, and was not an "Apache outbreak." Of course, the victims were white, and the occasion for this diatribe has its own life history. Florence residents were awaiting, with great anticipation, the impending execution of five Apaches accused of killing two white victims on the San Carlos Reservation in 1887. To the dismay of the prospective white audience, Gon-shay-ee, As-ki-say-la-la, and Pah-sla-gos-la cheated the gallows by committing suicide the night before the execution. After the execution of the two remaining Apaches, Kah-dos-lah and Na-con-qui-say, one or more sadistic individuals visited the graveyard, decapitated Gon-shay-ee, and fled with his head. The editor commented, "and to this hour it is believed that even Gon-sha [*sic*] has not missed the head he so mysteriously lost."[83] In a gloating manner the editor continued, "Gon-sha, [*sic*] the ex-chief, now lies in his grave a headless piece of clay. He cheated the gallows by committing suicide and in turn he has been cheated out of his cabeza."[84]

Such striking examples provide insights into the deep-seated hatred for Apaches exhibited by white settlers and miners, a hatred that also reached into the criminal justice system. Apaches experienced a decided disadvantage when confronted with different values and a foreign criminal justice system.

Native American Legal Tradition

William Seagle suggests that indigenous societies did not have courts, but he believes that "the popular conception of the primitive blood-feud as one of an endless series of homicides" is incorrect.[85] Seagle explains that "some very primitive societies . . . discovered methods of mitigating the blood-feud" without established courts. For example, Eskimos sometimes settled differences by means of a boxing match, and Mohave Indians occasionally used a tug-of-war match.[86]

E. Adamson Hoebel claims that "courts" could be found in Cheyenne military society.[87] "Can anyone deny that the Elk Soldiers were in effect sitting as a court for the entire tribe? The test is first, one of responsibility. . . . It is, second, one of authority. . . . and it is, third, one of method. Unhampered by a system of formal precedent which 'required' them to judge according to the past, they recognized that the rule according to which they were settling this case was new, and they so announced it."[88] Hoebel also notes that the concept of courts as defined by modern jurisprudence was not the real issue. "The really fundamental *sine quo non* of law in any society—primitive or civilized—is the legitimate use of physical coercion by a socially authorized agent."[89] Similarly, A. R. Radcliffe-Brown views law as "the maintenance or establishment of social order . . . by the exercise of coercive authority through the use, or the possibility of use, of physical force."[90] Finally, Hoebel concludes, "law may be defined in these terms: *A social norm is legal if its neglect or infraction is regularly met, in threat or in fact, by the application of physical force by an individual or group possessing the socially recognized privilege of so acting.*"[91] Law viewed within this context aids in understanding Native American methods of controlling homicide.

There was no unanimity among Native American tribal groups on the classification and punishment of homicide. In Cheyenne society, the tribal council held the ultimate authority in murder cases, and even they could not condemn the perpetrator to death. "The solution was exile, and this was the sentence. Thus homicide was made a crime against the people."[92] After the offender's banishment the Cheyenne performed the ritual of "Renewal of the Medicine Arrows" to purge them from any bad medicine brought on by the murder of a Cheyenne. After leaving the camp, the perpetrator continued his life in another area. However, the Cheyenne believed in rehabilitation, and if the kin of the victim did not object, the perpetrator could eventually return to the camp.

Intratribal homicide was not common among the Cheyenne. George Bird Grinnell believed that sixteen cases occurred between 1835 and 1879. With an estimated population of 8,500, that would be approximately 4.2 homicides per 100,000 population per year, a homicide rate that falls within the middle range for the nineteenth century.[93] This homicide rate would be comparable to New York City during the mid to late nineteenth century.[94]

John Phillip Reid claims that the Cherokee knew their criminal law well, that "it was ingrained in his legal consciousness, the bone and marrow of his social existence."[95] It was the "foundation of most primitive legal systems" and was necessary for maintaining the social structure of Native American societies. Reid further notes that "talionic justice was by no means an institution of uniform application."[96]

There was a wide variety of methods to deal with homicide. Plains Indians used the peace pipe as a means of persuasion to stop blood feuds. The Iroquois would convene a council to forestall the "retaliatory killing," and Hurons developed a compulsory compensation plan in the seventeenth century.[97] The methods available to deal with homicide are striking and not always conducive to mitigation. For example, Comanches believed that a man had the right to kill his wife "with or without good cause," and it was not considered to be murder.[98] To the Comanches, "homicide was not legally a tribal or public affair." It was a quarrel for the family to resolve and tribal government had no right to interfere.[99]

Apache Social Traditions

Western Apaches perceived homicide in a manner somewhat similar to that of Comanches. Apache leadership did not possess the Cheyenne tribal council tradition of strong central power. Instead, Apache band or clan chiefs had only nominal power and could not dictate or control clan behavior. Leaders were respected for their power and leadership, but if they did not satisfy the majority, they could be quickly deposed.[100] Chiefs were chosen for their ability to lead raiding and war parties against the enemy. If their tactics proved ineffective and resulted in casualties, another warrior could come forward and lead the band.[101] This diffuse leadership style may explain why the Apaches developed social-control mechanisms that paralleled the Comanche concept of murder as being a "family matter."

Among the Apaches, the clan acted as the "family." Apaches believed that a man had the right to cut off his wife's nose if she had been unfaithful, and it was acceptable to kill her as well. If someone raped his wife, he "would attempt to kill the other man, and in doing so, public sentiment . . . would be with him."[102] If someone accidentally killed another, or killed in anger, it was common to pay atonement. If accepted by the aggrieved party, the issue could be resolved. In such cases the close blood relatives of the injured party demanded and accepted such payments. The victim's family could kill the perpetrator if the atonement was insufficient or if the killing was accompanied by great anger.

Blood feuds were frequent in Apache culture and created a certain amount of instability. Apaches seemed to hold grudges and believed in "getting even." Once the loss became "equal," the feud could end, but in some cases the feuds escalated. In many ways Apache social controls for homicide parallel the Mediterranean feuding tradition discussed above. Among the Apaches, the wronged party, whether it be for a homicide, wife rape, or just an insult, might ambush the perpetrator without warning. Homicides were often committed "during or following drinking parties," where, under the influence of *tiswin*,[103] an alcoholic beverage made from corn, old grudges might be recalled and "settled." On numerous occasions the Indian agent at San Carlos complained about these drunken bouts. In his 1881 report to the commissioner of Indian Affairs, J. C. Tiffany claimed that his Indian police had been successful in destroying two thousand gallons of tiswin. However, he candidly admitted that he had not solved the drinking problem and reported that "several Indians [were] wounded in fights among themselves or at Tis-win parties" and these occurrences were common.[104] Eight years later another Indian agent admitted that tiswin drinking bouts continued to plague the San Carlos Reservation and usually ended in the killing of one or more participants.[105] Even as late as 1901 the San Carlos Indian agent complained that he was unable to suppress the drinking of tiswin. By that time, however, homicides related to tiswin parties had ceased to be a major problem.[106]

Grenville Goodwin reported a significant number of homicides involving tiswin during the late nineteenth century. An informant told Goodwin that "whenever one man had killed another, he continually carries weapons with him" hoping to prevent an ambush.[107] Goodwin observed that "too much stress cannot be placed on the clan nature of feuds. The opposing party was not spoken of as the enemy of the family . . . but as the enemy of the clan."[108] His informants recounted several revenge homicides that dramatically escalated out of control. In 1850 a group of Apaches participated in a game of hoop-and-pole and soon began to quarrel. One man fatally stabbed another. He jumped on his horse and galloped away. In a running battle he killed one of his pursuers. Within a few minutes he had killed four. In the ensuing melee "twenty-two men were killed."[109] Later, members of one of the clans discovered where the murderers had fled. An informant related that they surrounded the camp and that his father ordered his men, " 'Point your guns and arrows at all those men and don't miss any. Kill them all at once.' . . . The seven men who came out of the wickiup were shot down and killed right there."[110] The participants were "getting even" with the opposing clan.

Whites had difficulty dealing with Apache customs and traditions. Serving under General George Crook's command in Arizona, Britton Davis spent time with the Apaches in the 1880s and understood how some of them felt about white criticism. Davis recalled that General Crook had ordered all tiswin making at San Carlos to be stopped immediately. Davis called some of the chiefs in to talk to them about the tiswin problem. He began by discussing wife beating.

"Old Nana got up, said an angry sentence or two . . . and stalked out of the tent." Davis insisted that his Apache scout, Mickey Free, translate exactly what Nana had said. Reluctantly Free replied, "Tell the *Nantan Enchau* (stout chief) . . . that he can't advise me how to treat my women. He is only a boy. I killed *men* before he was born."[111] Davis understood and later reported Apache chief Chihuahua's observations that when the Apaches had made peace with the Americans,

> nothing had been said about their conduct among themselves; they were not children to be taught how to live with their women and what they should eat or drink. All their lives they had eaten and drunk what seemed good to them. The white men drank wine and whiskey, even the officers and soldiers at the posts. The treatment of their wives was their own business. They were not ill treated when they behaved. When a woman would not behave the husband had the right to punish her. . . . Now they were being punished for things they had a right to do so long as they did no harm to others.[112]

Although their belief system was quite different from that of white society, the Apaches possessed deep-rooted moral values that paralleled the white social code. "In fact, he [the Apache] adhered more strictly to his social code," Frank C. Lockwood observed, "than the white man does to his."[113] Apache society provided various rules to control social and criminal behavior.[114] The Apache lifestyle, however, posed insurmountable problems, and Arizona territorial officials refused to tolerate such behavior. Although based on centuries of existence, Apache social traditions were incompatible with white society.

The Gila County Criminal Justice System

The criminal justice system in Gila County operated under the dominant white society governed by rules established by the U.S. Congress and the territorial legislature. To address violent crime during the territorial period, it employed a joint control system with powers shared within federal and county jurisdictions. Originally the federal district courts possessed jurisdiction over criminal cases that occurred on federal military posts and Indian reservations. In 1883, however, the case of *Ex Parte Crow Dog* brought about an important change in Indian criminal law. Crow Dog had killed Spotted Tail, a popular Brulé Sioux chief, on the Sioux Reservation on August 5, 1881.[115] Families of the two parties negotiated a settlement based on tribal tradition. With the acceptance of compensation from Crow Dog, the issue was resolved. However, federal officials, unhappy

Members of the Gila County Sheriff's Department, 1907. *Left to right:* George Henderson, Ralph Sturgis, John Davis, Sheriff J. H. Thompson *(seated)*, Bill Voris, and Charley Edwards. Sheriff Thompson resigned after being indicted for murder, even though he was later acquitted. (Courtesy of Arizona Historical Society / Tucson, no. 22300)

with the outcome, prosecuted and convicted Crow Dog under federal law. On appeal, the U.S. Supreme Court ruled that the U.S. District Court of Dakota had no jurisdiction and overturned the conviction.[116] To rectify this discrepancy, Congress passed the Indian Appropriation Act of March 3, 1885, commonly called the Major Crimes Act, and eventually the U.S. Supreme Court decision *U.S. v. Kagama* (1886) clarified criminal jurisdiction. The Major Crimes Act placed seven serious crimes (including homicide) occurring on Indian reservations under the jurisdiction of the local territorial courts, which convened in the various county seats.[117]

The Arizona territorial criminal justice system mirrored the U.S. legal system, which had its origins in English law modified by the colonial experience and the establishment of federal and state systems. Although this modified system moved west with the settlers, it failed to educate or bring the previous occupants, such as Apaches and Hispanics, into its alien criminal justice system. Apaches had developed their own legal system over an extended period of time and saw no reason to change. They were unable to pursue their legal rights under this alien system, and they seldom received effective legal counsel. Their disadvantage is evident in the high number of plea bargains for Apaches compared to low rates for white defendants. The Apaches received inferior legal assistance, particularly during the period 1880–1900, which helps to explain the high conviction rates for Apache perpetrators.

Even though they committed acts that were accepted as reasonable behavior according to Apache standards, those same acts were perceived differently by white society. Two distinct cultures existed, one dominated by a complicated system of legal control, the other centered on social control dictated by centuries of tribal traditions. U.S. Supreme Court Justice Samuel F. Miller explained the Indians' predicament while describing how they were treated: "It [the court system] tries them not by their peers, nor by the customs of their people, nor the law of their land, but by superiors of a different race, according to the law of a social state of which they have an imperfect conception, and which is opposed to the traditions of their history . . . one which measures the red man's revenge by the maxims of the white man's morality."[118] Although addressing the treatment of Crow Dog, a Sioux, Justice Miller's observation of the unfairness of the criminal justice system is just as applicable to Apaches in Arizona Territory, where there were no attempts by San Carlos Reservation or county officials to bring Apaches fairly into this new complicated legal system.

Apache Interracial and Intraracial Homicides

During the late 1880s Arizona experienced a series of interracial killings. Apaches killed outside their race more than any other racial or ethnic group. Twenty-seven percent of their victims were white, and 2 percent Hispanic (the rest were Apache).[119] These interracial homicide cases provide a window through which we can evaluate the treatment of Apache defendants. Although forty-eight cases between 1880 and 1920 involved Apaches prosecuted for murder or manslaughter, only a few court transcripts still exist. Unless a case was appealed or a commutation was requested, most transcript notes were destroyed. These Apache trial transcripts exist only because they were appealed to the Arizona Territorial Supreme Court and eventually to the U.S. Supreme Court.[120]

An examination of several interracial homicide cases provides clues about the treatment of Apaches accused of killing whites. In the case discussed earlier, Nah-deiz-az (sometimes called "the Carlisle Kid") had just returned from

Carlisle Indian School, where he had spent a year or more developing farming skills. Upon his return Nah-deiz-az worked on his father's farm along the Gila River on the San Carlos Reservation. About the same time, Second Lieutenant Seward Mott received an assignment to San Carlos. Less than two years out of West Point, Mott knew little about Apaches or their customs and was unable to deal effectively with them. His appointment as acting head of the Indian Police seems misguided and improvident.[121] Little is known about him, but Mott exhibited arrogance and proved to be quarrelsome. His heavy-handed style did not sit well with some of the Apaches.

On March 10, 1887, Mott and the Indian Police arrested and jailed Nah-deiz-az's father for refusing to work the farm as ordered. Nah-deiz-az testified that "his father was helping him to work with one hand, only because he is crippled."[122] After finding out that his father had been locked in the guardhouse, Nah-deiz-az mounted a horse, raced after Mott, and confronted him. In an angry manner Nah-deiz-az shouted, "What did you put my father in the jail for?" One witness claimed that Mott "asked what he had said." Nah-deiz-az retorted, "Now, you want to put me in jail too? You will not put me in jail."[123] Nah-deiz-az drew a .45 Colt revolver and fired at Mott. The impact knocked the officer off of his horse. Mott jumped to his feet and ran down the hill with Nah-deiz-az in hot pursuit, firing as he ran. He also fired at Frank Porter, an employee at San Carlos, who retreated from the scene. Nah-deiz-az admitted firing "ten shots at the Lieutenant" inflicting three wounds. One proved fatal.[124]

This case typifies the tragedy that sometimes characterized reservation life. After returning from the Carlisle school Nah-deiz-az felt out of place on the reservation, where Apaches eyed him with suspicion. Typically Indians who returned from white schools were accepted by neither whites nor reservation Indians.[125] Given that the conflict involved an inexperienced army officer and a young Apache chafing from white arrogance, such a deadly encounter should not seem too surprising. In a one-day trial the jury found Nah-deiz-az guilty and sentenced him to life imprisonment.[126] (He was later retried and sentenced to death.)

Another case involving Apache defendants accused of killing a white appears to have been a miscarriage of justice. In October 1890, the Gila County prosecutor charged Guadalupe, Bat-dish, Back-el-cle, and Nat-tsin with murdering Edward Baker, a white rancher, on July 12 of that year. Baker lived in an isolated region in the Sierra Ancha Mountains northwest of the San Carlos Reservation. On Monday, July 14, a neighbor discovered his body with a bullet wound and "his head nearly severed from the trunk." Investigators observed moccasin

Nah-diez-az, also known as "the Carlisle Kid," was convicted and executed for killing Lieutenant Seward Mott on the San Carlos Reservation in March 1887. (Courtesy of Arizona Historical Society/Tucson, no. 19527)

tracks near the body and immediately suspected Apaches. Prosecutors believed that Guadalupe, his two sons, and Back-el-cle were the killers because they had been seen near the Sierra Ancha Mountains on the day of the murder. After a brief trial, a jury quickly found the defendants guilty of murder.[127]

In January 1891, W. H. Griffin and P. B. McCabe, attorneys for the defendants, appealed the conviction to the Arizona Territorial Supreme Court. In their brief the attorneys built a convincing case against the convictions. Guadalupe, Bat-dish, Back-el-cle, Nat-sin, and four family members had stopped at Patterson's ranch about 8 A.M. on July 12, the day Baker was killed. They had breakfast with Patterson and then camped about a half mile from the ranch.

Patterson passed their camp around noon "but did not see Guadalupe, Nat-tsin, or Bat-dish. About five or six o'clock, Patterson again rode into the Indian camp, and saw there all three of the defendants. . . . Patterson was in the camp when they were packing up; saw one or two deer that the Indians had killed; and saw nothing unusual about the camp."[128] Prosecutors theorized that the defendants left the camp, climbed the mountains, and killed Baker between the hours of 9 A.M. and 6 P.M. Patterson, however, noted that he had talked to all of the defendants and "saw nothing unusual; did not see Baker's horse; did not see any of Baker's property" when they left the camp. Defense counsel believed that "if they did not kill Edward Baker on Saturday afternoon, then they did not kill him at all."[129]

As corroborating evidence they offered the testimony of Al Sieber, former chief of Apache scouts, who tracked the killers from Baker's place. Sieber picked up the trail of three horse tracks—"two large, and one small one; one was shod"—and followed it to a recently abandoned campsite. Sieber and his scouts continued to follow the trail for about thirteen miles, to a place where the perpetrators had stopped again to camp, about six miles from Patterson's ranch. "The party took to the water of Cherry Creek, to hide the trail," Sieber testified, and "there we lost it, and I never found it any more."[130] The defense attorneys argued that J. H. Baker had testified that they owned "a very large *bare-footed horse. We didn't shoe him; we used him for cultivating.*"[131] Patterson, however, had not seen any similar horse in the Guadalupe camp. Furthermore, Sieber and his Apache scouts followed the killers' tracks, which did not cross or come near Guadalupe's trail where they entered and left Patterson's ranch. The defense attorneys concluded "that such evidence as has been offered by the prosecution, by all the legal rules, establishes the *innocence* of the three defendants, Nat-tsin, Bat-dish, and Guadalupe."[132] Despite vague circumstantial evidence offered by the prosecution that was often contradicted by the expert testimony of respected scout Al Sieber,[133] the jury found the Apaches guilty of first-degree murder and sentenced them to life in prison.[134] The appeal failed.

A case involving Captain Jack, although it did not involve white victims, had important implications for a series of Apache homicide cases involving white victims tried in Phoenix, Arizona Territory. In May 1888, the U.S. district attorney in Globe indicted Captain Jack, an Apache band chief, for murdering Nasson and Noh-chu-bre-con at San Carlos in Gila County.[135] Second U.S. District Court trial-transcript testimony suggests that Captain Jack did not kill either of the two victims. However, Te-te-che-le, Tzay-zin-tilth, Has-tin-du-to-dy, Ilth-kah, Lah-cohn, and Til-ly-chil-lay, co-indicted members of Captain Jack's

Al Sieber served as chief of scouts for General George Crook and in 1890 testified on behalf of Guadalupe, Batdish, Back-el-cle, and Nattsin, who were accused of murdering Edward Baker. (Courtesy of Arizona Historical Society / Tucson, no. 43419)

band, probably did kill them. Sometime previous to these homicides two or three of Captain Jack's band, possibly including his father and a brother, had been killed by members of a rival band led by Ca-sa-do-ra.[136] According to Apache tribal custom, if the aggrieved party did not receive an acceptable payment from the family or clan of the perpetrator of the homicide, Captain Jack, as chief, or a band member, was required to take retribution.

After several months Captain Jack became angered that a member of the offending band had not been killed. He approached Colonel Simon Snyder, a military officer at San Carlos Reservation, and explained his predicament. "It was customary among his people," Snyder testified, "that where an Indian had been killed in order to avenge him that relatives of the Indian were justified in killing one of the other band in satisfaction."[137] Snyder also noted that Captain Jack felt "very bad, he could not eat, he could not sleep thinking about this all the time and he thought that the time had come for him to take action in the matter and he was going to settle it to suit himself."[138] Snyder, of course, advised him against taking the law into his own hands. Court testimony reveals that Captain Jack did not actually participate in the killings, which appear to have been committed by four members of his band. Further evidence indicated that members of Ca-sa-do-ra's band were armed with rifles and poised to attack Captain Jack's people just prior to the retaliation.[139] Despite the testimony of Snyder and others, the Maricopa County jury, sitting for the Second U.S. District Court, found Captain Jack guilty and sentenced him to thirty years in prison. His codefendants received comparable prison terms.

In a similar case the Second U.S. District Court found Gon-shay-ee guilty of first-degree murder and sentenced him to death.[140] The twenty-five-page court transcript indicates that Gon-shay-ee probably committed the crime. The question of evidence, however, was not the key issue in this case. Legal counsel for Gon-shay-ee appealed to the U.S. Supreme Court claiming that the Second U.S. District Court, under which the proceedings occurred, lacked jurisdiction over this case as dictated by the Major Crimes Act of 1885.[141] Accordingly, defense counsels asked for a writ of *habeas corpus*. The Supreme Court agreed to hear the petitioners. In a case that held important implications for nine similar Apache homicide cases in Arizona Territory, Justice Samuel F. Miller carefully cited *Ex Parte Crow Dog, U.S. v. Kagama,* and the Major Crimes Act of 1885. Although the indictment did not cite specifically where the crime occurred, the law was clear: original jurisdiction resided in the territorial courts of Arizona. In this case, the territorial court system in Pinal County should have tried Gon-shay-ee.[142]

Although the five U.S. district courts held their sessions within the county seats and had the same judges as the county courts, they were to be maintained separately. The county sheriff should have secured the prisoner, the Pinal County grand jury should have issued the indictment, the county district attorney should have prosecuted the defendant, and the county judge should have heard the case. By assuming jurisdiction, the defense argued, the U.S. District Court had exceeded its powers. Justice Miller noted that "the Indian shall at least have all the advantages which may accrue from that change [Major Crimes Act], which transfers him, as to the punishment for these crimes, from the jurisdiction of his own tribe to the jurisdiction of the government of the Territory in which he lives."[143] They issued the writ, overturned his previous conviction, and remanded the case for retrial.

U.S. v. Gon-shay-ee and *U.S. v. Captain Jack* brought about the reevaluation of eleven Apache Indians convicted of murder in U.S. district courts in Arizona Territory. The U.S. Supreme Court remanded these cases to the Arizona Territorial Supreme Court, which reversed the convictions and returned them to the county courts for retrial. The overturning of the convictions did not assure that the defendants would go free. All were retried in the county courts, and most were convicted. However, Gila County authorities retried Captain Jack and found him not guilty. Four of his codefendants, Has-tin-du-to-dy, Te-te-che-le, Lah-cohn, and Til-ly-chil-lay, were also retried—and found guilty. The unfortunate Ilth-kah died in the Ohio Penitentiary before his appeal had been heard.[144]

Being sentenced to prison proved to be extremely deadly for Apaches. Yuma Territorial Prison records are incomplete, but six Apache defendants tried in Gila County court died in prison. This was an all too familiar experience for Native American inmates. An evaluation of Yuma Territorial Prison mortality statistics reveals that Native American death rates were much higher than those of either whites or Hispanics. Of the Apaches sentenced to Yuma for murder or manslaughter, 37 percent died after surviving an average of 4.8 years. By comparison, 10 percent (two inmates) of the whites died in prison. These figures parallel high death rates at San Quentin State Prison, California, where 43 percent of the Native American inmates convicted of murder or manslaughter died—most within four years. For reasons that remain unclear, incarceration appeared to be a death sentence for many Indians.[145] A few, such as Chaw Paw, Bac-el-cle, Mat-zin, and Nesho survived and eventually were released from prison.

High interracial murder rates among Apache defendants help explain their long terms of imprisonment. Gila County judges sentenced six Apaches to life imprisonment. In a one-day retrial Gila County officials also convicted and condemned to death Nah-deiz-az. The court's message was clear. Apaches who murdered whites could expect severe sentencing.[146]

Of course, Apaches were not guiltless; some did commit homicides. Most of their victims, however, were Apaches living on or near the reservation. In the 1880s the Indian agent at San Carlos experienced significant difficulty trying to help Apaches adjust. By 1886 they were confined to the reservation without a substitute for their old lifestyle of raiding for cattle and horses. One can only imagine the difficulty they experienced giving up the horse for the hoe. Apaches turned more and more to drinking tiswin as a way to relieve the drudgery of farming. The women normally prepared the tiswin while the men fasted for two or three days. Under these conditions the alcohol had a dramatic effect. These drinking episodes sometimes turned into wild melees resulting in fights and occasionally ending in death. Homicides were often committed under such inebriation.[147]

Gila County authorities indicted four white defendants accused of killing Apaches. Charges against three were dropped. A jury found Harry Jose, the fourth defendant, guilty. Jose received a life sentence. It is significant that this crime occurred in 1913, after the intense hatred for Apaches had subsided considerably.[148]

On February 18, 1906, Arizona Ranger J. B. Holmes attempted to arrest Matze in an Apache camp near Roosevelt. According to one observer, Holmes said, "Hi there, with that gun!"[149] Holmes immediately began firing and hit Matze five times at close range. Holmes was exonerated. In another case, D. E. Mabin accused Cole, an Apache, of trying to rob him on the streets of Globe. Claiming that Cole "went for his gun," Mabin used a shotgun to shoot his victim at close range. There was no gun found on or near the victim.[150] Gene Perry killed Jess, an Apache female, in April 1913. There was no coroner's inquest, and the charges were soon dropped.

Whites usually killed within their own racial or ethnic group. On October 21, 1890, Alex Graydon and D. A. Reynolds, both armed and dangerous, stepped on to Broad Street in Globe, Arizona, and shot it out. Graydon shot Reynolds four times. As usual, it was ruled self-defense.[151] Eight years later Charles Edwards and Charles Cadotte decided to settle a quarrel that had plagued them for several years. Both armed, they stepped into the streets of Globe and began to fire at each other. Cadotte fell mortally wounded. In this case, a jury found Edwards guilty.[152] In another case, Robert Tally and Jesse Danner became involved in a fist fight around midnight on a street in Miami, Arizona. Several men pulled them apart. Tally quickly pulled his revolver and fatally shot Danner four times at close range. Although charged with murder, a jury found him not guilty.[153] Other shoot-outs also occurred on the streets of Globe, Miami, and Winkelman.[154]

On October 17, 1906, A. J. Purvis approached Deputy Sheriff George Shanley on a train headed from San Carlos Reservation to Globe. Shanley had visited the reservation to arrest and return Harry F. Wilbur to the Gila County jail. Purvis walked up to Shanley and began a casual conversation. He asked Shanley if his prisoner was Wilbur, and Shanley replied, "Yes." Suddenly, without warning, Purvis pulled a revolver and shot Wilbur, the handcuffed prisoner, to death.[155] Purvis then put the gun to his head and committed suicide. The stunned Shanley immediately ordered the conductor to stop the train at Rice

Station, on the San Carlos Reservation, to obtain medical aid for Wilbur. The victim died of his wounds.[156]

In another unusual case Ben Olney told John Hawkins to get off his property and accused him of "insulting" his wife. As Hawkins began to back away from the house, Olney's daughter said, "Papa, don't shoot."[157] Olney fired several shots in rapid succession from a revolver, killing Hawkins instantly. Despite the fact that there were several witnesses and the victim was unarmed and backing away, no charges were filed against Olney. Such shootings were common in Gila County.

Gila County Lynchings

Despite the much-publicized tradition of lynch-mob activity in other parts of the West, only three examples of such collective violence can be identified in Gila County, Arizona.[158] Two of these incidents occurred in 1882, and the final one in 1910. Some authors have treated lynchings as though they were an acceptable means of "controlling lawlessness" on the frontier. There is little doubt that lynchings were homicides, yet virtually all of the perpetrators of these crimes avoided criminal prosecution. Few citizens perceived this kind of retributive "justice" as a crime; rather, it appeared to be a reasonable reaction to a crime committed by lawless citizens. All three of the lynchings occurred after homicides committed by the four victims.

Lynching was not strictly a rural phenomena. Although lynching victims make up only a small percentage of the total homicides committed (1.8 percent), they provide important insights into Gila County society. It is significant that all three of the lynching incidents occurred at night. Although there was little chance of being prosecuted for such a crime, the perpetrators apparently did feel some guilt for their violent actions and sought anonymity. Previous research has indicated that ethnic minorities are usually overrepresented in victim statistics of lynchings, but this was not the case in Gila County, where the lynching of whites suggests that life was cheap and that the concept of "taking the law" into one's hands was acceptable—as late as 1910.

The typical lynching in the West required a crime, a victim, and a group of citizens willing to take retribution against the alleged perpetrator of the offense. On August 20, 1882, Globe residents found Andrew Hall, a Wells Fargo driver, and Dr. W. F. Vail robbed and shot to death just outside of town.[159] Hall had been carrying a pouch with money at the time he was ambushed by bandits. Apparently Dr. Vail witnessed the crime and was shot to prevent him from identifying the robbers. Evidence suggested that Curtis Hawley, Lafayette Grimes, and Cicero Grimes committed the crime. Sheriff W. W. Lowther assembled a posse and quickly located and arrested the three suspects. Under heavy-handed interrogation Lafayette Grimes confessed, named Hawley as his partner, and implicated his younger brother Cicero. The sheriff locked them in jail to await a hearing and trial.[160]

Three days after the crime a crowd of about one hundred Globe citizens gathered to take action and marched on the jail. At first Sheriff Lowther resisted the mob, "but on learning that the jail would be stormed . . . he finally consented to the mob's demand."[161] Under the cover of darkness the mob assembled, held a quick "trial," and then at 1:30 A.M., August 24, 1882, they executed Lafayette Grimes and Hawley by hanging them from the "Hangman's Tree," a large sycamore on Broad Street.[162] At the last moment the mob agreed to spare Cicero Grimes. It had been established that he had not participated in the killings but only acted as a lookout. Arizona Territory newspapers gave their approval to the lynch-mob executions.[163]

Several months later, Constable Thomas Kerr began to celebrate Christmas in Pioneer, Arizona, about twenty miles south of Globe. He spent most of the day in the Wood and Wilman's Saloon drinking and gambling. Late in the evening, heavily under the influence of alcohol, he asked William Hartnett to join him in a drink, but Hartnett refused. Exploding with anger, Kerr whipped out his revolver and shot Hartnett dead. Several men grabbed Kerr and others sounded the alarm. Quickly a mob assembled, allowed Kerr to make out a will, and then hanged him from a sycamore tree.[164] The next morning, Sheriff Lowther arrived to investigate and found the frozen body of Constable Kerr still hanging from the tree. Despite questioning numerous citizens of Pioneer, the sheriff was unable to find a single person who would admit knowing who committed the hanging. The justice of the peace who held the inquest delivered a verdict: "name of deceased, Thomas P. Kerr; age, 40; nativity, United States; place of death, Pioneer; date of death, December 25, 1882; cause of death, hanged by neck; parties unknown."[165]

The third extralegal killing occurred in the Gila County jail in Globe on July 3, 1910. Kingsley Olds had been arrested and accused of causing the drowning death of two teenage sisters, Myrtle and Lou Goswich. The coroner's inquest revealed that there were no signs of criminal assault or rape on either victim's body and listed drowning as the cause of death.[166] The coroner theorized that the girls had gone bathing and one of them got in too deep. The other tried to save her, but could not. Olds, who witnessed their predicament, was too frightened to save them, so "he attempted suicide" with his handgun.[167] A grand jury viewed the circumstances in an entirely different manner. After hearing the witnesses, they concluded that Kingsley Olds had murdered the girls by drowning them.[168] The sheriff locked Olds in the jail to await a court hearing. Three days later someone waited in the judge's chambers on the third floor of the courthouse, which provided an unrestricted view of Olds in his jail cell. At about 4:20 A.M. on July 3, 1910, that person fired one shot from a rifle and killed Olds in his cell.[169] The sheriff was unable to identify the assassin.

Of course, mob action was not the only form of group killing used in Gila County. Posses provided another means that had legal sanction. For example, a sheriff's posse led by E. E. Hodgson attempted to arrest Marian Bagsley on the Salt River in August 1887. Bagsley drew his revolver and fired at the posse, who returned fire, killing him instantly. He had been accused of cattle rustling.[170] Two years later, the Apache Kid assassinated Sheriff Glen Reynolds while being transported to Yuma Prison. Jerry Ryan, the newly appointed sheriff, organized a posse to search for and capture the Apache Kid and several Apaches involved in the escape. Their attempts proved fruitless.[171]

Despite the long tradition of lynch-mob activity in the Far West and Arizona, Gila County proved to be an exception. Although at least sixty-nine men fell victim to lynch mobs in Arizona Territory, Gila County accounted for only four.[172] Equally interesting, the mob lynchings in Gila County do not appear racially motivated. Nevertheless, group violence played a role in Gila County just as it did in Douglas County, Nebraska, and Las Animas County, Colorado.

Indictment Data

Whites constituted the majority (46 percent) of the indictments for murder between 1880 and 1920 (fig. 5.1). The high percentage of Apache indictments parallels high black percentages in Douglas County. Although comprising less than 15 percent of the Gila County population, Apaches accounted for 35 percent of homicide indictments.[173] Most of the homicides committed by whites occurred in Globe and Miami, whereas Apache defendants usually killed their victims on or near the San Carlos and Fort Apache reservations[174] or, during the twentieth century, in the mining communities where they worked.

The conviction rate disparity between Apache and white defendants in Gila County indicates bias within the criminal justice system (fig. 5.2). Apache conviction rates were twice as high as white rates, paralleling data on blacks collected in Omaha, Nebraska.[175] Gila County judges and juries convicted 77

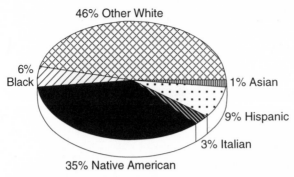

46% Other White

6%
Black

1% Asian

9% Hispanic

3% Italian

35% Native American

Fig. 5.1. Homicide indictments by race/ethnicity, Gila County, 1880–1920. *Source:* Registers of criminal action.

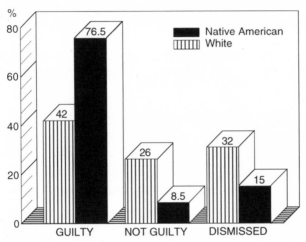

Fig. 5.2. Homicide verdicts in Gila County for Native Americans and whites, 1880–1920. *Source:* Registers of criminal action.

percent of the Apache defendants. Hispanics, Asians, and blacks also had significantly higher conviction rates than did whites. However, the relatively small number of cases (except those involving Hispanics) prevents meaningful analysis.[176] The not-guilty verdicts also suggest bias against Apaches. Only four Apaches were found not guilty, and these cases involved Apache victims. Not-guilty verdicts were reached three times as often for whites as for Apaches. The only dismissals of charges against Apache defendants involved Apache victims.

The Gila County homicide cases involving Apache perpetrators and white

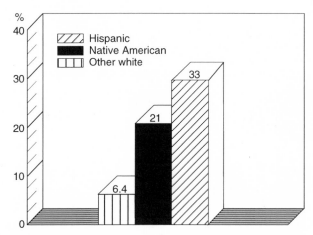

Fig. 5.3. Plea bargaining by race / ethnicity, Gila County, 1880–1920. *Source:* Registers of criminal action.

victims occurred within a short time span. Gila County attorneys prosecuted 50 percent of these Apache defendants in 1889, 40 percent in 1890, and the remaining defendant in 1897. In other words, the ten Apache defendants committed all of these interracial homicides within a ten-year period.[177] All of the Apache defendants indicted for killing whites were convicted. During this same period a significant number of whites were killed by Apaches in Pinal, Graham, and Apache counties, which along with Gila County shared portions of the San Carlos Reservation.[178] The cases involving Apache perpetrators and Apache victims are spread more evenly over the period studied. The percentages of such homicides per decade for Gila County from 1880 to 1920 were 39.5, 37.5, 12.5, and 10.5 percent, respectively. The peak period of 1896–97, when 23 percent of these homicides occurred, was followed by a significant decline. Seventy-three percent of these cases involved Apache male victims and usually included the use of tiswin.[179] This downward trend in Apache homicides suggests the influence of white domination and regimentation on residents of the San Carlos Reservation, including employment, education, and agricultural training. Apaches were finally adapting to the imposition of white control over their lives.

Another criterion for assessing conviction rates is plea bargaining, a common procedure for Apache defendants in Arizona Territory. District attorneys practiced it to resolve legal issues with minimal expense. Twenty-one percent of the plea bargains in the period 1880–1920 involved Apaches, compared to 6.4 percent for whites (fig. 5.3).[180] All Apache plea-bargain cases involved Apache

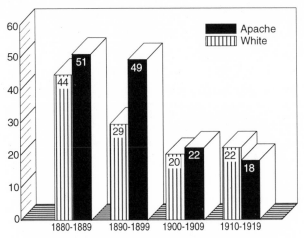

Fig. 5.4. Homicide indictment rates (per 100,000 population) for Apaches and whites in Gila County, 1880–1920. *Source:* Registers of criminal action.

victims and were evenly split between male and female victims. In five of the cases (45 percent) involving Apache female victims, the Apache defendants (all male) pleaded guilty. In one case the accused received a life sentence; all of the other plea bargains included reduced sentences.[181] Apache defendants understood little English and interpreters committed errors in translating from one language to another. Misinterpreting one or two words could have a dramatic effect on understanding what the district attorney or judge was explaining. The high rate of Apache plea bargains indicates that the system failed to provide them with adequate safeguards, such as legal counsel that would guarantee fairness.

Hispanics also plea-bargained at a high rate (33 percent). Three of the four Hispanic defendants who plea-bargained were indicted for killing other Hispanics. All three received reduced sentences. Joe Martínez, however, killed Edward Porter, another white. Although both men had been drinking and the fight occurred on a street in Christmas, Arizona, the plea bargain included a life sentence. The small sample (four cases) prevents any meaningful analysis.

Homicide indictment rates provide a useful measurement of violence levels in Gila County. Both white and Apache homicide indictment rates per 100,000 population were high during the years 1880 to 1920 (fig. 5.4). White indictment rates began with 44 per 100,000 during 1880–89, and then declined to 29 for the period 1890–99, 20 (1900–1909), and 22 (1910–19). Apache homicide indictment rates started with 51 per 100,000 in the first decade, declined to 49 during 1890–99, then dropped to 22 and 18 per 100,000, respectively, for the last two decades. Following the trend found in Douglas and Las Animas counties, Gila County's homicide indictment rates were significantly higher than those in eastern cities. This reflects the propensity to carry handguns (concealed or openly), the failure to enforce laws against carrying such weapons, the abuse of alcohol, the hostility of the criminal justice system toward Apaches, and the general instability of society within the mining camps in Gila County.

Conclusions

Gila County was a violent place for a variety of reasons. First, the clash of cultures—Apache versus Anglo—created a volatile situation that resulted in interracial homicides. These and other killings suggest that a regional culture of violence existed involving both societies. Second, white society brought with it other factors that increased the chances of lethal violence in Gila County. For example, the carrying of handguns seemed to be endemic in Globe and Miami. Apparently no man felt completely dressed unless he strapped on a Colt .45 Peacemaker or slipped a small-caliber handgun into one of his pockets. Data reveal that 94 percent of the white defendants used guns to kill their victims.

Third, the data indicate that the circumstances were right in Gila County to produce violent conditions. It was the critical convergence of a variety of factors that helped to create the conditions that existed within small, rural-based towns like Payson, Gisela, Globe, and Miami. These were new towns and villages that grew quickly with the development of copper mining and the cattle industry. The mix of various ethnic groups increased the volatility that may have already existed within the habits and personality makeup of the new inhabitants of Gila County.

Fourth, heavy drinking and the carrying of guns led to violence on the frontier, whether it was Lincoln County, New Mexico, or Gila County, Arizona.[182] There were numerous saloons catering to the miners in the Arizona copper mining towns. These factors created a deadly mix for anyone visiting Globe or Miami. The data verify that the mixing of handguns, petty grievances, and alcohol often proved lethal.

Finally, racial factors also appeared in Gila County. The intense Indian-hating in Arizona at the outset of Indian-white relations set the stage for future race relations. Patterns of direct and indirect, overt and covert prejudice by attorneys, judges, juries, and editors against Native American peoples legitimized their social, cultural, and legal oppression. Instead of providing justice within a new legal system, the Arizona territorial court system instituted a program of social control that was disparate, discriminatory, and predisposed to nineteenth-century versions of scientific racism. The region's educated elite set the tone for racial intolerance and sanctioned the perversion of a system designed to safeguard the rights of all Americans—including Native Americans.

❖6❖

Lethal Violence

An Appraisal

Our entertainment and our serious writing are suffused with violence to a
notorious degree; it is endemic in our history. . . .
    Ours is a gun culture—a thing without parallel among the industrial
nations of the world.
                                    —Richard Hofstadter, *American Violence*

Data comparison has demonstrated that high levels of lethal violence existed in
the American West, at least in Douglas, Las Animas, and Gila counties. But
what explains this behavior? More than any other issue, it is the rapid convergence of diverse cultures, industrialization, and differing social systems that
best accounts for high lethal-violence levels in the American West. Moving west,
each succeeding county was less settled, and the population more transient.
Influences of an ethnically diverse population accompanied by the rapid growth
associated with a boomtown phenomenon (the best indicator of critical convergence) created social instability, especially in Las Animas and Gila counties.

Settlement of Douglas County occurred much earlier than in Las Animas or
Gila counties. Although Omaha achieved relative social stability, it did suffer
interracial stress, perhaps best illustrated by the lynchings of black victims in
1891 and 1919. Whereas Douglas County reflected urban traits with a more

stable population, the transient nature of society strongly influenced both Las Animas and Gila counties. Omaha boasted a population of 181,000 by 1920, but Trinidad and Globe could only muster 10,906 and 7,044, respectively. The latter cities had grown rapidly, however, especially between 1900 and 1910, with Trinidad doubling and Globe more than tripling in population. Both cities resembled boomtowns in their rapid convergence of diverse ethnic groups and industrialization.

In one recent sociological study, William Freudenburg and Robert Jones suggest that a typical boomtown would be "a community that is not only small (under 10,000 persons), but also isolated, situated well over a hundred miles from the nearest metropolitan area."[1] Trinidad and Globe fit this criteria. Trinidad lies approximately two hundred miles south of Denver, the largest city in Colorado, and the most populous city near Globe is Phoenix, ninety miles west. Both counties were isolated during the study period, but especially Gila County. Freudenburg and Jones's study of modern-day boomtowns also reveals that criminal activities increase more rapidly than population, from 26 to 112 percent per year.[2] Recent boomtowns are usually associated with rapid energy-related economic growth similar to that of Trinidad between 1900 and 1910. Numerous other small boomtowns developed in Las Animas County near the coal mines, all with diverse ethnic populations and numerous saloons. Aguilar, Sopris, Delagua, Segundo, Primero, and Forbes, as well as the more populous Trinidad, proved to be hot spots for lethal violence. In Gila County, Globe and Miami became boomtowns as the copper industry grew. All of these towns lacked stability and experienced high homicide rates.[3]

The development of a subculture of violence in Douglas County and of regional cultures of violence in Las Animas and Gila counties provides a further explanation for high violence levels in the American West. In Douglas County, blacks played an important role in the levels of lethal violence. Fleeing southern violence, thousands of blacks migrated to Omaha seeking jobs and protection. They soon discovered that racial prejudice and discrimination restricted upward mobility, forcing them to fill the service-related and common laborer jobs. Having experienced violence in the South, a significant number of blacks carried handguns. Raised in a southern tradition, blacks held to the exaggerated honor common to the South and believed that any offensive remarks "are each equal to a blow, and any of them justifies an assault."[4] Seventy-six percent of those blacks indicted for homicide used handguns. Blacks, with homicide rates dramatically higher than whites (55 and 4.6 per 100,000 population, respectively), exhibited the presence of a subculture of violence in Douglas County.[5]

Although whites in Omaha had homicide rates higher than those in Boston, New York, and Philadelphia (see fig. 1.11), there is no indication that a subculture of violence existed among them.

Moving west to Colorado, one finds a dramatic increase in lethal-violence levels. Whereas homicide rates averaged 6 per 100,000 in Douglas County, in Las Animas County the average rate was 34 per 100,000. In the coal mining region around Trinidad, lethal violence became a common method for resolving disputes, and it was not restricted to any single ethnic or racial group. By 1900, Las Animas County had become an ethnically diverse region filled with Italians, Greeks, Bohemians, Austrians, Serbians, and a variety of other east Europeans joining with other whites, Hispanics, and a smaller number of blacks seeking employment in the coal mines.

By establishing company towns, the Colorado Fuel and Iron Company dominated society within the hinterland of Las Animas County surrounding Trinidad. They created an "artificial" society controlled by company guards, company-town marshals, and county deputy sheriffs who worked closely with the coal mine operators. It was a restrictive atmosphere that lacked a sense of community and bred discontent. Within this environment the company saloon became the center of activity and in some cases the only social gathering place available for young men. The mixing of diverse ethnic groups in the saloons helps to explain high inter-ethnic homicide rates in Las Animas County. Whites killed outside of their racial group in 31 percent of homicide cases, followed by Hispanics and blacks (22 and 18 percent, respectively). The data confirm the presence of a regional culture of violence in Las Animas County.[6]

Moving farther west to Gila County, Arizona, the homicide rates again rise dramatically, doubling to 70 per 100,000. Homicide rates were especially high during the first three decades (see fig. 1.10). During the period 1885 to 1889, homicide rates reached a phenomenal 133.5 per 100,000. Here, in one of the last frontier regions in the nineteenth-century American West, the clash of cultures formed a backdrop for violence. The intrusion of white society on Apache homelands elicited a violent reaction that resulted in the Apache wars and is reflected in high Apache interracial-homicide indictment rates. In Gila County 29 percent of the Apaches indicted for homicide had killed outside of their race; white and Hispanic perpetrators had killed outside of their race or ethnic group in 12 and 27 percent of homicide cases, respectively.

Another indication that Gila County had a regional culture of violence is the high homicide rate for whites. Although not as ethnically diverse as Las Animas County, Gila County developed a rather unstable transient society that included

Irishmen, Italians, Hispanics, and blacks. Whether in Globe, Miami, Payson, Gisela, or Pioneer, saloons played an important role in the social life of young men employed in copper mines or on ranches. When this diverse group of well-armed young men mixed socially, disagreements often escalated into lethal affairs. Exhibiting some of the aspects of a southern code of honor, armed men took their grievances into the streets, where they settled them with gunfire. Twenty-nine percent of the shootings in Gila County occurred in this fashion. An additional 21 percent of the homicides occurred on San Carlos Reservation. This high rate of homicides committed by Apaches and linked to tiswin parties provides further evidence of the existence of a regional culture of violence.

During the 1850s, settlement of the American West jumped over Las Animas and Gila counties to California and other western regions. Settlement within these two isolated counties occurred later than in Douglas County, Nebraska. Both Las Animas and Gila counties, however, experienced rapid albeit late growth, especially around 1900 to 1920. High homicide rates during this era (see figs. 2.9 and 2.10) reflect a general social instability that resulted in a regional culture of violence.

It should be noted that none of the three counties studied could be labeled a lawless frontier, because each had a criminal justice system. The data, however, reveal that the criminal justice systems were not colorblind. In Las Animas County the general acceptance of high levels of violence, at least by juries, resulted in low conviction rates for most groups, averaging 29 percent for Italians, Hispanics, and other whites; in contrast, there was a 79 percent conviction rate for blacks, which parallels high rates for black defendants in Douglas County. In Gila County, a similar pattern of conviction rates for whites and Native Americans (42 percent versus 76.5 percent) is strong evidence of racial distortion within that criminal justice system as well. For blacks and Native Americans, the chances of conviction were very high, regardless of the race of the victim or the cause of the killing.

One characteristic of many homicides was the minor nature of their origins. Although a wide variety of causal factors can be identified, the petty nature of many disputes deserves comment. A violent confrontation could occur in virtually any saloon in Douglas, Las Animas, or Gila counties, and statistics confirm that they often did. On numerous occasions individuals argued over "too much foam on the beer," drinks on credit, fifty-cent bets, pool wagers, and other minor issues. Given the incidence, also, of major conflicts such as vendettas, racial animosities, love triangles, domestic disputes, strikes, and police shootings, it is clear that these societies were prone to use lethal violence to resolve disputes.

Although not a causal factor, alcohol figured prominently in homicide scenarios. Perpetrators drank prior to committing homicide in 75 percent, 60 percent, and 71 percent of the cases in Douglas, Las Animas, and Gila counties, respectively. Victims consumed alcohol in similar numbers, averaging 62 percent for the three counties. The data suggest that a cultural tradition of drinking coupled with handguns proved deadly.[7]

It is the pervasive nature of gun culture, however, that best illustrates high levels of lethal violence in Douglas, Las Animas, and Gila counties. The existence of a strong gun culture increased the likelihood that disputes might turn lethal. It was an invitation to violence. Perpetrators ranging in age from fourteen to sixty-nine carried guns, and the consequences are reflected in a handgun-homicide rate that averaged 63 percent for the three counties, and in a combined gun rate (handguns, rifles, and shotguns) of 74.6 percent. Mirroring the pattern of increasing levels of violence from east to west in the three counties, the use of guns to commit homicide also increased. In Douglas County 63 percent of homicides were committed using guns, and in Las Animas and Gila counties, the rate increases to 79 and 82 percent, respectively.

John Shelton Reed, in speaking of the rural South, observed that "the availability of guns turns what otherwise would be shouting matches or fistfights into shooting affrays."[8] That certainly was the case in the American West, particularly in Las Animas and Gila counties. Both exhibited unstable conditions that included the presence of large numbers of guns. Douglas County also had its share of guns, however, exemplified by the high handgun-homicide indictment rates of 75 and 57 percent for black and white defendants, respectively. The 18 percent higher rate for blacks reflects a tradition they brought with them from the South, and also the presence of a subculture of violence.[9]

The fact that more than 30 percent of homicide perpetrators were in their twenties reveals that age played an important role in the homicide rates and indicates that youth was strongly intertwined with gun culture. Whether considering the fourteen-year-old who killed a sheep herder[10] with a gun in Las Animas County, or the three black youths who shot and killed a store owner in a robbery attempt in Omaha,[11] numerous examples demonstrate the propensity of men to use guns to commit homicides. Such incidents also indicate the existence of a regional culture of violence in Las Animas County, and a subculture of violence in Douglas County. Youth was not, however, a prerequisite for carrying or using firearms; in all three counties an average 10 percent of homicide perpetrators were fifty years or older, and 25 percent were at least forty.

Accused / Indicted Ratios

As suggested in the previous discussion, the hypothesis that ethnic minorities accused of committing homicides had a greater chance of being indicted was sustained, but the ratio is not overwhelming. The accused/indicted ratio refers to the percentage of those individuals who were accused and identified of a homicide and then actually indicted. This ratio reveals whether bias existed within the criminal justice system. Data collected from coroner's inquests, newspapers, and court records provide this composite. The average difference between the accused/indicted ratio of all ethnic minorities and whites accused of homicide is 11 percent (table 6.1). Since several of the ethnic-minority samples are relatively small, they may be unreliable. For example, the 100 percent indictment rate for Hispanics in Douglas County involves only four defendants. Similarly the black and Italian samples for Gila County include only ten and two defendants, respectively. The low rate (40 percent) for twenty Italians accused of homicide in Douglas County is distinctive. There is no apparent explanation for this curiosity. However, the strongest evidence of bias within the criminal justice system exists in the indictment percentages for blacks in both Douglas and Las Animas counties, for Apaches in Gila County, and for Hispanics in Las Animas County. These are large samples (103, 26, 47, and 84 cases, respectively), which would suggest reliability. Their combined average is 72 percent, or 12 percent higher than the average white rates for the same counties.

The homicide accused/indicted ratios indicate bias within the system. Once identified by authorities, ethnic minorities accused of homicide were more likely to be indicted than whites. The accused/indicted ratio had its greatest impact in Douglas County, where 32 percent of the victims of homicides committed by blacks were white. Also, the large number of indictments (sixty-seven) increased the bias effect. Although there were fewer blacks indicted in Gila County (eight cases), the 90 percent ratio reflects the presence of bias. The 72 percent ratio for Apaches in Gila County's forty-eight cases is even stronger evidence of bias. As well as leading to high conviction rates, this form of bias tended to result in more severe punishment for certain racial minorities, especially blacks and Native Americans, than for white citizens accused of homicide.

Table 6.1 Accused/Indicted Ratios, 1880–1920

County	Other white (%)	Hispanic (%)	Native American (%)	Black (%)	Italian (%)
Douglas	63	100	—	70	40
Las Animas	59	73	—	72	62
Gila	59	40	72	90	100
Average %	60	71	72	77	67

Sources: Coroner's inquests and registers of criminal action.

By combining coroner's inquests and court records to measure levels of lethal violence, this study has revealed the weakness of using only indictments to assess homicide rates. By establishing an accused/indicted ratio, it is possible to determine not only whether racial minorities were discriminated against during the trial phase, but also whether favoritism occurred during the preliminary stages up to, but not including, the indictment process. Although the data are not overwhelming, racial minorities were more likely to be indicted than whites (see table 6.1). African Americans and Native Americans experienced the highest ratios (averages of 77 and 72 percent, respectively), compared to 60 percent for whites.

A comparison of handgun-homicide rates obtained from indictment data and coroner's inquests reveals another dimension. In Douglas County, 66 percent of those indicted for homicide used handguns, yet the coroner's inquests list guns for 58 percent. A similar drop of 10 percent can be seen for Las Animas County, and a lesser amount (3 percent) was observed for Gila County. The data indicate that grand juries and prosecutors were more likely to indict perpetrators who employed handguns than those who used other means to kill their victims. Coroner's inquests offer a better method for measuring the real homicide rate of any given county over time. They are less likely to be racially biased and usually record the deaths of individuals in all categories, including lynchings, and in cases ruled as self-defense that might not reach the indictment stage.

More Evidence of Violence in the West

To further document the existence of a violent culture in the American West, a survey of homicide indictments in Dickinson County, Kansas, was completed. Dickinson County was selected for several reasons. First, it is situated in another

Great Plains state, south of Nebraska, but farther west than Douglas County. Second, it is a rural farming region with relatively few racial minorities—the population composition would suggest a stable society.[12] Finally, Dickinson County is famous for Abilene and its short-lived cattle-drive trade from Texas.

Abilene, the county seat, is located on the Kansas Pacific Railroad line in the central part of the state. The first herd of Texas longhorns arrived in 1867, but by 1872 Ellsworth and other towns farther west soon replaced Abilene as favored railroad junctions for cattle shipment. Although the cattle-drive period endured for a brief five years, it brought Abilene some notoriety for being a wide-open city with wild cowboys, brothels, gambling establishments, and, of course, William "Wild Bill" Hickok. During his short tenure as marshal of Abilene (April 15–December 13, 1871), Hickok managed to kill Phil Coe, a gambler, in a gun battle in front of the Alamo Saloon, and also Mike Williams, his deputy, by mistake, when he rushed to Hickok's aid on that same fateful night, October 5, 1871.[13] With the quick demise of the cattle-drive market, Abilene returned to a quiet town, and Dickinson County, with its rolling, fertile plains, turned to wheat production.

Robert R. Dykstra claims that during the cattle-drive period, Abilene, Dodge City, Ellsworth, Wichita, and Caldwell were not especially violent, and he cites an average 1.5 homicides per year.[14] Using Dykstra's data, however, statistical analysis indicates that the Dickinson County homicide rates for 1870, 1871, and 1872 (the peak period of the cattle drives) averaged 87.6 per 100,000. The highest rate (98.6 per 100,000) occurred during 1871. The cattle drives to Abilene ended after the 1871 season. The homicides that occurred after 1872 further refute Dykstra's contentions that homicide was an uncommon occurrence in cattle towns in the American West.[15]

With rapid population shifts, one might expect high violence levels in town during the cattle drives, but what would Abilene be like after they ended? A survey of criminal appearance dockets revealed a homicide indictment rate of 6.6 per 100,000 for Dickinson County for the period 1880–1920.[16] Since these are indictment rates (not homicide rates)[17] a comparison should be made with indictment rates in the three counties. The homicide indictment rates during the same period for white defendants in Douglas, Las Animas, and Gila counties averaged 3.8, 25.6, and 28.7 per 100,000, respectively. In other words, the 6.6 per 100,000 rate of Dickinson County confirms the high homicide indictments rates in the American West. Dickinson County data reinforce the contention that the American West was violent.

In a survey of seven California counties for the period 1850–1900, Santa

Barbara had the highest homicide rate (92 per 100,000), followed by San Diego (80.7), San Luis Obispo (70.3), Tuolumne (59.9), Calaveras (39.3), San Joaquin (26.3), and Sacramento (20.4), or an average for all seven counties of 55.5 per 100,000 for the five-decade period. Sacramento, the most urban county, had the lowest rates, while the counties dominated by more rural influences of ranching and farming had the highest rates, followed by the two gold-camp counties. During the most intensive gold rush phase, during the 1850s, Calaveras and Tuolumne counties exhibited very high homicide rates (48.6 and 95.5 per 100,000, respectively). Thereafter, both counties experienced significant population decline accompanied by a drop in the homicide rate. The firearm-homicide rate for these seven counties averaged 60 percent, and the handgun homicide rate averaged 51 percent. Although the time frame (1850–1900 versus 1880–1920) and geographical regions for the two studies are different, the results are strikingly similar.[18]

Finally, in reevaluating the data, it is important to note that the Dickinson County, Kansas, homicide indictment rate (6.6 per 100,000) was significantly lower than in Las Animas and Gila counties (25.6 and 28.7 per 100,000, respectively). The Abilene experience suggests that rural factors alone are not conducive to high lethal-violence levels. It is believed that Las Animas and Gila counties are representative of the American West, because virtually every state and territory had regions where such diverse factors converged quickly. If one were to survey homicide rates in other counties in California, Montana, Wyoming, Arizona, Oregon, North Dakota, Kansas, Washington, South Dakota, and Idaho where such factors existed, it is likely that similar high homicide rates would be discovered. The data convincingly prove that in the American West—especially in Las Animas and Gila counties—lethal violence was common.

Notes

CI = *Coroner's Inquests*

Chapter 1. Critical Convergences in the American West

1. Richard Maxwell Brown, "Historiography of Violence in the American West," in Michael P. Malone, ed., *Historians and the American West* (Lincoln: Univ. of Nebraska Press, 1983), 253–54.

2. Robert M. Utley, *High Noon in Lincoln: Violence on the Western Frontier* (Albuquerque: Univ. of New Mexico Press, 1987), 179.

3. See Marvin Wolfgang and Franco Ferracuti, *The Subculture of Violence: Towards an Integrated Theory of Criminology* (London: Tavistock, 1967); and Raymond D. Gastil, "Homicide and the Regional Culture of Violence," *American Sociological Review* 36 (June 1971): 412–27; and *Cultural Regions of the United States* (Seattle: Univ. of Washington Press, 1975).

4. For a discussion of such convergences and how they define the American West, see Patricia Nelson Limerick, "What on Earth is the New Western History?," 86; and Walter Nugent, "Frontiers and Empires in the Late Nineteenth Century," 162, in Patricia Nelson Limerick, Clyde A Milner II, and Charles E. Rankin, eds., *Trails: Toward a New Western History* (Lawrence: Univ. Press of Kansas, 1991); and Richard Maxwell Brown, "Violence," 422, in Clyde A. Milner II, Carol A. O'Connor, and Martha A. Sandweiss, eds., *The Oxford History of the American West* (New York: Oxford Univ. Press, 1994).

5. For a discussion of western films and the portrayal of violence, see John H. Lenihan,

"Classics and Social Commentary: Postwar Westerns, 1946–1960," *Journal of the West* 22 (Oct. 1983): 34–42; Martin M. Winkler, "Classical Mythology and the Western Film," *Comparative Literature Studies* 22 (winter 1985): 516–40; Richard T. Jameson, "'Deserve's got nothin' to do with it': *Unforgiven*," *Film Comment* 28 (Sept.–Oct. 1992): 12–14; Henry Sheehan, "Scraps of Hope: Clint Eastwood and the Western," *Film Comment* 28 (Sept.–Oct. 1992): 16–27; and Alexander Mackendrick, "Dead Man's Clothes: The Making of *The Wild Bunch*," *Film Comment* 30 (May–June 1994): 44–57.

6. Scholars not discussed here but who also suggest the American West was violent include James Truslow Adams, "Our Lawless Heritage," *The Atlantic Monthly* 142 (July–Dec. 1928): 732–40; Stanley Vestal, *Queen of Cowtowns: Dodge City* (E. Dutton and Company, Inc., 1928); R. W. Mondy, "Analysis of Frontier Social Instability," *Southwestern Social Sciences Quarterly* 24 (Sept. 1943): 167–77; Mabel A. Elliott, "Crime and the Frontier Mores," *American Sociological Review* 9 (Apr. 1944): 185–92; W. C. Holden, "Law and Lawlessness on the Texas Frontier, 1875–1890," *Southwestern Historical Quarterly* (Oct. 1940): 188–203; C. L. Sonnichsen, *I'll Die Before I'll Run: The Story of the Great Feuds of Texas* (New York: Devin-Adair, Company, 1962); Nyle H. Miller and Joseph W. Snell, *Why the West Was Wild: A Contemporary Look at the Antics of Some Highly Publicized Kansas Cowtown Personalities* (Topeka: Kansas State Historical Society, 1963); and Gary L. Roberts, "Violence and the Frontier Tradition," in Forrest R. Blackburn et al., eds., *Kansas and the West* (Topeka: Kansas State Historical Society, 1976), 96–111; and "The West's Gunmen," *The American West* 8 (Jan. 1971): 10–15, 64; (Mar. 1971): 18–23, 61–62.

7. Joe B. Frantz, "The Frontier Tradition: An Invitation to Violence," in Hugh Davis Graham and Ted Robert Gurr, eds., *The History of Violence in America: Historical and Comparative Perspectives* (New York: Frederick A. Praeger, Publishers, 1969), 127–54.

8. Ibid., 145.

9. Joseph G. Rosa, *The Gunfighter: Man or Myth?* (Norman: Univ. of Oklahoma Press, 1969), 198.

10. Ibid., 64.

11. Harry Sinclair Drago, *The Great Range Wars: Violence on the Grasslands* (Lincoln: Univ. of Nebraska Press, 1970), 97.

12. Richard Maxwell Brown, *Strain of Violence: Historical Studies of American Violence and Vigilantism* (New York: Oxford Univ. Press, 1975). See also David A. Johnson, "Vigilance and the Law: The Moral Authority of Popular Justice in the Far West," *American Quarterly* 33 (1981): 558–86.

13. Brown, "Historiography of Violence," 234.

14. Ibid.

15. Ibid., 253–54.

16. Brown, "Violence," 393–425.

17. Richard Maxwell Brown, *No Duty to Retreat: Violence and Values in American History and Society* (New York: Oxford Univ. Press, 1991).

18. Ibid., 400, 410–11.

19. Ibid., 423.

20. See Lynn I. Perrigo, "Law and Order in Early Colorado Mining Camps," *Mississippi Valley Historical Review* (June 1941); Michael N. Canlis, "The Evolution of Law Enforcement in California," *The Far-Westerner* (July 1961); and Harry N. Anderson, "Deadwood, South Dakota: An Effort at Stability," *Montana: The Magazine of Western History* (Jan. 1970).

21. Robert R. Dykstra, *The Cattle Towns* (New York: Alfred A. Knopf, 1968), 146.

22. Ibid., 144.

23. Ibid., 146.

24. Frank Richard Prassel, *The Western Peace Officer: A Legacy of Law and Order* (Norman: Univ. of Oklahoma Press, 1972), 8.

25. Ibid., 8, 22.

26. W. Eugene Hollon, *Frontier Violence: Another Look* (New York: Oxford Univ. Press, 1974), ix–x.

27. Lawrence M. Friedman and Robert V. Percival, *The Roots of Justice: Crime and Punishment in Alameda County, California, 1870–1910* (Chapel Hill: Univ. of North Carolina Press, 1981), 27–28.

28. Ibid., 137.

29. Roger McGrath, *Gunfighters, Highwaymen, and Vigilantes: Violence on the Frontier* (Berkeley: Univ. of California Press, 1984), 254.

30. Book review by Robert R. Dykstra in *The Annals of the American Academy* 48 (Sept. 1985): 189.

31. Book review by Ron Limbaugh, *The Journal of American History* 72 (June 1985): 160.

32. McGrath, *Gunfighters*, 253.

33. Patricia Nelson Limerick, *The Legacy of Conquest: The Unbroken Past of the American West* (New York: W. W. Norton and Company, 1987).

34. Richard White, *"It's Your Misfortune and None of My Own": A New History of the American West* (Norman: Univ. of Oklahoma Press, 1991), 329.

35. Ibid., 330.

36. For example, see his discussion of Sheriff Henry Plummer in Montana, Dykstra's statistics on cattle towns, and the Ludlow massacre.

37. For a discussion about defining homicide, see Marvin E. Wolfgang and Rolf B. Strohm, "The Relationship between Alcohol and Criminal Homicide," *Quarterly Journal of Studies on Alcohol* 17 (June 1956): 411.

38. For a discussion of self-defense, see Brown, *No Duty to Retreat*.

39. Many researchers have adopted the criminal indictment or information filed by the prosecutor as the measure of homicide. Roger Lane suggests that "only one satisfactory measure of homicide remains: the number of indictments prepared for the grand juries each year." The coroner's inquests were unavailable for his study. See Lane, *Violent Death in the City: Suicide, Accident, and Murder in Nineteenth-Century Philadelphia* (Cambridge: Harvard Univ. Press, 1979), 58. For a fuller discussion of indictments as a measure of

homicide, see Lane, "Urban Homicide in the Nineteenth Century: Some Lessons for the Twentieth," in James A. Inciardi and Charles E. Faupel, eds., *History and Crime: Implications for Criminal Justice Policy* (Beverly Hills: Sage Publications, 1980), 91–109; Robert H. Tillman, "The Prosecution of Homicide in Sacramento California, 1853–1900," *Southern California Quarterly* 68 (summer 1986): 167–81; and Friedman and Percival, *The Roots of Justice*, 17, 166–69.

40. For another view arguing against the use of coroner's inquests, see Margaret A. Zahn, "Homicide in the Twentieth Century United States," in Inciardi and Faupel, eds., *History and Crime*, 114–15.

41. Eric Mottram, " 'The Persuasive Lips': Men and Guns in America, the West," *American Studies* 10 (Apr. 1976): 82.

42. James Buchanan Given, *Society and Homicide in Thirteenth-Century England* (Stanford: Stanford Univ. Press, 1977), 1.

43. For methodology on using state and local records, see Richard Crawford and Clare V. McKanna, Jr., "Crime in California: Using State and Local Archives for Crime Research," *Pacific Historical Review* 55 (May 1986): 284–95.

44. See Bruce Smith, *Rural Crime Control* (New York: Institute of Public Administration, 1933), 180–217; Walter H. Anderson, *A Treatise on the Law of Sheriffs, Coroners, and Constables with Forms* (Buffalo: Dennis & Company, Inc., 1941), vol. 1: 23–33 and vol. 2: 697–707; Thomas Rogers Forbes, "Crowner's Quest," *Transactions of the American Philosophical Society* 68 (1978): 2–50; George H. Weinmann, "A Compendium of the Statute Law of Coroners and Medical Examiners in the United States," *Bulletin of the National Research Council* 83 (Aug. 1931): 1–136; and R. F. Hunnisett, *The Medieval Coroner* (Cambridge: Cambridge Univ. Press, 1961).

45. On plea bargaining, see Lawrence M. Friedman, "Plea Bargaining in Historical Perspective," *Law and Society Review* 13 (winter 1979): 247–60; and Mark H. Haller, "Plea Bargaining: The Nineteenth-Century Context," *Law and Society Review* 13 (winter 1979): 273–79.

46. Friedman and Percival, *Roots of Justice*, 185; and Clare V. McKanna, Jr., "Four Hundred Dollars Worth of Justice: The Trial, Conviction, and Execution of Indian Joe, 1892–1893," *Journal of San Diego History* 33 (fall 1987): 197–212.

Chapter 2. Murder Most Foul

1. H. C. Brearley, *Homicide in the United States* (Montclair: Patterson Smith, 1969 [1932]), 5. This is the first study to examine homicide from a national perspective.

2. Marvin Wolfgang, *Patterns in Criminal Homicide* (Philadelphia: Univ. of Pennsylvania Press, 1958). Wolfgang assembled his data set from the Philadelphia Police Department homicide-squad investigation files. He concludes that this information from initial investigations can "provide a more comprehensive and valid description of the crime, the victim, and the offender than any other source" (13).

3. Ibid., 12.

4. Ibid., 5. For a recent critique of Wolfgang, see Per-Olof H. Wikstrom, "Cross-National Comparisons and Context-Specific Trends in Criminal Homicide," *Journal of Crime and Justice* 14(2) (1991): 71–95.

5. Lane, *Violent Death*.

6. Ibid., 10.

7. Ibid., 56, 58.

8. See Andrew F. Henry and James Short, Jr., *Suicide and Homicide: Some Economic, Sociological, and Psychological Aspects of Aggression* (New York: Free Press, 1954); Alex D. Porkorny, "A Comparison of Homicides in Two Cities," *Journal of Criminal Law, Criminology and Police Science* 65 (Dec. 1965): 479–87; Theodore N. Ferdinand, "The Criminal Patterns of Boston Since 1849," *American Journal of Sociology* 73 (July 1967): 84–99; Richard Block, *Violent Crime: Environment, Interaction, and Death* (Lexington, Mass.: Lexington Books, 1977); and Ted Robert Gurr, Peter N. Grabosky, and Richard C. Hula, *The Politics of Crime and Conflict: A Comparative History of Four Cities* (Beverly Hills: Sage Publications, 1977).

9. The accused/indicted ratio is the pairing of statistics for those identified and accused of a homicide with indictment data from a grand jury or information from the prosecutor. These data have been collected from coroner's inquests, newspapers, and court records.

10. *Trinidad Chronicle-News*, Aug. 12, 1908.

11. *Trinidad Chronicle-News*, Aug. 12 and Aug. 13, 1908.

12. *Trinidad Chronicle-News*, Aug. 13, 1908.

13. Data compiled for this study do not allow for any significant evaluation of motivation by the perpetrators beyond general comments on similarities of patterns displayed within the three counties. See Wolfgang, *Patterns in Criminal Homicide*, 5.

14. See Lane, *Violent Death* , 79.

15. See Philip Jordan, *Frontier Law and Order* (Lincoln: Univ. of Nebraska Press, 1970), 1–22.

16. If the victim survived the shock of being shot, infection remained a great danger due to the nature of the wound. Medical practice during this period was not well equipped to deal with massive trauma caused by gunshot wounds, which often led to peritonitis. For high-risk factors associated with firearms, see David McDowall, "Firearm Availability and Homicide Rates in Detroit, 1951–1986," *Social Forces* 69 (June 1991): 1085–1101; and Gary Kleck and Karen McElrath, "The Effects of Weaponry on Human Violence," *Social Forces* 69 (Mar. 1991): 669–92.

17. A. W. F. Taylerson, *Revolving Arms* (New York: Walker and Company, 1967), 32–44; Geoffrey Boothroyd, *The Handgun* (London: Cassell, 1970), 221–24, 345–57. One could purchase handguns through Sears, Roebuck for less than two dollars. See *The Sears, Roebuck Catalog* (Chicago: Sears, Roebuck and Company, 1902), 316–21.

18. For a listing of gun shops and pawn shops, see *McAvoy's Omaha Street Directory for*

1901 (Omaha: Omaha Printing Company, 1901), 919; and *Omaha Street Directory 1911* (Omaha: Omaha Directory Company, 1911), 1381, 1430.

19. Black newspapers ran editorials complaining about the carrying of handguns in Omaha. One suggested that "any boy who pleases can find someone to sell him a gun." See the *Omaha Monitor,* Sept. 4, 1919, and Aug. 21, 1919. Also see Jordan, *Frontier Law and Order,* 1–22; and Lee Kennett and James LaVerne Anderson, *The Gun in America: The Origins of a National Dilemma* (Westport, Conn.: Greenwood Press, 1975), 133–64.

20. The large number of shootings with rifles during the 1913–14 coal miners' strike was eliminated from figure 2.4 because it would have distorted the percentage, increasing it to 19 percent.

21. Jordan, *Frontier Law and Order,* 7.

22. See 1902 *Sears, Roebuck Catalog,* 316–21.

23. Zahn, "Homicide," 111–31; and "Homicide in the Twentieth Century: Trends, Types, and Causes," in Ted Robert Gurr, ed., *Violence in America: The History of Crime,* vol. 1 (Newbury Park, Calif.: Sage Publications, 1989), 216–34.

24. Arizona, Gila County, *Coroner's Inquests (CI),* body of State Jones, Oct. 11, 1906, RG 103, Phoenix.

25. *Trinidad Chronicle-News,* Sept. 10, 1902.

26. *Trinidad Chronicle-News,* Mar. 15, 1908.

27. *CI* (Gila Co.), body of Roderick McContach, Dec. 1, 1895, RG 103.

28. *CI* (Gila Co.), body of Charles Dye, Oct. 24, 1898.

29. *CI* (Las Animas Co.), bodies of Giovanni Raino and Garlano Falsetti, July 25, 1905, Trinidad City Library, Trinidad, Colo.

30. Whether the victim was already dead is not known. See *CI* (Gila Co.), body of Frank Thompson, June 4, 1916.

31. The fact that Rose Myers was a prostitute may explain why charges were not filed against Bert Anderson. Facts surrounding the Martínez case suggests a lover's triangle. See *CI* (Las Animas Co.), bodies of Rose Myers and Lucita Martínez, Mar. 30 and Apr. 10, 1906.

32. *CI* (Gila Co.), body of Jack Lane, Feb. 1, 1910.

33. *Trinidad Daily News,* Sept. 5, 1894.

34. See *Trinidad Daily News,* Feb. 10, 1902; Feb. 23, 1903; and Sept. 12 and 28, 1909; and *Arizona Silver Belt* (Globe), Jan. 31, 1885; Mar. 14, 1885; Oct. 30, 1886; Mar. 2, 1889; Nov. 11, 1902; and May 4, 1918.

35. *CI* (Las Animas Co.), body of D. B. Munroe, Apr. 3, 1902.

36. *Trinidad Chronicle-News,* Nov. 22, 1906.

37. *Trinidad Chronicle-News,* Aug. 12, 1908.

38. Tafoya's father served as Las Animas County sheriff and "was killed by a drunken Texan who shot him down without warning in a billiard hall." See *Trinidad Chronicle-News,* Feb. 18, 28, and Mar. 15, 1907.

39. *Trinidad Chronicle-News,* Sept. 9, 1917.

40. *Omaha World-Herald*, Aug. 16, 1913.

41. *CI* (Douglas Co.), body of Alfred Jones, May 6, 1914, "Coroner's Inquest Logs," Douglas County Coroner's Office, Omaha, Nebr.

42. There is no apparent explanation for the low figure for Las Animas County.

43. These figures do not include the Ludlow massacre shootings by the Colorado National Guard. Those killings are treated separately since the National Guard is a military organization rather than a law enforcement body.

44. See Larry D. Ball, *Desert Lawmen: The High Sheriffs of New Mexico and Arizona, 1846– 1912* (Albuquerque: Univ. of New Mexico Press, 1992), 50–51.

45. *Trinidad Chronicle-News*, Aug. 17, 1913.

46. See Ball, *Desert Lawmen*, 38–54, 89–105, and 179–201.

47. *Trinidad Chronicle-News*, Dec. 12, 1902.

48. *CI* (Gila Co.), body of Tom Dagoney, July 9, 1906.

49. *CI* (Gila Co.), body of Antonio Mendoza, Apr. 12, 1905.

50. *CI* (Gila Co.), body of John W. Nelson, Nov. 1, 1907.

51. *Trinidad Chronicle-News*, Apr. 21, 1906.

52. *Trinidad Chronicle-News*, Jan. 18 and 20, 1912.

53. *Trinidad Chronicle-News*, Aug. 31, 1912.

54. See, for example, *Trinidad Chronicle-News*, Mar. 16, 1908; Aug. 17, 1915; *Arizona Silver Belt*, Mar. 15, 1911; Nov. 22, 1913; and Sept. 17, 1916.

55. *Trinidad Chronicle-News*, May 16, 1899.

56. *Trinidad Chronicle-News*, Nov. 9, 1908.

57. *Trinidad Chronicle-News*, Mar. 28, 1911.

58. *Arizona Silver Belt*, Apr. 20, 1909.

59. *Arizona Silver Belt*, Jan. 23, 1911.

60. Arizona, Gila County, District Court, *Territory of Arizona v. S. Y. Hawkins* (1911), Fifth Judicial District of the Territory of Arizona, Case No. 965, RG 103, Arizona State Archives, Phoenix.

61. *Arizona Silver Belt*, Dec. 23, 1911.

62. Arizona, Gila County, Superior Court, *State of Arizona v. John H. Thompson and Harry Temple* (1911), Case No. 1044, RG 103, Arizona State Archives, Phoenix. This was an unfortunate incident that blemished a long, distinguished career in law enforcement. See Jess G. Hayes, *Sheriff Thompson's Day: Turbulence in the Arizona Territory* (Tucson: Univ. of Arizona Press, 1968), 180–82.

63. *Arizona Silver Belt*, Dec. 7, 1895; and Hayes, *Sheriff Thompson's Days*, 53–55.

64. *CI* (Gila Co.), body of Matze, an Indian, Feb. 19, 1906, 1.

65. Ibid., 2–15.

66. *Omaha World-Herald*, Aug. 14, 1899.

67. Ibid.

68. *Omaha World-Herald*, Feb. 9, 1904.

69. *Trinidad Daily News*, Mar. 28, 1889.

70. *Trinidad Daily News,* Nov. 21, 1895.

71. *Trinidad Chronicle-News,* Apr. 7, 1908.

72. See *CI* (Gila Co.), body of Edward Shanley, Oct. 3, 1906.

73. See *CI* (Gila Co.), body of Charles B. Edwards, Jan. 12, 1908.

74. See *CI* (Gila Co.), body of Thomas Kerr, Dec. 26, 1882; and Jess G. Hayes, *Boots and Bullets* (Tucson: Univ. of Arizona Press, 1967), 124–25.

75. *Arizona Silver Belt,* Jan. 10, 1911.

76. *Trinidad Chronicle-News,* Aug. 11 and 12, 1911; and *CI* (Las Animas Co.), body of William Walker, Aug. 11, 1911.

77. *Trinidad Chronicle-News,* Jan. 25, 1918.

78. *Omaha World-Herald,* Jan. 15, 1909.

79. *Omaha World-Herald,* Feb. 20, 1909.

80. *Omaha World-Herald,* Mar. 22 and 23, 1909.

81. *Omaha World-Herald,* Feb. 11, 1915.

82. *CI* (Gila Co.), body of John Bowers, Oct. 4, 1899.

83. See *CI* (Gila Co.), body of Chil-chu-a-na, Sept. 15, 1909.

84. *CI* (Las Animas Co.), body of an unidentified Negro male, Apr. 29, 1902.

85. *Trinidad Chronicle-News,* Oct. 16, 1907.

86. Ibid.

87. *Trinidad Chronicle-News,* Mar. 10, 1916.

88. *Trinidad Chronicle-News,* Aug. 18, 1917.

89. McGrath, *Gunfighters,* 254.

Chapter 3. Seeds of Destruction

This chapter originally appeared in the *Journal of American Ethnic History*.

1. For examples, see Howard Chudacoff, *Mobile Americans: Residential and Social Mobility in Omaha, 1880–1920* (New York: Oxford Univ. Press, 1972); Thomas C. Cox, *Blacks in Topeka, Kansas, 1865–1915: A Social History* (Baton Rouge: Louisiana State Univ. Press, 1982); Norman L. Crockett, *The Black Towns* (Lawrence: Regents Press of Kansas, 1979); Kenneth Marvin Hamilton, *Black Towns and Profit: Promotion and Development in the Trans-Appalachian West, 1877–1915* (Urbana: Univ. of Illinois Press, 1991); and Nell Irvin Painter, *Exodusters: Black Migration to Kansas after Reconstruction* (New York: Alfred A. Knopf, 1977).

2. Roger Lane, *Roots of Violence in Black Philadelphia, 1860–1900* (Cambridge: Harvard Univ. Press, 1986).

3. See Derral Cheatwood, "Black Homicides in Baltimore 1974–1986: Age, Gender, and Weapon Use Changes," *Criminal Justice Review* 15 (autumn 1990): 192–207; Darnell F. Hawkins, ed., *Homicide Among Black Americans* (Washington, D.C.: Univ. Press of America, 1986); Thomas F. Pettigrew and Rosalind Barclay Spier, "The Ecological Structure of Negro Homicide," *American Journal of Sociology* 67 (May 1962): 621–29; Harold M.

Rose and Paula D. McClain, *Race, Place, and Risk: Black Homicide in Urban America* (Albany: State Univ. of New York Press, 1990); and Wolfgang, *Patterns in Criminal Homicide*.

4. See E. M. Beck, James L. Massey, and Steward E. Tolnay, "The Gallows, the Mob, and the Vote: Lethal Sanctioning of Blacks in North Carolina and Georgia, 1882 to 1930," *Law and Society Review* 23(2) (1989): 317–31; W. Fitzhugh Brundage, *Lynching in the New South: Georgia and Virginia, 1880–1930* (Urbana: Univ. of Illinois Press, 1993); Barry Crouch, "A Spirit of Lawlessness: White Violence–Texas Blacks, 1865–1968," *Journal of Social History* 18 (winter 1984): 217–32; Michael S. Hindus, "Black Justice Under White Law: Criminal Prosecutions of Blacks in Antebellum South Carolina," *Journal of American History* 63 (Dec. 1976): 575–99; and Stewart Tolnay and E. M. Beck, "Black Flight: Lethal Violence and the Great Migration, 1900–1930," *Social Science History* 14 (fall 1990): 347–70; Stewart E. Tolnay and E. M. Beck, *A Festival of Violence: An Analysis of Southern Lynchings, 1882–1930* (Urbana: Univ. of Illinois Press, 1992); Gilles Vandal, " 'Bloody Caddo': White Violence Against Blacks in a Louisiana Parish, 1865–1876," *Journal of Social History* 25 (winter 1991): 373–88; and George C. Wright, *Racial Violence in Kentucky, 1865–1940: Lynchings, Mob Rule, and "Legal Lynchings"* (Baton Rouge: Louisiana State Univ. Press, 1990).

5. See Wolfgang and Ferracuti, *Subculture of Violence*.

6. *Omaha World-Herald*, Apr. 4, 1903.

7. Ibid. This racial term used by the white observer may help to explain the volatility of this and other situations between blacks and whites. The newspaper did not repeat verbatim the words used by the white victim.

8. Ibid.

9. For a discussion of ethnic demographics, see Kathleen Fimple, "An Analysis of the Changing Spatial Dimensions of Ethnic Neighborhoods in Omaha, Nebraska, 1880–1900," Ph.D. dissertation, Univ. of Nebraska-Lincoln, 1989.

10. Chudacoff, *Mobile Americans*, 13–23.

11. The 1891 lynching of George Smith, a black, at the Douglas County Court House proved to be the exception.

12. The author surveyed a 20 percent random sample of heads of household to determine sex, age, nativity, place of residence, and occupation of Omaha's black population. Most were concentrated in the third ward in 1900 but showed a marked shift northward by 1910. See U.S. Bureau of Census, RG 513, Nebraska State and Federal Census; SG 2, Federal Census, 1900 and 1910, U.S. Bureau of the Census, Washington, D.C.

13. H. Donald, "The Negro Migration of 1916–1918," *Journal of Negro History* 6 (Oct. 1921): 383–498; Thomas J. Woofter, Jr., *Negro Migration: Changes in Rural Organization and Population of the Cotton Belt* (New York: W. D. Gray, 1920); and Louise V. Kennedy, *The Negro Peasant Turns Cityward: Effects of Recent Migration to Northern Centers* (New York: Columbia Univ. Press, 1930).

14. Howard N. Rabinowitz, "The Conflict between Blacks and the Police in the Urban South, 1865–1900," *The Historian* 39 (Nov. 1976): 72. Rabinowitz discovered a

significant number of examples of "the effective use of intimidation by blacks against white policemen."

15. Ibid., 69. Similar research in seven nineteenth-century California counties revealed that county district attorneys seldom prosecuted police for killing citizens.

16. Tolnay and Beck, "Black Flight," 360–61.

17. NAACP, *Thirty Years of Lynching in the United States, 1889–1918* (New York: National Association For the Advancement of Colored People, 1919), 31. See also Arthur F. Raper, *The Tragedy of Lynching* (Chapel Hill: Univ. of North Carolina Press, 1933); Robert Ingalls, "Lynching and Establishment Violence in Tampa, 1858–1935," *Journal of Southern History* 53 (Nov. 1987): 613–44; James M. SoRelle, "The 'Waco Horror': The Lynching of Jesse Washington," *Southwestern Historical Quarterly* 86 (Apr. 1983): 517–37; and Ray Stannard Baker, "What Is a Lynching?: A Study of Mob Justice, South and North," *McClure's Magazine* 24 (1904–5): 300–314.

18. Raper, *Tragedy of Lynching*, 33. See also Tolnay and Beck's discussion of how southern courts "victimized blacks and represented a lethal threat" ("Black Flight," 357).

19. Chudacoff, *Mobile Americans*, 14–16.

20. Ibid., 127. Chudacoff notes that "the housing market began to push blacks into the Near North Side" with the segregation index increasing from "36.5 in 1910 to 47.9 in 1920" (155). At the same time Jim Crow discrimination against blacks began to increase.

21. Ibid., 20.

22. See the U.S. Bureau of Census, RG 513, Nebraska State and Federal Census, SG 2, Federal Census, 1900 and 1910. The third ward proved to be the location of virtually all the brothels. Information collected included name, age, race, address, nativity, and occupation.

23. Ibid. Blacks constituted 3 and 3.5 percent of the total population in 1900 and 1910, respectively. See Anne M. Butler, *Daughters of Joy, Sisters of Misery: Prostitutes in the American West, 1865–90* (Urbana: Univ. of Illinois Press, 1985); and Clare V. McKanna, Jr., "Prostitutes, Progressives, and Police: The Viability of Vice in San Diego, 1900–1930," *Journal of San Diego History* 35 (winter 1989): 44–65.

24. Black ghettos that formed in northern cities often developed around red-light districts. See George E. Haynes, "Conditions Among Negroes in the Cities," *Annals of the American Academy of Political and Social Science* 49 (Sept. 1913): 105–19.

25. *McAvoy's Omaha Street Directory for 1901* (Omaha: Omaha Printing Company, 1901), 965–67; and *Omaha Street Directory, Including South Omaha, 1911* (Omaha: Omaha Directory Company, 1911), 1454–56.

26. *Omaha Monitor,* Aug. 5, 1910.

27. See Eric Monkkonen, *The Dangerous Class: Crime and Poverty in Columbus, Ohio, 1860–1885* (Cambridge: Harvard Univ. Press, 1975); and Charles Loring Brace, *The Dangerous Classes of New York, and Twenty Years Working Among Them* (New York: Wynkoop and Hallenbeck, 1872).

28. *Omaha Monitor,* Jan. 14, 1910.

29. *Omaha Monitor,* Mar. 18, 1910; Feb. 24, 1911.

30. *Omaha Monitor,* Aug. 17, 1919.

31. *Omaha Monitor,* Apr. 19, 1919.

32. *Omaha Monitor,* Jan. 20, 1919.

33. *Omaha Monitor,* Mar. 11, 1910.

34. *Omaha Monitor,* Dec. 19, 1919. Cities in many northern states developed Jim Crow policies that segregated the races in theaters, restaurants, and other accommodations. In some cases there were no city ordinances, just the policy of the businesses, and no one paid any attention to protests by blacks. See also Allan Spear, "The Origins of the Urban Ghetto, 1870–1915," in Nathan I. Huggins, Martin Kilson, and Daniel M. Fox, eds., *Key Issues in the Afro-American Experience,* vol. 2 (New York: Harcourt, Brace, Jovanovich, 1971), 153–66.

35. See U.S. Bureau of Census, RG 513, Nebraska State and Federal Census, SG 2, Federal Census, 1900 and 1910. The 20 percent sample provided a total of 136 and 155 households for 1900 and 1910, respectively. Males listed as heads of household remained consistent for the two decades (77 and 76 percent, respectively).

36. W. E. B. DuBois, in his 1896–97 study of blacks in Philadelphia's predominately black seventh ward, discovered that 75 percent of black males held jobs categorized as "laborer" or "domestic-related employment" such as porters, messengers, and handymen in saloons. See W. E. Burghardt DuBois, *The Philadelphia Negro: A Social Study* (Philadelphia: Univ. of Pennsylvania, 1899), 97–103.

37. *Omaha Monitor,* Dec. 9, 1916.

38. *Omaha Monitor,* Sept. 16, 1916.

39. *Omaha Monitor,* Nov. 6, 1919. This suggests the tactics of rousting, which have long been a sore point among minority citizens.

40. The editorial mentioned that officers Noah, George Thomas, Joseph Balleau, and Harry Buford had served well in the capacity of police detectives and noted that they "apprehend all lawbreakers, white or black."

41. Nebraska, Douglas County, District Court, *Criminal Appearance Dockets, 1880–1920,* Douglas County Courthouse, Omaha, Nebr.

42. Lane, *Roots of Violence,* 166; and Wolfgang, *Patterns in Criminal Homicide,* 308–09.

43. Nebraska, Douglas County, District Court, *Criminal Appearance Dockets, 1880–1920.*

44. *Omaha Daily Bee,* Feb. 16, 1888.

45. Ferguson died in the Nebraska State Penitentiary on Feb. 15, 1890, after serving two years. See Nebraska, State Prison, *Descriptive Records to Inmates, 1880–1920,* inmate no. 1384, RG 86, Nebraska State Historical Society, Lincoln, Nebr.

46. *Omaha World-Herald,* Dec. 14, 1907; and Nebraska, State Prison, *Descriptive Records to Inmates,* no. 5005.

47. *Omaha World-Herald,* Oct. 19, 1913; and Nebraska, State Prison, *Descriptive Records to Inmates,* inmate no. 6285.

48. *Omaha World-Herald,* July 28, 1905; and Nebraska, State Prison, *Descriptive Records to Inmates, 1880–1920,* inmate no. 4542.

49. *Omaha World-Herald,* Aug. 16, 1913.

50. *Omaha World-Herald,* June 23, 1915.

51. *CI* (Douglas Co.), body of Juan Gonzalez, June 23, 1915.

52. *Omaha World-Herald,* Mar. 17, 1900; *CI* (Douglas Co.), body of Jacob Williams, Mar. 17, 1900.

53. *Omaha World-Herald,* May 15, 16, 1906.

54. See Nebraska, State Prison, *Descriptive Records to Inmates, 1880–1920,* inmate no. 5005.

55. *Omaha World-Herald,* Aug. 28, 1919; and Nebraska, State Prison, *Descriptive Records to Inmates,* inmates nos. 7567, 7568, and 7569.

56. *Omaha Bee,* July 7, 1880.

57. Nebraska, Douglas County, District Court, *Criminal Appearance Dockets, 1880–1920,* Case No. 5-349.

58. *Omaha Bee,* Dec. 14, 1895.

59. Nebraska, Douglas County, District Court, *Criminal Appearance Dockets, 1880–1920,* Case No. 54-2.

60. *Omaha World-Herald,* July 30, 1893.

61. *Omaha World-Herald,* Aug. 24, 1900.

62. *Omaha Daily Bee,* July 2, 1907.

63. *Omaha World-Herald,* Feb. 20, 1917.

64. *Omaha World-Herald,* Sept. 5, 1908.

65. *Omaha World-Herald,* Oct. 27, 1893.

66. Ibid.

67. *Omaha World-Herald,* Feb. 9, 1909.

68. *Omaha World-Herald,* May 13, 1906; Aug. 25, 1910.

69. *Omaha World-Herald,* Dec. 14, 1895; Dec. 11, 1899.

70. Saloons were abundant in Omaha, numbering 285 in 1891, 284 in 1901, and 293 in 1911. See *Omaha City and South Omaha City Directory for 1891* (Omaha: J. W. Wolfe and Company, Publishers, 1891), 1045–48; *Omaha City Directory for 1901,* 965–67; and *Omaha City Directory, 1911,* 1454–56.

71. Newspapers and criminal case files often do not provide information on the condition of the victim or perpetrator. For cocaine use, see the case involving William Miles in *Omaha World-Herald,* July 28, 1905.

72. Hispanics had 100 percent conviction rates, but there were only six cases, a rather small sample upon which to base any meaningful conclusions.

73. Lane, *Roots of Violence,* 88. However, Lane concluded that "the Philadelphia records show no consistent differences of any kind."

74. Friedman, "Plea Bargaining in Historical Perspective," 249 (emphasis in the original text).

75. Haller, "Plea Bargaining," 278.

76. See *Omaha World-Herald* May 15, 16, 1906; Aug. 28, 1919.

77. Fifty percent of the Hispanic defendants (three cases) also plea-bargained.

78. *Omaha World-Herald*, Mar. 11, 1906.

79. In two homicide studies on Arizona and California during a similar time period, the author found that many Native American defendants who could not afford legal counsel at the preliminary-hearing stage plea-bargained to the same or a lesser charge. Some divulged facts about their actions or, in some cases, admitted guilt while being questioned at the preliminary hearing. Eighteen and 20 percent of Native American defendants in Arizona and California, respectively, plea-bargained, whereas whites plea-bargained in 5 and 3 percent of homicide cases. Plea bargaining in all three regions was relegated to the indigent defendants who often did not understand their rights. See McKanna, "Treatment of Indian Murderers," 65–77.

80. Lane, *Roots of Violence*, 142–43; and H. C. Brearley, *Homicide in the United States* (Montclair, N.J.: Patterson Smith, 1969), 99. Brearley uses homicide statistics (actual homicides) collected from the federal government, not homicide indictments.

81. For other comparisons and differing analysis see Rose and McClain, *Race, Place, and Risk: Black Homicide in Urban America*. See also Zahn, "Homicide," 111–32; William Wilbanks, *Murder in Miami: An Analysis of Homicide Patterns and Trends in Dade County (Miami) Florida, 1917–1983* (New York: Univ. Press of America, 1984); and Wolfgang, *Patterns in Criminal Homicide*, 361–83.

82. The data are incomplete, however: there were five black cases with unknown victims or locations, and one white and four black victims with unknown locations.

83. Lane, *Roots of Violence*, 173. For an earlier study on homicide and aggressive behavior that Lane used to develop his conclusions, see Martin Gold, "Suicide, Homicide, and the Socialization of Aggression," *American Journal of Sociology* 58 (May 1958): 651–61.

84. *Omaha Enterprise*, Mar. 11, 1910; *Omaha Monitor*, Sept. 16, 1919; Dec. 9, 1916, and Dec. 18, 1919. Such examples of discrimination were not unusual in the Great Plains region. See for example, Cox, *Blacks in Topeka*, particularly 115–25; and Spear, "Origins of the Ghetto, 1870–1915," 153–66.

85. See Vandal, "Bloody Caddo," 373–88; Tolnay and Beck, "Black Flight," 347–70; Edward L. Ayers, *Vengeance and Justice: Crime and Punishment in the Nineteenth-Century American South* (New York: Oxford Univ. Press, 1984); Rabinowitz, "Conflict between Blacks and Police," 62–76; and Michael S. Hindus, "Black Justice Under White Law: Criminal Prosecutions of Blacks in Antebellum South Carolina," *Journal of American History* 63 (Dec. 1976): 575–99.

86. See U.S. Bureau of Census, RG 513, Nebraska State and Federal Census, SG 2, Federal Census, 1900 and 1910.

87. See Wolfgang and Ferracuti, *Subculture of Violence*.

88. See Thomas F. Pettigrew and Rosalind Barclay Spier, "The Ecological Structure of Negro Homicide," *American Journal of Sociology* 68 (May 1962): 621–29.

89. Sheldon Hackney, "Southern Violence," *American Historical Review* 74 (Feb. 1969): 908.

90. Gastil, "Homicide," 416.

91. Ibid., 491. Gastil discovered that "the correlation of Southernness with homicide was obviously high . . . and there were also high correlations with Negro mobility when the homicidal culture index was held constant" ("Homicide," 421).

92. Lane, *Roots of Violence*, 148–49, 164–66; and DuBois, *Philadelphia Negro*, 74–79.

93. See Wilbur J. Cash, *The Mind of the South* (New York: Vintage Books, 1940); and Hackney, "Southern Violence," 920.

94. Ayers, *Vengeance and Justice*, 177–81. See also Bertram Wyatt-Brown, *Southern Honor: Ethics and Behavior in the Old South* (New York: Oxford Univ. Press, 1982).

95. Ayers, *Vengeance and Justice*, 266.

96. Ibid., 267.

97. John Shelton Reed, "Below the Smith and Wesson Line: Reflections on Southern Violence," in Merle Black and John Shelton Reed, *Perspectives on the American South*, vol. 1 (New York: Gordon and Breach Science Publishers, 1981), 12.

98. Ayers, *Vengeance and Justice*, 269–70.

99. Ibid., 274.

100. Ibid.

101. Ibid., 275.

102. DuBois, *Philadelphia Negro*, 261, 257.

103. Ibid., 261, 253.

104. W. E. B. DuBois, *Souls of Black Folk* (New York: American Library, 1969), 201, as quoted in Ayers, *Vengeance and Justice*, 183. Roger Lane suggests that DuBois "spent several months in 1897–1898 living and taking notes in the Seventh Ward. The resulting study, *Philadelphia Negro*, is arguably the best piece of sociology written by an American in the nineteenth century." DuBois used this research for *Souls of Black Folk*. See also Lane, *Roots of Violence*, 148; Herbert Shapiro, *White Violence and Black Response: From Reconstruction to Montgomery* (Amherst: Univ. of Massachusetts Press, 1988), 91–157; and Woofter, *Negro Migration*, 141–44.

105. See Gold, "Suicide, Homicide," 651–61.

106. All five cases involving black perpetrators with the victim's race unknown resulted in convictions.

107. For a study on interracial homicides in California that confirms this thesis, see McKanna, "Red, White, and Dead," 1–25.

108. See Arnold M. Paul, *Conservative Crisis and the Rule of Law: Attitudes of Bar and Bench, 1887–1895* (Ithaca, N.Y.: Cornell Univ. Press, 1960); and Benjamin B. Ringer and Elinor R. Lawless, *Race-Ethnicity and Society* (New York: Routledge, 1989), 152–57.

109. Thomas F. Gossett, *Race: The History of an Idea in America* (Dallas: Southern Methodist Univ. Press, 1963), 286.

110. For discussions and statistics on lynching and racial riots, see NAACP, *Thirty Years*

of Lynching; Mary Frances Berry, *Black Resistance / White Law: A History of Constitutional Racism in America* (New York: Appleton-Century-Crofts, 1971), 103–35; Elliott M. Rudwick, *Race Riot at East St. Louis, July 2, 1917* (Carbondale: Southern Illinois Univ. Press, 1964); Robert V. Haynes, *A Night of Violence: The Houston Riot of 1917* (Baton Rouge: Louisiana State Univ. Press, 1976); and William Tuttle, Jr., *Race Riot: Chicago and the Red Summer of 1919* (New York: Atheneum, 1970).

111. *Omaha Daily Bee*, Oct. 10, 1891.

112. Ibid.

113. Ibid.

114. Ibid.

115. *Omaha World-Herald*, Oct. 10, 1891.

116. At a preliminary hearing to determine whether members of the mob should be indicted for murder, Dr. Carl C. Allison, who performed the autopsy, suggested that Smith had died before the hanging. He testified that "the condition of the body tends to show that he died of fright, and it is my opinion that this is the cause and not strangulation." This testimony was controversial and may have been introduced to suggest that the defendants should not be charged with murder. See the *Omaha World-Herald*, Oct. 20, 1891.

117. *Omaha Daily Bee*, Oct. 10, 1891.

118. Ibid. The reporter's characterization within this passage suggests the writer's attitude—if not society's in general—toward minority members of the Omaha community.

119. Ibid.

120. Ibid.

121. Ibid.

122. *Omaha World-Herald*, Oct. 13, 1891.

123. *Omaha Daily Bee*, Oct. 10, 1891. Three days after the lynching, Mrs. Smith, wife of victim, walked up the county jail steps and banged softly on the iron door. She had come to claim her husband's clothes and personal effects. A reporter noted that "she appeared to be still dazed by the terrible fate of the man who once claimed her as his wife." See *Omaha World-Herald*, Oct. 13, 1891.

124. The newspaper account was filled with racial stereotypes. For example, it refers to Smith as the "fiend," "the brute," "the black villain," "the nigger," and "the colored ravisher." No one could clearly identify Smith as the attacker. Even Mrs. Yates, the mother of the victim of the alleged assault, hedged and said that she "would not be willing to swear positively as to his identity, but she firmly believed that he [Smith] was the brute who had assaulted her child." The girl was unable to identify Smith as her attacker. *Omaha Daily Bee*, Oct. 10, 1891.

125. *Omaha World-Herald*, Mar. 16, 1906.

126. Ibid.

127. *Omaha World-Herald*, Aug. 27, 1917. Florence is located a few miles north of Omaha in Douglas County.

128. See Orville D. Menard, "Tom Dennison, the *Omaha Bee,* and the 1919 Omaha Race Riot," *Nebraska History* 68 (winter 1987): 152–65.

129. *Omaha Monitor,* Aug. 17, 1919. See also *Omaha Monitor,* Sept. 4, 1919.

130. *Omaha Daily Bee,* Sept. 26, and 27, 1919.

131. This same procedure of taking the alleged assailant to the victim's house for identification had been used in the 1891 lynching of George Smith (see *Omaha World-Herald,* Oct. 10 and 13, 1891). In both cases, after the identification, word spread rapidly throughout the city and the results, of course, were disastrous.

132. *Omaha World-Herald,* Sept. 29, 1919.

133. Ibid.

134. Ibid. For a fuller discussion of the political and racial implications of this lynching, see particularly the *Omaha Monitor's* coverage, Oct. 2, 9, 16, and 23, 1919. See also Menard, "Tom Dennison, the *Omaha Bee,*" 152–65; and Michael L. Lawson, "Omaha, A City in Ferment: Summer of 1919," *Nebraska History* 58 (fall 1977): 395–417.

135. See the *Omaha World-Herald,* Oct. 10, 1891.

136. In the 1919 lynching, the alleged perpetrator had robbed the victim's boyfriend and had taken a watch and other items that could be identified. A search of his person and residence would have provided "real" proof to connect him to the crime. See *Omaha Daily Bee,* Sept. 27, and 28, 1919.

137. Tolnay and Beck, "Black Flight," 354.

Chapter 4. The Violent West

1. For example, see Mario Barrera, *Race and Class in the Southwest: A Theory of Racial Inequality* (Notre Dame, Ind.: Univ. of Notre Dame Press, 1979); Alberto Camarillo, *Chicanos in a Changing Society: From Mexican Pueblos to American Barrios in Santa Barbara and Southern California, 1848–1930* (Cambridge: Harvard Univ. Press, 1979); Arnoldo De León, *Ethnicity in the Sun Belt: A History of Mexicans in Houston* (Houston: Mexican American Studies Program, Univ. of Houston, 1989); *They Called Them Greasers: Anglo Attitudes Toward Mexicans in Texas, 1821–1900* (Austin: Univ. of Texas Press, 1983); Mario Garcia, *Desert Immigrants: The Mexicans of El Paso, 1880–1920* (New Haven, Conn.: Yale Univ. Press, 1981); Richard Griswold del Castillo, *The Los Angeles Barrio, 1850–1900: A Social History* (Berkeley: Univ. of California Press, 1979); *La Familia: Chicano Families in the Urban Southwest, 1848 to the Present* (Notre Dame, Ind.: Univ. of Notre Dame Press, 1984); Carey McWilliam, *North From Mexico: The Spanish Speaking People of the United States* (Philadelphia: Lippincott, 1961); David Montejano, *Anglos and Mexicans in the Making of Texas, 1836–1986* (Austin: Univ. of Texas Press, 1987); Richard L. Nostrand, *The Hispano Homeland* (Norman: Univ. of Oklahoma Press, 1992); Alex M. Saragoza, "Recent Chicano Historiography: An Interpretive Essay," *Aztlán: A Journal of Chicano Studies* 19 (1988–90): 1–77; and William B. Taylor and Elliott West, "Patrón Leadership at the Crossroads: Southern Colorado in the Late Nineteenth Century," *Pacific Historical Review* 42 (Aug. 1973): 335–57.

2. For the Italian experience, see Richard D. Alba, *Italian Americans: Into the Twilight of Ethnicity* (Englewood Cliffs, N.J.: Prentice-Hall, 1985); Alan Balboni, "From Laborer to Entrepreneur: The Italian-American in Southern Nevada, 1905–1947," *Nevada Historical Society Quarterly* 34 (spring 1991): 257–72; Lawrence A. Cardoso, "Nativism in Wyoming, 1868 to 1930: Changing Perceptions of Foreign Immigrants," *Annals of Wyoming* 58 (spring 1986): 20–38; Dino Cenel, *From Italy to San Francisco: The Immigrant Experience* (Stanford: Stanford Univ. Press, 1982); Luciano J. Iorizzo and Salvatore Mondello, *The Italian-Americans* (New York: Twayne Publishers, 1971); Jerre Mangione and Ben Morreale, *La Storia: Five Centuries of the Italian American Experience* (New York: Harper Collins, 1992); Andrew F. Rolle, *The Immigrant Upraised: Italian Adventurers and Colonists in an Expanding America* (Norman: Univ. of Oklahoma Press, 1968); and Arthur C. Todd, *The Cornish Miner in America* (Glendale, Calif.: Arthur H. Clark Company, 1967). For other ethnic groups, see Louis James Cononelos, *In Search of Gold Paved Streets: Greek Immigrant Labor in the Far West, 1900–1920* (New York: AMS Press, 1989); Zeese Papanikolas, *Buried Unsung: Louis Tikas and the Ludlow Massacre* (Lincoln: Univ. of Nebraska Press, 1991); Mary Kasilometes Scott, "The Greek Community in Pocatello, 1890–1941," *Idaho Yesterday* 28 (fall 1984): 29–36; Evangelos C. Vlachos, *The Assimilation of Greeks in the United States* (Athens: Ex-Social Sciences Centre, 1968); Anna Zellick, "Fire in the Hole: Slovenians, Croatians and Coal Mining on the Musselshell," *Montana: The Magazine of Western History* 40 (spring 1990): 16–31; and David M. Emmons, *The Butte Irish: Class and Ethnicity in an American Mining Town, 1875–1925* (Urbana: Univ. of Illinois Press, 1989).

3. Sarah Deutsch, *No Separate Refuge: Culture, Class, and Gender on an Anglo-Hispanic Frontier in the American Southwest, 1880–1940* (New York: Oxford Univ. Press, 1987).

4. Ibid., 105. For a discussion of life in the Colorado Fuel and Iron Company's coal-company towns in Las Animas County, see Eric Margolis, "Western Coal Mining as a Way of Life: An Oral History of the Colorado Coal Miners to 1914," *Journal of the West* 24 (July 1985): 1–115.

5. See Gastil, *Cultural Regions*, 97–116.

6. For examples of research on crime in eastern urban areas, see Wolfgang, *Patterns in Criminal Homicide;* Monkkonen, *The Dangerous Class;* Samuel Walker, *Popular Justice: A History of American Criminal Justice* (New York: Oxford Univ. Press, 1980); Lane, *Violent Death* and *Roots of Violence;* and Gurr, *Violence in America,* vol. 1.

7. The newspaper erred in suggesting that Disalvo was the victim of a "secret order" assassination. Americans have become enamored with the concept of the "mafia," but this and other cases all display the symptoms of family-related vendettas or feuds, and there is no hint of a mafia plot.

8. *Trinidad Chronicle-News,* July 18, 1911.

9. For a discussion of the development and consequences of Mediterranean vendettas or feuds, see Stephen Wilson, *Feuding, Conflict, and Banditry in Nineteenth-Century Corsica* (Cambridge: Harvard Univ. Press, 1988); Jacob Black-Michaud, *Cohesive Force: Feud in the Mediterranean and the Middle East* (Oxford: Basil Blackwell, 1975); and Franco Ferracuti,

Renato Lazzari, and Marvin E. Wolfgang, eds., *Violence in Sardinia* (Rome: Mario Bulzoni, 1970).

10. Limerick's *Legacy of Conquest* has sparked an ongoing debate about interpreting western history. See Larry McMurtry's essay "How the West Was Won or Lost," *New Republic* 203 (Oct. 22, 1990): 32–37; and Limerick, *Legacy of Conquest*. It should be noted that Limerick barely touches the topic of violence in her new western history, except where it involves minorities. See also White, *"It's Your Misfortune."*

11. The indictment data consist of 282 cases during the period 1880–1920. See Colorado, Las Animas County, *Registers of Criminal Action, 1880–1920,* Las Animas County Courthouse, Trinidad, Colo.

12. The term "other whites" in this study refers to northern Europeans. Because of the large number of Italians and Hispanics, this allows the separation of ethnic groups for data interpretation.

13. The term "Hispanic" will be used in this study because it is difficult to determine whether defendants were recent migrants from Mexico or had lived their entire lives in New Mexico or Colorado as Spanish Americans. Although there is recent preference for "Latino," Hispanic has the advantage of being gender neutral.

14. Luis Baca, "The Guadalupita Colony of Trinidad," *Colorado Magazine* 21 (Jan. 1944): 22–27; and Morris F. Taylor, *A Sketch of Early Days on the Purgatory* (Trinidad, Colo.: Risley Printing Company, 1959), 35–37. See also A. W. McHendrie, "Trinidad and Its Environs," *Colorado Magazine* 6 (Sept. 1929): 166; and "Place Names in Colorado (T)," *Colorado Magazine* 20 (Jan. 1943): 35.

15. Richard Patterson, *Historical Atlas of the Outlaw West* (Boulder, Colo.: Johnson Books, 1985), 48; and Ralph C. Taylor, *Colorado South of the Border* (Denver: Sage Books, 1963), 472–82.

16. Patterson, *Historical Atlas,* 49; and Taylor, *Colorado,* 478–82.

17. Richard L. Nostrand, *The Hispano Homeland* (Norman: Univ. of Oklahoma Press, 1992), 117, 143; Baca, "Guadalupita Colony," 24–25; and McHendrie, "Trinidad," 166–68.

18. Deutsch, *No Separate Refuge,* 35.

19. Taylor, *Colorado,* 284–85.

20. Deutsch, *No Separate Refuge,* 101–03; and Carl Abbott, *Colorado: A History of the Centennial State* (Boulder, Colo.: Colorado Univ. Associated Press, 1976), 46–47.

21. Margolis, "Western Coal Mining," 37–39.

22. Alba, *Italian Americans,* 21.

23. Ibid., 25.

24. Ibid., 52–54.

25. Iorizzo and Mondello, *The Italian-Americans,* 40–48.

26. Ibid., 47–50.

27. U.S. Bureau of the Census, *Twelfth Census of the United States, 1900,* vol. 1 (Wash-

ington, D.C.: U.S. GPO, Office, 1901), 740; *Thirteenth Census of the United States, 1910,* vol. 2 (Washington, D.C.: U.S. GPO, 1913), 222; and Mangione and Morreale, *La Storia,* 187. By 1910 Colorado had a population of approximately 40,000 Italians.

28. Rolle, *The Immigrant Upraised,* 174–75.

29. Vlachos, *Assimilation of Greeks,* 57.

30. See Cononelos, *Gold Paved Streets,* 139–85.

31. The 1910 census of Las Animas County lists 163 people born in Greece. See U.S. Bureau of the Census, *Thirteenth Census, 1910,* vol. 2, 222. On the Greek role in labor organizations in mining in the West, see particularly Cononelos, *Gold Paved Streets,* 196–211.

32. See Papanikolas, *Buried Unsung.*

33. Margolis, "Western Coal Mining," 42–44.

34. See Eugene S. Gaddis, "Gaddis Exhibit," *The Colorado Coal Miners' Strike,* in *Industrial Relations: Final Report and Testimony* (Washington, D.C.: U.S. GPO, 1916), vol. 9, 8905–6 (hereinafter cited as *Final Report*). The list includes such ethnic origins as English, Scotch, Welsh, Irish, German, Swedish, Bohemian, French, Croatian, Russian, and Serbian.

35. Deutsch, *No Separate Refuge,* 87–90.

36. On the coal company's attempt to control county coroners, see "Doyle Exhibit No. 2," in *Final Report,* vol. 8, 7344–47; and George S. McGovern and Leonard F. Guttridge, *The Great Coalfield War* (Boston: Houghton Mifflin, 1972), 28–34.

37. James B. Allen, *The Company Town in the American West* (Norman: Univ. of Oklahoma Press, 1966), 156–60. See also H. Lee Scamehorn, *Mill and Mine: The CF&I in the Twentieth Century* (Lincoln: Univ. of Nebraska Press, 1992), 197.

38. Barron B. Beshoar, *Out of the Depths: The Story of John R. Lawson, a Labor Leader* (Denver: Golden Bell Press, 1980), 2. Beshoar's father practiced medicine in and around the camps during this era. As a young boy Barron often accompanied his father on trips to the company towns.

39. Comment by Eugene S. Gaddis, "Gaddis Exhibit," in *Final Report,* vol. 9, 8910.

40. Ibid., 8912.

41. Scamehorn, *Mill and Mine,* 86.

42. Margolis, "Western Coal Mining," 41.

43. Company stores were located in Berwind, Cuatro, Engle, Morley, Primero, Segundo, Sexto, Tabasco, Tercio, and Valdéz. The Berwind and Tabasco stores also served the company towns of Forbes and Delagua.

44. Written, published, and recorded by Merle Travis in 1947, *Sixteen Tons* (American Music, Inc., 1947) did not become a hit until Tennessee Ernie Ford recorded it for Capitol Records in 1955. It became an overnight sensation and reached number one within a few weeks. Travis was the son of a Kentucky coal miner. See Nat Shapiro, *Popular Music: An Annotated Index of American Popular Songs, 1940–1960,* vol. 2 (New York: Adrian Press, 1965), 236.

45. Gaddis, *Final Report*, vol. 9, 8910. These were typical fees collected from underground workmen for the period 1913–14.

46. Scamehorn, *Mill and Mine*, 111; and Margolis, "Western Coal Mining," 66.

47. Scamehorn, *Mill and Mine*, 117. Scamehorn's work is the authorized company history, written mainly from Colorado Fuel and Iron Company records.

48. Gaddis, *Final Report*, vol. 9, 8913. Gaddis, an ordained minister, had a great dislike for alcohol and its effects on family life. For similar conditions in the coal counties of Lackawanna, Luzerne, and Schuylkill, Pennsylvania, see Peter Roberts, *Anthracite Coal Communities: A Study of the Demography, the Social, Educational and Moral Life of the Anthracite Regions* (New York: Macmillan, 1904), 222–43.

49. See also Robert E. Popham, "The History of the Tavern," in Yedy Israel et al., eds., *Research Advances in Alcohol and Drug Problems*, vol. 4 (New York: John Wiley and Sons, 1978), 281–95; and Mark E. Lender and James K. Martin, *Drinking in America* (New York: Free Press, 1982), 102–33, 205–6.

50. Gaddis, *Final Report*, vol. 9, 8914–15.

51. Ibid., 8927.

52. Dan DeSantis, as quoted in Margolis, "Western Coal Mining," 63.

53. Ibid., 63–64.

54. Scamehorn, *Mill and Mine*, 85.

55. Gaddis, *Final Report*, vol. 9, 8919.

56. See Scamehorn, *Mill and Mine*, 80–90; and "Farr Exhibit," in *Final Report*, vol. 8, 7304–8.

57. Beshoar, *Out of the Depths*, 2.

58. Scamehorn, *Mill and Mine*, 90.

59. Beshoar, *Out of the Depths*, 2.

60. For a discussion of their methods, see Winthrop D. Lane, "The Labor Spy in West Virginia," *The Survey* 47 (Oct. 22, 1921): 110–12; and "West Virginia: The Civil War in Its Coal Fields," *The Survey* 47 (Oct. 29, 1921): 177–83.

61. Police shootings were not limited to company towns. Trinidad and Aguilar also experienced a significant number of police homicides (eleven and four, respectively).

62. See Colorado, Las Animas County, *Coroner's Inquests, 1906–1915*, Trinidad City Library, Trinidad, Colo.

63. At Cripple Creek, county officials indicted "thirty-seven striking miners" for committing acts of violence and "tarred and feathered" a union attorney. In a similar strike at Telluride in 1901, mine owners employed strikebreakers to crush strikes that ended with "violence and deaths." See Percy Stanley Fritz, *Colorado: The Centennial State* (New York: Prentice-Hall, 1941), 369–71.

64. See Deutsch, *No Separate Refuge*, 87–106; and Abbott, *Colorado*, 103–41.

65. Abbott, *Colorado*, 133.

66. Ibid., 125.

67. Ibid., 135.

68. See *CI* (Las Animas Co.), bodies of 75 victims found within the Primero, Colorado, mine, Feb. 1, 1910.

69. Margolis, "Western Coal Mining," 13–14, 25; and James Whiteside, *Regulating Danger: The Struggle for Mine Safety in the Rocky Mountain Coal Industry* (Lincoln: Univ. of Nebraska Press, 1990), 74–75, 132–33. Another explosion occurred at the Cokedale mine, Feb. 9, 1911. Colorado miners suffered 1,708 casualties between 1884–1912, and an additional 1,307 deaths between 1913 and 1933, most of the latter occurring in the first decade.

70. Victor Bazanelle claimed that "the fire boss was drunk all the time. . . . They were drunk when they went in." See Margolis, "Western Coal Mining," 25. Actually, most victims died from other mine-related accidents such as cave–ins, exposure to dangerous equipment, or being run over by coal cars, but explosions were more dramatic and focused attention on the mines.

71. "Doyle Exhibit," *Final Report,* vol. 7, 7345. See also Deutsch, *No Separate Refuge,* 89; and Papanikolas, *Buried Unsung,* 37.

72. *Trinidad Chronicle-News,* Feb. 10, 1902.

73. *Trinidad Chronicle-News,* Feb. 23, 1903.

74. *CI* (Las Animas Co.), body of Aldridge Clifton, Apr. 12, 1903.

75. *Trinidad Chronicle-News,* Jan. 14, 1908; and Sept. 12, 1908.

76. For similar cases, see *Trinidad Chronicle-News,* Sept. 23, 1912; Nov. 26, 1912; Apr. 28, 1913; and Feb. 9, 1917.

77. Because of the Ludlow massacre, the one-year period August 1913 to August 1914 will be treated separately. Most of these indictments were multiple in nature (492 names, often reoccurring and listing the same victim), and because virtually all were dismissed, these 132 cases have been excluded from the data and will be discussed only for general homicide-rate comparisons. The fact that all of those indicted were United Mine Workers indicates that this was a form of harassment by the prosecutor, encouraged by the Colorado Fuel and Iron Company. See Cases No. 6746 to 6804 and 6929 to 6955 in Colorado, Las Animas County, *Registers of Criminal Action, 1880–1920.*

78. McGovern and Guttridge, *Great Coalfield War,* 27.

79. Recent research in Arizona, California, and Nebraska resulted in quite different results. Native American and black conviction rates averaged 80 percent compared to about 40 percent for whites. See Clare V. McKanna, Jr.: "Life Hangs in the Balance: The U.S. Supreme Court's Review of *Ex Parte Gon-Shay-Ee,*" *Western Legal History* 3 (summer/fall, 1990): 197–211; and "Treatment of Indian Murderers," 55–67.

80. See Clare V. McKanna, Jr., "Red on White: Inter-Racial Homicides in Arizona and California, 1880–1912," paper presented at the Western History Conference, Austin, Tex., Oct. 1991. Native Americans who killed whites had very high rates of convictions and death sentences.

81. See Eric Monkkonen, "Diverging Homicide Rates: England and the United States, 1850–1875," in Gurr, *Violence in America*, vol. 1, 86–87; Roger Lane, "On the Social Meaning of Homicide Trends in America," in Gurr, 66; and Neil Alan Weiner and Margaret A. Zahn, "Violence Arrests in the City: The Philadelphia Story, 1857–1980," in Gurr, 108, 113.

82. These figures, however, do not include the homicides that occurred during the 1913–14 coal miners' strike, when the Colorado National Guard, Baldwin-Felts company guards, and heavily armed strikers made Las Animas County look like a war zone. Because of the nature of that cataclysmic event, including the Ludlow massacre, these data have been treated separately. The homicide rate (not the indictment rate) for that one-year period (Aug. 1913 to Aug. 1914) skyrocketed to 226 per 100,000. See *CI* (Las Animas Co.), 1913–14.

83. The national average for homicide rates from 1900 to 1920 increased from 2.6 per 100,000 to 8. (The national rates may reflect higher levels of southern and western violence.) See Brearley, *Homicide in the United States*, 15–16; Lane, *Violent Death*, 60; Monkkonen, "Diverging Homicide Rates," 84–88; Theodore N. Ferdinand, "The Criminal Patterns of Boston since 1849," *American Journal of Sociology* 63 (July 1967): 84–99; and Allen, *Homicide*, 120–39.

84. All of the latter counties started with rates as high as 72 to 125 per 100,000 (none below 20) in the 1850s, but declined by the 1890s. See McKanna, "Homicide, Race, and Justice in California, 1850–1900," manuscript in preparation, 1–18. In a study of a region on the border of Kentucky and Tennessee, one researcher found that homicide rates averaged 51 per 100,000 for a similar time period. See William Lynwood Montell, *Killings: Folk Justice in the Upper South* (Lexington: Univ. of Kentucky Press, 1986), 164.

85. *Webster's New World Dictionary* (New York: Simon and Schuster, 1988), 1480.

86. In 1848, 207 homicides occurred in Corsica. See Wilson, *Feuding, Conflict, and Banditry*, 15.

87. Ibid., 54.

88. Ibid., 92–93, 100–01.

89. Black-Michaud, *Cohesive Force*, xiii–xiv. It should be noted that these were viewed not as murders but as justified "revenge killings" within the accepted social practices of many Mediterranean cultures. See also Christopher Boehm, *Blood Revenge: The Anthropology of Feuding in Montenegro and other Tribal Societies* (Lawrence: Univ. Press of Kansas, 1984), 66.

90. See Boehm, *Blood Revenge*, 112–13.

91. Wilson, *Feuding, Conflict, and Banditry*, 107.

92. See primarily Boehm, *Blood Revenge*, 91–120; and Wilson, *Feuding, Conflict, and Banditry*, 91–127, 177–205.

93. *Trinidad Chronicle-News*, July 18, 1911.

94. *Trinidad Chronicle-News*, July 19, 1911. See Wilson, *Feuding, Conflict, and Banditry*, 190–203.

95. *Trinidad Chronicle-News,* July 22, 1918; and *CI* (Las Animas Co.), body of Dominic Pistone, July 22, 1918.

96. See *CI* (Las Animas Co.), bodies of Bartolo Sylvestri, May 9, 1899; Guiseppe Maniscala, Nov. 17, 1907; and Vincenzo Provenzo, Aug. 24, 1915; *Trinidad Chronicle-News,* Nov. 21, 1907, and Aug. 24, 1915.

97. *CI* (Las Animas Co.), body of Vincenzo Provenzo, Aug. 26, 1915, 17. Doctor G. W. Robinson testified, "Whoever did the shooting must have been shooting upward, the wound on the side was caused when the man fell off the horse, or after he was on the ground" (2).

98. Ibid., 25–26.

99. Ibid., 9.

100. *Trinidad Chronicle-News,* Apr. 8, 1905.

101. Ibid.

102. Ibid.

103. Colorado, Las Animas County, District Court, *People v. Barneycastle,* case no. 8076, "Statement by W. Tom Barneycastle," 3, Las Animas County Courthouse, Trinidad, Colo.

104. Ibid.

105. Colorado, State Prison Records, *Records of Convicts, 1850–1920,* W. T. Barneycastle, inmate no. 10557, RG 83-267, Colorado State Archives, Denver.

106. Colorado, Las Animas County, *Coroner's Inquests,* body of Jakimo Parlapiano, May 9, 1906.

107. *Trinidad Chronicle-News,* Jan. 31, 1908; May 31, 1908.

108. *Trinidad Chronicle-News,* Jan. 14, 1909.

109. *Trinidad Chronicle-News,* Mar. 2, 1909.

110. *Trinidad Chronicle-News,* Mar. 6, 1902.

111. *Trinidad Chronicle-News,* Dec. 18, 1916, and Mar. 24, 1917.

112. *Trinidad Chronicle-News,* Sept. 9, 1917.

113. Colorado, Las Animas County, District Court, *People v. J. Avelino Vigil,* case no. 132. Penitentiary Mittimus issued to Las Animas County Sheriff John J. Marty, Sept. 24, 1917, Las Animas County courthouse, Trinidad, Colo.

114. *Trinidad Chronicle-News,* Dec. 25, 1896.

115. *Trinidad Chronicle-News,* Oct. 15, 1908.

116. Quoted on the cover of Beshoar, *Out of the Depths.*

117. H. M. Gitelman, "Perspectives on American Industrial Violence," *Business History Review* 47 (spring 1973): 17.

118. See "Doyle Exhibit," *Final Report,* vol. 8, 7345. It was common for county officials to side with business interests throughout the United States during this era. They viewed it as an economic issue and cared little for the concerns of miners, legitimate or otherwise, particularly those of recently arrived immigrants who did not share their cultural heritage. Baldwin-Felts had the reputation for recruiting enough men to do the

job. In 1912 they put "some 2,500 Baldwin-Felts men" into Kanawha County, West Virginia, to suppress a strike. See Edward Levinson, *I Break Strikes!: The Technique of Pearl L. Bergoff* (New York: Robert M. McBride and Company, 1935), 151.

119. *CI* (Las Animas Co.), bodies of Gerald Lippiatt and George W. Belcher, Aug. 17 and Nov. 21, 1913. Seven years later, Albert C. Felts, one of the Baldwin-Felts directors known for his gun play, was killed by Chief of Police Sid Hatfield during a coal mining strike in Matewan, West Virginia. See Papanikolas, *Buried Unsung,* 69; and Margolis, "Western Coal Mining," 72–73. John Sayles's 1987 film *Matewan* provides a poignant, although somewhat biased, portrayal of union attempts to organize in Mingo County, West Virginia. Police Chief Sid Hatfield and the mayor met the Baldwin-Felts detectives on the streets of Matewan. A gun battle ended with the deaths of seven "detectives," two miners, the mayor, and a "boy bystander." Credited with killing all seven Baldwin-Felts gunmen, the shootout in Matewan made "two-gun" Sid Hatfield an instant folk hero. Less than a year later he was caught unarmed on the steps of a courthouse in an adjacent county, and he was shot fifteen times by Baldwin-Felts gunmen who went unpunished for the killing. See Virgil C. Jones, *The Hatfields and the McCoys* (Chapel Hill: Univ. of North Carolina Press, 1948), 233–45; Lon Savage, *Thunder in the Mountains: The West Virginia Mine War, 1920–21* (Pittsburgh: Univ. of Pittsburgh Press, 1990), 3–23; Altina L. Waller, *Feud: Hatfields, McCoys, and Social Change in Appalachia, 1860–1900* (Chapel Hill: Univ. of North Carolina Press, 1988), 244–46; and John L. Spivak, *A Man in His Time* (New York: Horizon Press, 1967), 89–93.

120. Coroner Sipe selected inquest jurors sympathetic to the company. Between Jan. 1, 1910, and Mar. 1, 1913, "in 30 cases; 24 of these had the same man, a gambler and bartender by the name of J. C. Baldwin, as foreman of the jury." See Samuel Yellen, *American Labor Struggles* (New York: Harcourt, Brace and Company, 1936), 209.

121. Ibid., 208.

122. Testimony before the House Committee on Mines and Mining as quoted in the *New York Times,* Apr. 7, 1914. It should be noted that most of the coal miners walked out of the mines. At least 8,000 men supported the strike (221).

123. Eugene O. Porter, "The Colorado Coal Strike of 1913: An Interpretation," *The Historian* 12 (autumn 1949): 27.

124. Yellen, *American Labor Struggles,* 212.

125. Las Animas County Sheriff Grisham deputized 348 of these guards as "special" deputies. See "Farr Exhibit," in *Final Report,* vol. 8, 7304–08.

126. *Denver Post,* May 6 and 13, 1914.

127. Yellen, *American Labor Struggles,* 222–23.

128. See John A. Fitch, "Law and Order: The Issue in Colorado," *The Survey,* 33 (Dec. 5, 1914): 254–57.

129. This seems unusual since the coroner had always supported the company's claims in any investigations (*The Denver Post,* Apr. 22, 1914; Yellen, *American Labor Strug-*

gles, 236). The Las Animas County Coroner conducted inquests on the bodies and concluded that union-organizer Louis Tikas suffered three bullet wounds—all in the back—and had his head bashed severely with a rifle wielded by Linderfelt. Most of the women and children died during the fire that swept the camp. They were hiding from gunfire in a small underground dugout, where they suffocated. Dr. Aca Harvey, one observer at Ludlow, noticed several National Guardsmen standing by the tents. At the coroner's inquest he was asked what became of the tents. He replied, "It looked as though they [National Guard] were pouring coal oil on them." After hearing several corroborating witnesses, authorities determined that the National Guard had indeed set the fire. See *Final Report*, vol. 8, 7363–73.

130. "Lindsay Exhibit No. 2," in *Final Report*, vol. 8, 7363–65; *Denver Post*, Apr. 25, 26, 27, and 29, 1914; and *New York Times*, Apr. 26, 27, and 28, 1914. See particularly the headline from the Apr. 25, 1914, edition of the *Denver Post*: "500 women storm capitol, corner squirming governor, and demand strike war end. Undaunted by a driving rain storm, the women picketed the capitol demanding to see the governor."

131. Yellen, *American Labor Struggles*, 240.

132. The indictments issued by the grand jury during this session are chaotic. Since they did not have sufficient evidence to charge a specific individual with a particular homicide, they chose to use a multiple-indictment method, listing from two to twenty or more names on an individual indictment involving the death of one person. This method was employed to intimidate and coerce the coal miners by allowing the sheriff to arrest and detain a larger number of strikers in an effort to cripple their will to continue the strike (Colorado, Las Animas County, *Criminal Registers, 1913–1914*, Las Animas County Courthouse, Trinidad, Colo.

133. Belcher, a Baldwin-Felts agent known for his gunplay, had killed George Lippiatt just two months before being shot in Trinidad on Nov. 20, 1913. Although the newspaper account of the Nimmo shooting listed him as a deputy sheriff, Nimmo was from Denver, not Las Animas County, and it is more likely that he was a "special" deputy hired by the Baldwin-Felts agency. See the *Denver Post*, Oct. 27, 1913, and *Trinidad Chronicle-News*, Nov. 21, 1913.

134. Colorado, Supreme Court, *Lawson v. the People*, 63 Colorado 275 (1917).

135. Colorado, Supreme Court, *Zancannelli v. the People*, 63 Colorado 254 (1917).

136. Ibid., 255.

137. Ibid., 256.

138. Ibid., 256–57.

139. Ibid., 257.

140. Ibid., 258.

141. Ibid., 261.

142. Ibid., 262.

143. Ibid., 265.

144. Ibid.

145. Conversation between Edward Doyle and John R. Lawson, as quoted in Beshoar, *Out of the Depths,* 357.

146. Gastil, *Cultural Regions,* 102.

147. Ibid., 103. There are critics of Gastil's thesis. See Colin Loftin and Robert H. Hill, "Regional Subculture and Homicide: An Examination of the Gasti–Hackney Thesis," *American Sociological Review* 39 (Oct. 1974): 714–24; Steven F. Messner, "Regional and Racial Effects on the Urban Homicide Rate: The Subculture of Violence Revisted," *American Journal of Sociology* 88 (Mar. 1983): 997–1007; Christopher G. Ellison, "An Eye for an Eye? A Note on the Southern Subculture of Violence Thesis," *Social Forces* 69 (June 1991): 1223–39; and Donald J. Shoemaker and J. Sherwood Williams, "The Subculture of Violence and Ethnicity," *Journal of Criminal Justice* 15(6) (1987): 461–72.

148. Gastil, *Cultural Regions,* 102.

149. Ibid., 105.

150. Ibid.

151. Ibid., 251.

152. Bat Masterson, as quoted in Bill O'Neal, *Encyclopedia of Western Gun–Fighters* (Norman: Univ. of Oklahoma Press, 1979), vii. It is interesting to note that Masterson seldom became involved in gunfights and is recorded to have killed only three men. See Richard O'Connor, *Bat Masterson* (Garden City, N.Y.: Doubleday, 1957), 176–92; and O'Neal, *Encyclopedia,* 219–22.

Chapter 5. Red versus White

1. Sidney L. Harring, *Crow Dog's Case: American Indian Sovereignty, Tribal Law, and United States Law in the Nineteenth Century* (New York: Cambridge Univ. Press, 1994).

2. See Ronet Bachman, *Death and Violence on the Reservation: Homicide, Family Violence, and Suicide in American Indian Populations* (New York: Auburn House, 1992); Bachman, "An Analysis of American Indian Homicide: A Test of Social Disorganization and Economic Deprivation at the Reservation County Level," *Journal of Research in Crime and Delinquency* 28 (Nov. 1991): 456–71; Rita Bienvenue and A. H. Latif, "Arrests, Disposition, and Recidivism: A Comparison of Indians and Whites," *Canadian Journal of Criminology and Corrections* 16(2) (1974): 105–16; Vine Deloria, Jr., "Laws Founded in Justice and Humanity: Reflections on the Content and Character of Federal Indian Law," *Arizona Law Review* 31(2) (1989): 203–24; William Hagan, *Indian Police and Judges: Experiments in Acculturation and Control* (New Haven, Conn.: Yale Univ. Press, 1966). K. N. Llewellyn and E. Adamson Hoebel, *The Cheyenne Way: Conflict and Case Law in Primitive Jurisprudence* (Norman: Univ. of Oklahoma Press, 1941); Ken Peak and Jack Spencer, "Crime in Indian Country: Another 'Trail of Tears,' " *Journal of Criminal Justice* 15(6) (1987): 485–94; Archie and Bette Randall, "Criminal Justice and the American Indian," *The Indian*

History 11 (spring 1978): 42–48; John Phillip Reid, *A Law of Blood: The Primitive Law of the Cherokee Nation* (New York: New York Univ. Press, 1970); and Charles F. Wilkinson, *American Indians, Time, and the Law: Native Societies in a Modern Constitutional Democracy* (New Haven, Conn.: Yale Univ. Press, 1987).

3. *Arizona Silver Belt* (Globe), Dec. 28, 1889.

4. See also the Florence *Arizona Weekly Enterprise*, Nov. 16, 1889, and Dec. 7, 1889.

5. Wolfgang, *Patterns in Criminal Homicide*, 222–23; Lane, "Urban Homicide," 91–110; and Ted Robert Gurr, "Historical Trends in Violent Crime: Europe and the United States," in Gurr, *Violence in America* , 21–54.

6. The exceptions are Richard L. Carrico, "Spanish Crime and Punishment: The Native American Experience in Colonial San Diego, 1769–1830," *Western Legal History* 3 (winter/spring, 1990): 21–33; McKanna, "Four Hundred Dollars Worth of Justice," 197–212; McKanna, "Life Hangs in the Balance," 197–211; and McKanna, "Murderers All: The Treatment of Indian Defendants in Arizona Territory, 1880–1920," *American Indian Quarterly* 17 (summer 1993): 359–69.

7. For crime research techniques, see Crawford and McKanna, "Crime in California," 284–95. For methodological information, see also Lane, *Violent Death*, 154–159; Wolfgang, *Patterns in Criminal Homicide*, 298–313; and McKanna, "Ethnics and San Quentin Prison Registers: A Comment on Methodology," *Journal of Social History* 18 (Mar. 1985): 477–82; and "The Nameless Ones: The Ethnic Experience in San Quentin," *Pacific Historian* 31 (spring 1987): 21–33.

8. Arizona, Gila County, District Court, *Registers of Criminal Action, 1880–1920,* Arizona State Archives, Phoenix. Kathy Jones suggests, "Unless the record of aggregate behavior is linked with individual-level data, we cannot reach any firm conclusions about the social history of murder." See Jones, "Changing Patterns of Criminal Homicide in the West: San Diego, 1870–1900," paper presented at the Western Association of Women Historians meeting, Huntington Library, San Marino, Calif., Apr. 15, 1984.

9. *Graham County Bulletin* (Solomonville, Ariz.), Aug. 1897.

10. T. E. Farish, *Southeastern Arizona: Its Varied Climate and Wonderful Resources* (Phoenix: Arizona Gazette, 1889), 42–45.

11. Henry G. Alsberg, ed., *Arizona: The Grand Canyon State* (New York: Hastings House, 1956), 91; and *Graham County Bulletin* (Solomonville, Ariz.), Aug., 1897.

12. Dan Rose, *Prehistoric and Historic Gila County, Arizona* (Phoenix: Republic and Gazette Printery, 1935), 30.

13. Todd, *Cornish Miner*, 264.

14. Malcolm L. Comeaux, *Arizona: A Geography* (Boulder, Colo.: Westview Press, 1981), 291.

15. Todd, *Cornish Miner*, 261.

16. "Report of the Governor of Arizona," in *Annual Report of the Department of the Interior, 1898* (Washington, D.C.: U.S. GPO 1898), 281–84.

17. Univ. of Arizona, *Arizona and Its Heritage* (Tucson: Univ. of Arizona, 1936), 171–73.

18. Frank C. Lockwood, *Frontier Days in Arizona: From the Spanish Occupation to Statehood* (New York: Macmillan Company, 1932), 215–16.

19. Copper-mining management did not introduce safety hats and shoes in Arizona until the late 1920s. For Arizona copper-mining accident statistics, see Ronald C. Brown, *Hard-Rock Miners: The Intermountain West, 1860–1920* (College Station: Texas A&M Univ. Press, 1979), 60 and appendix B.

20. Alsberg, *Arizona,* 97.

21. Ibid., 99. See James R. Kluger, *The Clifton-Morenci Strike: Labor Difficulties in Arizona, 1915–1916* (Tucson: Univ. of Arizona Press, 1970); Richard H. Peterson, "Conflict and Consensus: Labor Relations in Western Mining," *Journal of the West* 12 (Jan. 1973): 1–17; Philip Taft, "The Bisbee Deportation," *Labor History* 13 (winter 1972): 3–40; and Arthur L. Walker, "Early Day Copper Mining in the Globe District," *Engineering and Mining Journal* 125 (Apr. 14, 1928): 604–08; (Apr. 28, 1928): 694–98.

22. Richard J. Perry, *Western Apache Heritage: People of the Mountain Corridor* (Austin: Univ. of Texas Press, 1991), 185.

23. William Y. Adams, "Wage Labor and the San Carlos Apache," in Keith H. Basso and Morris E. Opler, eds., *Apachean Culture History and Ethnology* (Tucson: Univ. of Arizona Press, 1971), 119.

24. George D. Corson to Commissioner of Indian Affairs, Sept. 28, 1901, in *Annual Report, Interior, 1901* (Washington, D.C.: U.S. GPO, 1902), 190.

25. Statement by Edward Arhelger as quoted in Dan L. Thrapp, *Al Seiber: Chief of Scouts* (Norman: Univ. of Oklahoma Press, 1964), 337.

26. C. L. Sonnichsen, "The Ambivalent Apache," *Western American Literature* 10 (summer 1975), 99.

27. Ibid., 114.

28. Reuben Gold Thwaites, ed., *The Jesuit Relations and Allied Documents: Travels and Explorations of the Jesuit Missionaries in New France,* vol. 348 (Cleveland: Burrows Brothers, 1898), 147.

29. Ignaz Pfefferkorn, *Sonora: A Description of the Province* (Albuquerque: Univ. of New Mexico Press, 1949), translated and annotated by Theodore E. Treutlein, 148–49.

30. Ibid., 145.

31. Ibid., 149.

32. Samuel Woodworth Cozzens, *The Marvellous Country; or Three Years in Arizona and New Mexico, The Apaches' Home* (Minneapolis: Ross and Haines, 1967), 110.

33. Ibid., 110–11.

34. Patrick Hamilton, *The Resources of Arizona* (San Francisco: A. L. Bancroft, 1884), 293.

35. Ibid., 293–94.

36. Ibid., 294.

37. Cozzens, *Marvellous Country,* 90.

38. Bil Gilbert, *Westering Man: The Life of Joseph Walker* (New York: Atheneum, 1983), 263.

39. Ibid., 268.

40. Ibid., 274.

41. Ibid.

42. Ibid., 275.

43. Ibid.

44. Ibid.

45. Elie Reclus, *Primitive Folk: Studies in Comparative Ethnology* (London: Walter Scott, 1891), 124.

46. Ibid., 128.

47. Ibid., 129.

48. Ibid., 134–35.

49. Ibid., 136.

50. Ibid., 141.

51. Thomas Cruse, *Apache Days and After* (Lincoln: Univ. of Nebraska Press, 1987), 69.

52. Ibid., 187.

53. John C. Cremony, *Life Among the Apaches* (Lincoln: Univ. of Nebraska Press, 1983), 85.

54. Ibid., 266.

55. Ibid., 267.

56. D. C. Cole, *The Chiricahua Apache, 1846–1876: From War to Reservation* (Albuquerque: Univ. of New Mexico Press, 1988), 62.

57. *Memorial and Affidavits showing Outrages Perpetrated by the Apache Indians, in the Territory of Arizona, for the Years 1869 and 1870* (San Francisco: Francis and Valentine, 1871), 13.

58. Ibid., 8–9, 16.

59. *New York Times,* May 16, 1866.

60. Dispatch from General George Crook to Adjutant General, Military Division of the Pacific, Sept. 27, 1883, in *Annual Report of General George Crook, U.S. Army, Department of Arizona* (Prescott: Arizona, 1883), 9.

61. Ibid., 10.

62. See Ralph A. Smith, "The Scalp Hunter in the Borderlands, 1835–1850," *Arizona and the West* 6 (spring 1964): 5–22; William B. Griffen, *Utmost Good Faith: Patterns of Apache-Mexican Hostilities in North Chihuahua Border Warfare, 1821–1848* (Albuquerque: Univ. of New Mexico Press, 1989), 54, 118–19; and William B. Griffen, *Apaches at War and Peace: The Janos Presidio, 1750–1858* (Albuquerque: Univ. of New Mexico Press, 1988), 223–28; and William Cochran McGaw, *Savage Scene: The Life and Times of James Kirker, Frontier King* (New York: Hastings House, 1972).

63. Morris Edward Opler, *An Apache Life-Way: The Economic, Social, and Religious Institutions of the Chiricahua Indians* (Chicago: Univ. of Chicago Press, 1941), 349.

64. Ibid., 350.

65. Richard J. Perry, *Apache Reservation: Indigenous People and the American State* (Austin: Univ. of Texas Press, 1993), 103.

66. Ibid.

67. J. Dunn, Jr., *Massacre of the Mountains* (New York: Archer House, 1958), 339.

68. Perry, *Apache Reservation*, 104.

69. Bancroft, *History of Arizona and New Mexico, 1530–1888*, 559. Bancroft claims that only eight massacre victims were men. According to some the "troops who took part in the burial details wept unabashed as they buried the mutilated bodies." See Irene Burlison, *Yesterday and Today in the Life of the Apaches* (Philadelphia: Dorrance and Company, 1973), 19.

70. Odie B. Faulk, *Crimson Desert: Indian Wars of the American Southwest* (New York: Oxford Univ. Press, 1974), 166.

71. Henry F. Dobyns, "Inter-Ethnic Fighting in Arizona: Counting the Cost of Conquest," *Journal of Arizona History* 35 (summer 1994): 176.

72. See Clyde A. Milner II, "The Shared Memory of Montana Pioneers," *Montana: The Magazine of Western History* 37 (winter 1987): 2–13.

73. John H. McCallum, ed., *Francis Parkman: The Seven Years War* (New York: Harper Torchbooks, 1968), 43.

74. Robert Shulman, "Parkman's Indians and American Violence," *Massachusetts Review* 12 (spring 1971): 222.

75. Ibid., 226.

76. Ibid., 228.

77. *Arizona Silver Belt* (Globe), Nov. 2, 1889.

78. Ibid., Dec. 28, 1889. Some believe he meant that he was leaving a hell created by white men.

79. Ibid.

80. Hayes, *Apache Vengeance*, 126.

81. *Arizona Champion* (Flagstaff), June 18, 1887.

82. *Arizona Weekly Enterprise* (Florence), Nov. 16, 1889.

83. Ibid., Dec. 7, 1889.

84. Ibid. For further documentation, see also *Arizona Silver Belt* (Globe), Nov. 2, 1889; *Arizona Weekly Enterprise* (Florence), Oct. 19, 26, and Nov. 16, 1889; *San Francisco Examiner*, Dec. 7, 1889; and especially the editorial on the impending executions in the *Arizona Champion* (Flagstaff), Oct. 26, 1889.

85. William Seagle, *The Quest for Law* (New York: Alfred A. Knopf, 1941), 36.

86. Ibid., 39.

87. E. Adamson Hoebel, *The Law of Primitive Man: A Study in Comparative Legal Dynamics* (New York: Atheneum, 1970), 24.

88. Ibid.

89. Ibid., 26.

90. Quoted in Hoebel, *Law of Primitive Man*, 26.

91. Hoebel, *Law of Primitive Man*, 28. Emphasis in the original.

92. Ibid., 158. See K. N. Llewellyn and E. Adamson Hoebel, *The Cheyenne Way: Conflict and Case Law in Primitive Jurisprudence* (Norman: Univ. of Oklahoma Press, 1941), 132–68.

93. Hoebel, *Law of Primitive Man*, 159.

94. See Monkkonen, "Diverging Homicide Rates," 86–87.

95. John Phillip Reid, *A Law of Blood: The Primitive Law of the Cherokee Nation* (New York: New York Univ. Press, 1970), 73.

96. Ibid., 100.

97. Ibid., 45, 101.

98. Hoebel, *Law of Primitive Man*, 139.

99. Ibid., 141.

100. See L. Bryce Boyer, *Childhood and Folklore: A Psychoanalytic Study of Apache Personality* (New York: Library of Psychological Anthropology, 1979), 30–32.

101. The U.S. government discovered this in its attempts to obtain approval from Apache bands to sign peace agreements. These agreements were not considered binding by other bands or, in some cases, by the band whose chief signed the agreement. This helps to explain the nature and consequences of the Apache wars.

102. Grenville Goodwin, *The Social Organization of the Western Apache* (Chicago: Univ. of Chicago Press, 1942), 393.

103. Ibid., 398. The exact nature of *tiswin* is not clear. An alcoholic beverage made from corn, it is commonly called *tulapai* or *tulabai* by Apaches. James L. Haley claims that tiswin and tulabai are not one and the same. Tiswin "was prepared from mescal plants" similar to *pulque,* a common alcoholic beverage used by Mexican peasants (*Apaches: A History and Culture Portrait* [Garden City, N.Y.: Doubleday, 1981], 98); John G. Bourke, "Distillation by Early American Indians," *American Anthropologist* 7 (July 1894): 297–99; Winfred Buskirk, *The Western Apache: Living with the Land Before 1950* (Norman: Univ. of Oklahoma Press, 1986), 216–18; and Britton Davis, *The Truth About Geronimo* (New Haven: Yale Univ. Press, 1929), 115, 145–46.

104. J. C. Tiffany, U.S. Indian agent, to the commissioner of Indian Affairs, Sept. 6, 1881, in *Annual Report of the Commissioner of Indian Affairs, 1881* (Washington, D.C.: U.S. GPO, 1881), 7, 11 (hereinafter cited as *Annual Report*).

105. Captain John L. Bullis, acting U.S. Indian agent to the commissioner of Indian Affairs, Aug. 26, 1889, in *Annual Report*, 122. See also Indian agent reports for 1888 and 1892. In 1887 the commissioner of Indian Affairs reported that a "few San Carlos Apaches" under the influence had "killed one or two men" but had been punished. He suggested that they were not on the "war path" but that "they were drunken desperadoes, like thousands of drunken desperadoes of our cities and towns." Apparently he understood neither the nature of tiswin nor the fact that it served a socializing function for Apaches. See *Annual Report, 1887*, xxxiv.

106. See George D. Corson, U.S. Indian agent, to the commissioner of Indian Affairs, Sept. 28, 1901, in *Annual Report*, 192.

107. Goodwin, *Social Organization of the Western Apache*, 402.

108. Ibid., 404.

109. This is an exceptional case, but it indicates that retaliation in such feuds could be explosive. Ibid., 406.

110. Ibid., 408.

111. Davis, *The Truth About Geronimo*, 145–46. At that time Nana was in his eighties. Just three years earlier Nana, with only a handful of men and women, led a famous breakout and raid that frightened settlers and exhausted the U.S. Cavalry, which fought and lost a series of engagements. See Dan L. Thrapp, *The Conquest of Apacheria* (Norman: Univ. of Oklahoma Press, 1967), 211–16.

112. Davis, *The Truth About Geronimo*, 145.

113. Lockwood, *The Apache Indians*, 44.

114. Grenville Goodwin's *Social Organization of the Western Apache* provides the best appraisal of Apache custom, particularly chapter 7, "Social Adjustments," 374–427. See also Morris E. Opler, *An Apache Life Way* (Chicago: The Univ. of Chicago Press, 1941), 140–85, 336–53, and 406–14; Cremony, *Life among the Apaches*, 187–90 and 285–97; and John G. Bourke, "Medicine-Men of the Apache," in *Ninth Annual Report of the Bureau of Ethnology* (Washington, D.C.: U.S. GPO, 1892).

115. The definitive discussion of the Crow Dog case is Harring, *Crow Dog's Case*. See also William Seagle, "The Murder of Spotted Tail," *The Indian Historian* 3 (fall 1970): 10–22.

116. See *Ex Parte Crow Dog*, 190 U.S. 556 (1883).

117. The U.S. Supreme Court overturned Crow Dog's murder conviction, creating a great uproar. In response to intense pressure from white citizens, Congress passed the Major Crimes Act as a part of the general Indian appropriations bill in 1885. In *U.S. v. Kagama*, 118 U.S. 375–385 (1886) the U.S. Supreme Court held that Congress had a right to pass such legislation to control behavior on Indian reservations; therefore, the Major Crimes Act was legal and binding. See U.S. *Statutes At Large*, 341: 365–85 (Dec. 1883–Mar. 1885).

118. Opinion of U.S. Supreme Court Justice Samuel F. Miller, in *Ex Parte Crow Dog*, 109 U.S. 571–572 (1883).

119. Similar research in Douglas County, Nebraska, reveals comparable patterns for blacks in Omaha, who killed white victims 32 percent of the time, while whites killed black victims in only 4 percent of cases.

120. See Arizona, Territorial Supreme Court, *U.S. v. Captain Jack, Gon-shay-ee, Say-es, Miguel, et al., and Bat-dish, et al.*, case nos. 48-57 and 67, *Criminal Case Files, 1871–1912*, RG 92, Arizona State Archives, Phoenix.

121. Mott, ranked 114 in his class at West Point, received an appointment to Adjutant Commanding Company "A" Indian Scouts effective Dec. 21, 1886. See *Letters Received by the Office of the Adjutant General*, Main Series, 1881–89, in "Reports of General Nelson A. Miles, Commander at San Carlos Reservation," National Archives, Washington, D.C.;

and *Official Register of the U.S. Containing a List of Officers and Employees in the Civil, Military, and Naval Service on the First of July, 1885*, vol. 1 (Washington, D.C.: U.S. GPO, 1885), 399, 436.

122. Arizona, Territorial Supreme Court, *U.S. v. Nah-deiz-az*, Second U.S. District Court, RG 92, 14, Arizona State Archives, Phoenix.

123. Ibid., 15. From the testimony at the trial it is unclear what Lieutenant Mott said to Nah-deiz-az. Frank Porter and Kay-zay claimed that they did not hear Mott's rejoinder to Nah-deiz-az. However, Nah-deiz-az's reaction suggests that Mott threatened to jail him.

124. Ibid., 16. One secondary account erroneously claims that he fired only one shot at Mott. See Jess G. Hayes, *Apache Vengeance* (Albuquerque: Univ. of New Mexico Press, 1954), 13. Dr. T. B. Davis, who examined the body, claimed that "he had three wounds. One in the arm, one in the thigh, and the third in the buttock, penetrating the pelvic cavity." He further testified that the latter wound, the deadly one, occurred while Mott was running from Nah-deiz-az (11–12).

125. See Wilbert H. Ahearn, "Assimilationist Racism: The Case of the 'Friends of the Indian,'" *Journal of Ethnic Studies* 4 (summer 1976): 23–32; Ronald M. Johnson, "Schooling the Savage: Andrew S. Draper and Indian Education," *Phylon* 35 (Mar. 1974): 74–82; Bruce Rubenstein, "To Destroy a Culture: Indian Education in Michigan, 1855–1900," *Michigan History* 60 (summer 1976): 151–60; and Robert H. Keller, Jr., "American Indian Education: An Historical Context," *Journal of the West* 13 (Apr. 1974): 75–82.

126. See *U.S. v. Nah-deiz-az*, 24; and Arizona, Prison Records, *Yuma Territorial Prison Register, 1887*, RG 85, Arizona State Archives, Phoenix.

127. Arizona, Territorial Supreme Court, *Brief and Argument*, in *The Territory of Arizona v. Bat-dish, Back-el-cle, Nat-tsin, and Guadalupe*, RG 92, Arizona State Archives, Phoenix.

128. Ibid., 6.

129. Ibid., 7.

130. Ibid., 9.

131. Ibid., 11. Emphasis in original.

132. Ibid., 12. Emphasis in original.

133. Al Sieber believed that Ma-si committed this homicide and other crimes in the same vicinity. See Thrapp, *Al Sieber*, 347.

134. Guadalupe, age fifty, and his son Bat-dish, twenty, both died in the Arizona Territorial Prison in Yuma after seven years of incarceration. See Arizona, Prison Records, *Yuma Territorial Prison Registers, 1880–1912*, RG 85, Arizona State Archives, Phoenix.

135. See Arizona, Territorial Supreme Court, *U.S. v. Captain Jack*, (1888), Second U.S. Judicial District, Maricopa County, Arizona Territory, case no. 48, RG 92, Arizona State Archives, Phoenix.

136. Ibid., 6.

137. Ibid., 23.

138. Ibid., 24; *U.S. v. Captain Jack* 130 U.S. (1889) 354. Colonel Snyder's comments

provide context for the Apache male's attitude toward an enemy who has killed a member of his band.

139. Arizona, Territorial Supreme Court, *U.S. v. Captain Jack* (1888), No. 48, RG 92, Arizona State Archives, 10–19, 25–38.

140. Arizona, Territorial Supreme Court, *U.S. v. Gon-shay-ee* (1889), case no. 49, RG 85, Arizona State Archives, Phoenix. See also case nos. 48–57 and 67. Federal law dealing with homicide recognized only first-degree murder, which called for the death penalty. One can understand, then, why the Supreme Court justice suggested that the defendant was entitled to the same trial as other citizens in the various county jurisdictions, which recognized first- and second-degree murder. See *Revised Statutes of the United States, 1873–74* (Washington, D.C.: U.S. GPO, 1878), 18, Sec. 5339, Pt. 1: 1038.

141. See McKanna, "Life Hangs in the Balance," 198–211.

142. See *Ex Parte Crow Dog,* 109 U.S. 556 (1883); *U.S. v. Kagama,* 118 U.S. 375 (1886); and Chapter 341, *Statutes At Large,* 341: 363–85 (1885).

143. *U.S. v. Gon-shay-ee,* 130 U.S. (1889) 353.

144. Ilth-kah, along with Hah-skin-gay-gah-lah, a fellow Apache prisoner, died from a lung infection. See Ohio, Prison Records, *Register of Prisoners and Index, Dec. 1886–Feb. 1889,* Series 1536, Ohio State Historical Society, Columbus.

145. Without medical case files, it is impossible to explain adequately this dramatic death rate. For some observations on Native American deaths in California, see Sherburne F. Cook, *The Population of the California Indians, 1769–1870* (Berkeley: Univ. of California Press, 1976), 104–42. See also McKanna, "Treatment of Indian Murderers," 65–77.

146. Recent research suggests that even today a defendant's chance of receiving the death penalty depends more on the race of the victim than the race of the defendant. See Samuel R. Gross and Robert Mauro, *Death and Discrimination: Racial Disparity in Capital Sentencing* (Boston: Northeastern Univ. Press, 1989).

147. The various army officers who worked for the San Carlos Agency complained that the Apache men refused to stop drinking tiswin. Most reported that it led to numerous quarrels and fights that sometimes ended in killings. By 1893, Indian agents claimed that Apaches seemed to be drinking moderately, but the data suggest otherwise. See particularly Captain F. E. Pierce, acting agent, "Report on San Carlos Agency," *Annual Report, 1886,* 40; and Brevet Lieutenant-Colonel Lewis Johnson, "Report on San Carlos Agency," *Annual Report, 1893,* 122.

148. Arizona, Gila Co., District Court, *Criminal Case Files, 1881–1920,* RG 103, Arizona State Archives, case no. 870.

149. See *CI* (Gila Co.), body of Matze, Feb. 18, 1906, RG 103, Arizona State Archives, Phoenix.

150. See *CI* (Gila Co.), body of Cole (Apache TA 24), Oct. 23, 1909.

151. *CI* (Gila Co.), body of D. A. Reynolds, Oct. 22, 1890.

152. *CI* (Gila Co.), body of Charles Cadotte, Dec. 1, 1898.

153. *Arizona Silver Belt* (Miami), Nov. 19, 1913.

154. See, for example, *CI* (Gila Co.), bodies of Red Bronen, Jim Haskill, and Byron Williams, Oct. 23, 1909; Apr. 21, 1917; and Nov. 14, 1917.

155. *CI* (Gila Co.), body of Harry F. Wilbur, Oct. 18, 1906.

156. *Arizona Silver Belt* (Globe), Oct. 18, 1906.

157. *Arizona Silver Belt* (Miami), Feb. 24, 1918.

158. The number of lynchings is confirmed by Larry D. Ball, who developed a list of lynchings that occurred in Arizona and New Mexico (*Desert Lawmen,* 382).

159. *CI* (Gila Co.), bodies of Andrew Hall and W. F. Vail, Aug. 21, 1882.

160. Hayes, *Boots and Bullets,* 38–39.

161. Ibid.

162. *Arizona Silver Belt* (Globe), Aug. 24 and Sept. 2, 1882.

163. *Arizona Silver Belt* (Globe), Sept. 2, 1882.

164. Hayes, *Boots and Bullets,* 124–26.

165. Ibid., 126.

166. *CI* (Gila Co.), bodies of Myrtle and Lou Goswich, June 24, 1910.

167. Hayes, *Boots and Bullets,* 96. The wound was self-inflicted, but Olds insisted that a man shot him and frightened the girls, who then jumped in the river.

168. Ibid., 99.

169. *Arizona Silver Belt* (Globe), July 3, 1910.

170. Guy Anderson, ed., *Honor the Past, Mold the Future* (Globe, Ariz.: n.p., 1976), 35.

171. Ibid.

172. See Ball, *Desert Lawmen,* 382.

173. Population statistics for Native Americans are sketchy and unreliable. For example, the San Carlos Reservation figures for 1880, 1890, 1900, 1910, and 1920 are 3,000, 3,212, 729, 2,508, and 843, respectively. Further, only a portion of San Carlos Reservation fell under Gila County legal jurisdiction. Given these factors, it seems safe to say that Apaches never comprised more than 15 percent of the Gila County population.

174. Congress passed a bill in 1897 to divide White Mountain Reservation into Fort Apache Reservation in the north, and San Carlos in the south. See Captain Albert L. Myer's comments in "Report of San Carlos Agency," *Annual Report, 1897,* 114.

175. See chapter 2.

176. There were twelve, eight, and two cases, respectively, for Hispanics, blacks, and Asians. See Arizona, Gila Co., District Court, *Registers of Criminal Actions, 1881–1920,* RG 103, Arizona State Archives, Phoenix.

177. Ibid.

178. For a discussion of these cases, see McKanna, "Murderers All," 358–69.

179. Arizona, Gila County, District Court, *Criminal Case Files, 1881–1920,* RG 103, Arizona State Archives, Phoenix.

180. The small number of Hispanics cases may render any analysis of the data unreliable.

181. See Arizona, Gila County, District Court, *Criminal Case Files, 1881–1920,* nos. 178, 206, 241, 256, 268, and 280, RG 103, Arizona State Archives, Phoenix.

182. Gary L. Roberts, "Violence and Frontier Tradition," in Forrest R. Blackburn et al., eds., *Kansas and the West: Bicentennial Essays in Honor of Nyle H. Miller* (Topeka: Kansas State Historical Society, 1976), 109.

Chapter 6. Lethal Violence

1. William R. Freudenburg and Robert Emmett Jones, "Criminal Behavior and Rapid Community Growth: Examining the Evidence," *Rural Sociology* 56 (winter 1991): 620.

2. Ibid., 638. Areas studied included rural counties in Arizona, Colorado, Utah, Wyoming, and Washington.

3. Current sociological research indicates that during the past few decades, the "rural murder rate exceeds the rates for most cities" (Kenneth Wilkinson, "A Research Note on Homicide and Rurality," *Social Forces* 63 [Dec. 1984]: 445). That certainly was the case in Las Animas and Gila counties.

4. Ayers, *Vengeance and Justice,* 267.

5. See Wolfgang and Ferracuti, *Subculture of Violence.*

6. See Gastil, "Homicide," 416.

7. See Gary G. Forrest and Robert H. Gordon, *Substance Abuse, Homicide, and Violent Behavior* (New York: Gardner Press, 1990), 1–15; and Robert Nash Parker, "Alcohol and Theories of Homicide," in Fred Adler and William S. Laufer, eds., *New Directions in Criminological Theory,* vol. 4 (New Brunswick, N.J.: Transaction Publishers, 1993), 113–41.

8. John Shelton Reed, "To Live—and Die—in Dixie: A Contribution to the Study of Southern Violence," *Political Science Quarterly* 86 (Sept. 1971): 433.

9. See U.S. Bureau of Census, RG 513, Nebraska State and Federal Census, SG 2, Federal Census, 1900 and 1910.

10. See *CI* (Las Animas Co.), body of Jakimo Parlopiano, May 9, 1906; and *Omaha World-Herald,* Aug. 28, 1919.

11. Douglas County had the youngest homicide perpetrators (49 percent under thirty), followed by Las Animas and Gila counties (45 and 39 percent, respectively).

12. See *Thirteenth Census of the United States, 1910: Reports by States with Statistics for Counties, Cities,and other Civil Divisions, Alabama–Montana,* vol. 2 (Washington, D.C.: U.S. GPO, 1913), 678.

13. For the escapades of Hickok, see Nyle H. Miller and Joseph W. Snell, *Great Gunfighters of the Kansas Cowtowns, 1867–1886* (Lincoln: Univ. of Nebraska Press, 1963), 130–34; and Dykstra, *The Cattle Towns* (New York: Alfred F. Knopf, 1968), 143.

14. See Dykstra, *Cattle Towns,* 7, 146. The major weakness of Dykstra's analysis is his failure to place homicides in proper context. His comment that "the average number of homicides per cattle town trading season amounted to only 1.5 per year" (146) fails to show the ratio per 100,000 population, the common method of measuring homicide.

Further, Dykstra counts only the homicides that occurred within the cattle towns during the actual cattle-drive season. For additional criticism, see McGrath, *Gunfighters,* 268.

15. Dykstra, *Cattle Towns,* 142–47.

16. Twenty-one defendants were indicted for murder or manslaughter between 1880 and 1920. Kansas, Dickinson County, *Criminal Appearance Dockets, 1880–1920* (Dickinson County Courthouse, Abilene).

17. A search of the Dickinson County Courthouse and the Dickinson County Historical Society archives failed to reveal any coroner's inquests. The county clerk, district court clerk, and historical society archivist all believe that they may have been destroyed in a fire in the courthouse.

18. See McKanna, "Homicide, Race, and Justice in California, 1850–1900," manuscript in preparation. This study includes 1,317 homicide cases.

Index

About the Author

Clare V. McKanna, Jr., received his Ph.D. in history from the University of Nebraska-Lincoln in 1993. His articles on violence and crime have appeared in *Western Historical Quarterly, American Indian Quarterly, Western Legal History, Journal of Social History, Journal of American Ethnic History,* and other journals. He is currently researching homicide in nineteenth-century California, and lecturing on Native American and Latin American history at San Diego State University.